CONTEMPORARY
CULTURAL
THEORY

306·01 MIL

CORNWALL COLLEGE
LEARNING CENTRE

D0277383

CONTEMPORARY CULTURAL THEORY

Andrew Milner

UCL
PRESS

© Andrew Milner 1994

This book is copyright under the Berne Convention.
No reproduction without permission.
All rights reserved.

First published in 1994 by UCL Press
Second impression 1995

UCL Press Limited
University College London
Gower Street
London WC1E 6BT

The name of University College London (UCL) is a registered trade
mark used by UCL Press with the consent of the owner.

ISBN: 1-85728-127-6

British Library Cataloguing-in-Publication Data

A catalogue record for this book is available from the British Library.

Typeset in Baskerville.
Printed and bound by
Athenæum Press Ltd, Gateshead, Tyne & Wear.

CONTENTS

ACKNOWLEDGEMENT

As ever, I am indebted to Verity Burgmann, my partner in life and labour, for all the truly important things. I am grateful to our sons, David, James and Robert, just for being there, and also, let it be admitted, for sometimes not being there. I am indebted too to friends, colleagues and students in the Centre for Comparative Literature and Cultural Studies at Monash University and in the Centre for Cultural Studies at the University of Leeds, and to staff at the Monash University Library and the Brotherton Library. Comparisons are always invidious, but special thanks are due to Marie Maclean, David Roberts, Philip Thomson, Gail Ward and Chris Worth at Monash, Zygmunt Bauman, Griselda Pollock and Adrian Rifkin at Leeds. I am grateful to Stephen Mennell for suggesting a second edition of the book and to Nicholas Esson and Steven Gerrard for the enthusiasm with which they greeted that suggestion. For reasons many and various, thanks are due also to Sue Cockerill, Ann Dudgeon, Sheila Jones, Andrew Keogh, David Lockwood, Richard Milner, Joyce and Phil Morton, Colin Sparks and Kathy Türnier.

To the memory of my mother, Dorothy Milner, who died of cancer on 27 November 1988; to my father John Milner, who nursed her through that last illness; to the future of my sons, David, James and Robert; and to whatever connections we may yet be able to make between our respective biographies.

Introduction
The rise of cultural theory

Media and cultural studies have emerged as one of the more significant academic growth industries over the past quarter of a century, and more especially so during the past decade. In many universities, both "new" and "old", there are now separate courses or departments explicitly designated as such. Probably the best known is the Department of Cultural Studies, a successor institution to the earlier, highly respected Centre for Contemporary Cultural Studies, at the "old" University of Birmingham. The Birmingham department teaches courses at both graduate and undergraduate levels, actively promotes research in the field, and since 1991 has also published the annual journal, *Cultural Studies from Birmingham*. One could almost as easily cite the School of Communication Studies at the "new" Westminster University, however: it too teaches comprehensive programmes in media studies, it houses a research centre for communication and information studies, and publishes one of the leading journals in the area, *Media, Culture and Society*. Even where such institutional autonomy doesn't formally exist, the subject is still often taught, but as a part either of sociology or of "English". The new Teesside University, for example, provides a home both for cultural studies and for *Theory, Culture and Society*, again a leading journal in the field, in its School of Health, Policy and Social Studies. Cultural studies remains similarly indebted to sociology at the old University of Lancaster. But at both the old University of Southampton and the new Manchester Metropolitan University, the subject is effectively incorporated into "English studies". Elsewhere, it may appear as an adjunct to anthropology or to the visual arts: at the University of Leeds, for example, the Centre for Cultural Studies is actually attached to the Department of Fine Art. There are learned journals and learned societies devoted to the subject, both in Britain and overseas. There is even an international journal, *Cultural Studies*, with editorial groups in Britain, the United States and Australia, which has been published by Methuen and then by Routledge since 1987. Apparently, there is at least one draft GCE "A" level syllabus already in circulation.[1] If cultural studies is still not yet a fully organized discipline within British higher education, then it is nonetheless well on the way to becoming so.

As currently constructed both in Britain and elsewhere this "proto-discipline" of cultural studies still remains deeply indebted to the work of the Birmingham Centre. Originally founded in 1964, as a gradu-ate research unit under the directorship of Richard Hoggart, the Centre became, for much of the 1970s and 1980s, the intellectually pre-eminent institutional location for cultural studies in the English-speaking world. Antony Easthope, for example, now Professor of English and Cultural Studies at Manchester Metropolitan University, judges the Centre's work the most important "intervention in cultural studies in Britain".[2] Lawrence Grossberg, from the University of Illi-nois, agrees that: "there remains something like a center – to be pre-cise, the tradition of British cultural studies, especially the work of the Centre for Contemporary Cultural Studies".[3] Graeme Turner, a founding editor of the *Australian Journal of Cultural Studies* and a key fig-ure in the development of cultural studies in that country, echoes this view: "the Birmingham Centre . . . can justifiably claim to be the key institution in the history of the field".[4] The emergence and expansion of what eventually became known as "cultural studies" (which con-tinues apace, despite the politically motivated antipathy of the Con-servative government toward the old Birmingham Centre itself) has constituted one of the most exciting intellectual developments engen-dered by the protracted crisis of post-war Britain.

British cultural studies became the site for a sustained encounter between an earlier English tradition of "literary" cultural criticism on the one hand, and a variety of French structuralist and more gener-ally continental Western Marxist (and sociological) traditions on the other. This encounter has been theorized as that between "structur-alism" and "culturalism" by two subsequent directors of the Birming-ham Centre, Stuart Hall and Richard Johnson.[5] In each case, an empiricist culturalism is contrasted with a theoreticist structuralism. Hall's account in particular has been very widely influential. For Hall, culturalism elides the distinction between active consciousness and relatively "given" determinate conditions; it thus becomes susceptible to a general "experiential pull" and to an "emphasis on the creative", which constructs "experience" itself as the "authenticating test".[6] By contrast, structuralism recognizes the presence of constraining relations of structure; it thus acknowledges the importance of different levels of theoretical abstraction and successfully replaces the category of experience with that of ideology.[7] But insofar as the stress here falls upon the supposedly atheoretical nature of British culturalism, it seems to me that Hall misconstrues the situation. Indeed, he himself has elsewhere observed of Raymond Williams's *The Long Revolution*, one of the seminal culturalist texts, that: "It attempted to graft on to an idiom and mode of discourse irredeemably particular, empirical and moral in emphasis, its own . . . kind of 'theorizing' . . . The difficult, somewhat abstract quality of the writing . . . can largely be ascribed to its status as a 'text of the break'".[8]

Even then, Hall seriously underestimates the properly "theoretical" content of the culturalist tradition as it had evolved before Williams. If the mode of exposition of, for example, Leavisite literary criticism (perhaps, the single most important instance of culturalist thought) is indeed irredeemably particular, its intellectual content – as for example in the debate about industrialization and cultural decline or in that over the "dissociation of sensibility" – remains highly theoretical. There is nothing especially particular nor even especially empirical about Leavis's own insistence that the disintegration of the pre-industrial organic community is "the most important fact of recent history".[9] The discourse about culture, or better perhaps the various discourses about culture, which developed in Britain and Germany, France and Italy, Russia and the United States, essentially as a series of sustained reflections on the nature of cultural modernization, have *all* been irretrievably "theoretical" in nature, no matter how apparently "empirical" their particular reference points. Hence the invariable accompaniment of courses in cultural studies by parallel courses in cultural theory. Hence, too, the subject matter of this book.

Discourses become self-consciously theoretical, which is another way of saying that they become self-reflexive, as a general rule only when their subject matters become in some significant sense problematic. And it is only in the modern period itself that "culture", however defined, does indeed become such. The available definitions of this term are many and various, and we shall have cause to consider some of them in detail in what follows. For the moment, let me offer a rough working "non-definition" of "culture" as referring to that entire range of institutions, artefacts and practices which make up our symbolic universe. The term thus embraces art and religion, science and sport, education and leisure, and so on. By convention, however, it does not similarly embrace that range of activities normally deemed "economic" or "political". This threefold distinction between the economics of the market, the politics of the state and the culture of what is sometimes referred to as civil society, is a recurrent motif in modern social theory: it occurs, for example, in Marx as the distinction between mode of production, political superstructure and social consciousness,[10] and in Weber as that between class, party and status.[11] But it is clear that in each case, as in a whole range of parallel instances drawn from a wide range of discourses, consciousness/status/culture (ideology/discourse etc.) are largely residual categories, defined as much as anything by the negative property of not being economics or politics. In this very negativity we find the trace of the inherently problematic status of all modern concepts of culture.

Premodern societies, such as the feudalisms of medieval Europe or the hunting and gathering communities of tribalism, clearly exhibit behaviours that we would easily recognize as "cultural", whether religious or artistic, "scientific"[12] or educational. But this is our retrospective understanding, not their own. Precisely because culture, and perhaps especially religion, is indeed central to the life of most types of society other than that of the modern Occident, those societies typically possess no sense of the cultural as "different" and "residual", such as is conveyed by our modern Western usages. In short, culture has become a theoretical problem for us only because it is already socially problematic. It is because culture is not similarly central to our lives, or at least to the institutionally received accounts of our lives, that culture becomes so "theoretical" a concept. Cultural theory is not, then, simply a particular, specialist academic discourse, the guiding hand behind a particular set of empirical, substantive research problems; it is also, and more interestingly, itself the repressed "other" of a society the official rhetoric of which is provided almost entirely by what was once known as "political economy", and what are now the separate disciplines of economics and political science. Cultural theory is, in fact, one of the central discontents of our civilization.

But if culture has indeed become so problematic, then why has this been so? The short answer lies in the nature of socio-cultural modernization itself, and in particular in the rise to dominance of a distinctively capitalist system of economic organization. Sociologists, historians and economists typically use the term "capitalism" to describe a kind of economy in which goods and services are produced only in order to be sold as commodities in a more or less competitive market; in which production is organized by individual or collective "capitalists", who advance the capital (in the form either of machinery or of money) necessary for production, and who are motivated in principle only by the pursuit of the maximum possible profit; and in which labour is itself a commodity that the capitalist is able to purchase at the price of salaries or wages. Capitalism defined thus clearly represents the dominant "mode of production" in the modern world.

Capitalism is also, however, the dominant form of organization of modern *cultural* production. Indeed, a strong case can be made for the view that the book trade was in fact the first modern capitalist industry: as Febvre and Martin observe, "the printer and the bookseller worked above all and from the beginning for profit".[13] This historically novel mode of cultural production required for its eventual success not only the general development of capitalist forms of organization but also a number of factors quite specific to cultural production itself: the transformation of culture into a form of commodifiable personal property through, for example, the design of practically enforceable laws of copyright; the commercialization and professionalization of writing and publishing which such commodification permits; the development of techniques of "mechanical reproduction",[14] in the first place printing, but later also recording, film and broadcasting; and the expansion of the cultural market as a result, for example, of increases in literacy. This unprecedented commercialization of cultural production brought about an equally unprecedented transformation in the social position and status of cultural producers such as writers, artists, priests and teachers, those whom we might today designate as, collectively, "the intelligentsia".

In tribal societies, insofar as any specialist rôle existed at all for the intellectual, it was what Williams terms that of the "instituted artist",[15] a communally sponsored particular rôle, typically that of prophet-seer. In medieval and early modern Europe, by contrast, cultural production was organized according to one or another form of patronage system, that is: "the support of a writer by a person or institution that protects him but that, in return, expects satisfaction".[16] Such patronage systems – and there are a number of important sub-variants[17] – provide some real guarantee for the material security of the intellectual, but only at the price of a radical subordination of intellectual life to the often quite immediate cultural needs either of the church or of the aristocratic or royal court. The "sacral art" of the High Middle Ages "is wholly integrated into the social institution 'religion'", explains Peter Bürger. The "courtly art" of the early modern absolutist monarchies, he continues, "serves the glory of the prince and the self-portrayal of courtly society. Courtly art is part of the life praxis of courtly society, just as sacral art is part of the life praxis of the faithful".[18] Cultures thus organized require no specifically cultural theory, but rather only a theology or a politics respectively.[19]

But in capitalist society, according to Bürger, "the separation of art from the praxis of life becomes the decisive characteristic of the autonomy of bourgeois art".[20] In this context, the term "autonomy" denotes both (relative) freedom from social control and a corresponding social irrelevance.[21] At a slightly different level of analysis, that of the producer rather than the product, it denotes also both the freedom to write or to paint or to think much as one pleases and the freedom to starve as the price of so doing. And as the logics of capitalist development proceed, such autonomy comes to apply not only to "bourgeois" high art, but also to the newer arts of the newly culturally enfranchised "masses'; not only to art, but also to other cultural forms, even to religion in the more pluralist of post-Reformation, Protestant societies. These autonomies have never appeared either unproblematic or uncontestable, either to the cultural producers themselves or to others. Hence the various forms of political and religious intervention into the cultural commodity market, for example censorship, subsidy and education. The cultural conflicts thereby instigated are evidence, according to Williams, "of the most significant modern form of asymmetry"[22] between capitalist mechanical reproduction on the one hand, and the older established institutions of cultural and social reproduction on the other. As one consequence amongst many, such asymmetries as these have prompted the emergence of contemporary cultural theory, not as a single body of authoritative discourse, but as a set of competing, often mutually exclusive, often internally contradictory, almost always deeply troubled, narrative paradigms. For, insofar as the modern intelligentsia can be said to inhabit any particular social space, it is that locatable somewhere in the nexus between the commodified culture industries and state and church endowed institutions of cultural regulation.

The Italian Marxist theoretician Antonio Gramsci contrasted the "traditional" intellectuals, such as philosophers, priests, scholars and scientists, with "organic" intellectuals, such as engineers, economists and, as we should add today, TV journalists, script writers and advertising consultants.[23] The contrast is well taken, but only so long as we appreciate that these traditional intellectuals are not very traditional at all, though they may well often imagine themselves as such. The modern higher education system provides both the central training ground and continuing employment for both types of intellectual. And despite the customary rhetoric of the older at least of the universities, this system is itself an essentially recent social invention: of the 76 universities in England and Wales, 33 date only from 1992, and only three from before 1832. The expansion thus indicated is not simply quantitative but qualitative; it is overwhelmingly recent; and it reflects the social growth and professionalization of both types of intelligentsia. Cultural theory is not, then, the preserve of some near-archaic, traditional cultural élite, but rather the discursive articulation of a set of characteristically contemporary social contradictions, which continue to structure the lived experiences of characteristically contemporary kinds of intellectual. And, in a society as thoroughly encultured as is ours, such theories become, by turn, the property not only of specialist groups of intellectuals, but also of the collective lives of whole communities. They are, then, matters of no small consequence.

Chapter 1
UTILITARIANISM

The cultural contradictions of utilitarianism

By a strange irony, most courses in cultural theory taught in British institutions of higher education manage carefully to ignore what is almost certainly the single most influential such theory available to our culture, that is, utilitarianism. Historically, utilitarianism was the first of all modern cultural theories, chronologically prior to the whole range of competing successor paradigms. But it also almost certainly still represents the preferred paradigm of the vast majority of members of the contemporary business and political élite, and, as such, exercises an enduring influence over a great deal of cultural policy formation. Utilitarianism has typically been the intellectual property, however, of organic rather than traditional intellectuals, whereas it has been the latter who have typically organized the teaching of cultural theory in both the new and the old universities. Hence the peculiar mismatch by which an actually dominant paradigm is persistently misrepresented as either marginal, archaic, or even simply non-existent.

But what exactly is utilitarianism? I mean by the term "utilitarianism" a view of the social world as consisting, ideally or factually, in a plurality of discrete, separate, rational individuals, each of whom is motivated, to all intents and purposes exclusively, by the pursuit of pleasure (or "utility") and the avoidance of pain. The good society is thus one organized so as least to inhibit the individual in pursuit of his or her (but normally his) pleasures, one in which markets are as freely competitive as possible, and in which governments exist only so as to establish the legal framework within which such markets can freely function. It is a view which has its origins in 17th century England. Its evolution can be traced from the social contract theories of politics propounded by Thomas Hobbes (1588–1679) and John Locke (1632–1704), and the empiricist philosophical systems of David Hume

(1711–76), through to the political economy of Adam Smith (1723–90) and David Ricardo (1772–1823), and on to the self-proclaimed utilitarianism of Jeremy Bentham (1748–1832) and John Stuart Mill (1806–73).

It is an overwhelmingly British intellectual tradition, but one which certainly found echoes in 18th century French thought. Its political correlate is liberalism, in the 19th century sense of the term. Utilitarianism has provided the single most powerful justification for the forms of social organization characteristic of modern capitalist society: that they guarantee the greatest happiness of the greatest number. It has provided the intellectual underpinnings for two important academic disciplines, both of which are firmly entrenched within the modern university curriculum: economics in particular, but also, if to a lesser extent, political science. In its most recent manifestation, as "economic rationalism", it has provided the major analytical framework for the policy making of governments in Britain and the United States, Australia and New Zealand. There is in utilitarianism, moreover, not only a theory of the market and of the state, but also a quite explicit theory of culture.

The Canadian political philosopher, C. B. Macpherson, described utilitarianism as a "theory of possessive individualism", and argued that from Hobbes onwards it had presupposed a model of "possessive market society". Macpherson himself identifies eight essential features of this model, but only three need concern us here: that there is no authoritative allocation of work; that there is no authoritative provision of rewards for work; and that all individuals seek rationally to maximize their utilities.[24] As Macpherson's gloss on each of these serves to elaborate, this implies, respectively, that "individuals are free to expend their energies, skills and goods as they will"; that "individuals are not given or guaranteed, by the state or the community, rewards appropriate to their social functions"; and that individuals "seek to get the most satisfaction they can for a given expenditure".[25]

Macpherson's own interests were in the implications of this model, and of its real basis in social fact, for a theory of political obligation. But what we need to note are its implications for cultural theory. If individuals are free to expend their energies as they will, if rewards are not guaranteed by the state or the community, and if individuals seek to maximize their own satisfaction (again, as they will), then it requires only the further postulate that objects of cultural preference,

9

be they literary genres or religious doctrines, can be treated as commodities for sale in the market place (and this is as factually true of
market society as are any of Macpherson's own postulates) to lead us
to the conclusion that each man (and woman?) is entitled to whatever
cultural pleasures they may please, for so long as they are practically
procurable in the cultural market place. Thus each man (and woman?)
becomes his (or her?) own church or court.

If this is indeed the logic of cultural utilitarianism, it is nonetheless
not one which the early utilitarian philosophers chose to embrace with
any great enthusiasm. Obliged by general utilitarian principles to insist that "the principles of taste be universal, and nearly . . . the same
in all men", Hume, for example, hurriedly proceeded to the qualification that: "The organs of internal sensation are seldom so perfect
as to allow the general principles their full play . . . They either labour
under some defect, or are vitiated by some disorder; and by that means
excite a sentiment, which may be pronounced erroneous".[26] All preferences may be equal, then, but some (cultural) preferences are more
equal than others. Now, the possibility of defect or disorder in the organs of internal sensation is clearly one which threatens the logical credence of any utilitarian system. If the individual's natural capacities
are either physically or mentally defective, then there is no good reason at all to suppose that the free exercise of such capacities will lead
either to the greatest happiness of that individual or to that of the
greatest number of other individuals. Which is why utilitarianism typically discounts such defects and disorders as, to use a contemporary
phrase, not statistically significant. Except in the matter of "taste", of
course.

The problem is that Hume wishes to assert the desirability of that
natural equality which capitalist society promotes in opposition to feudalism, and that he wishes nonetheless to secure the continued existence of certain enduring standards of taste: "Whoever would assert
an equality of genius and elegance between Ogilby and Milton . . . it
appears an extravagant paradox, or rather a palpable absurdity, where
objects so disproportioned are compared together".[27] That asymmetry between capitalist production for profit on the one hand, and cultural and social reproduction on the other, which we noted earlier, is
thus inscribed within the deep structures of Hume's text. This internal contradiction, this inner tension, is not, however, a necessary consequence of the logic of utilitarianism itself. It is perfectly possible to

abandon, at least in theory and perhaps even in practice, any notion of standards, so as to proceed to a thoroughgoing, consistently utilitarian cultural theory. Such is exactly the position taken by Bentham, in deliberate defiance of Hume, when he insists that people are entitled to want whatever it is that they want: "push-pin is of equal value with . . . poetry".[28] But for all its logical consistency, Benthamism never actually becomes in any sense hegemonic within utilitarianism.

John Stuart Mill would later attempt to save utilitarianism from the more or less explicit "philistinism" of Benthamism, and from the charge that it is a "doctrine worthy only of swine" with the argument that: "It is better to be . . . Socrates dissatisfied than a fool satisfied".[29] Like Hume, Mill appeals to the notion that only some individuals are properly fit to judge in such matters. But, unlike Hume, he attempts to ground this "unfitness" in the presence or absence of prior experience: if the fool is of a different opinion, this is because fools "only know their own side of the question. The other party to the comparison knows both sides".[30] The problem here, as any English teacher can attest, is that there are those who have indeed read both, and who nonetheless prefer to Milton, if not Ogilby, then some contemporary equivalent. Prior experience *per se* is not, then, sufficient: ultimately, proper judgement can be made between two pleasures only "by those who are competently acquainted with both".[31] Thus Mill's solution comes exactly to replicate that of Hume.

Commendable though Mill's implied preference for poetry over push-pin must seem to those who would value poetry (or philosophy), it remains nonetheless intellectually incoherent: on strictly utilitarian grounds it can *never* be better to be dissatisfied than satisfied. Qualitative definitions of experiential value, such as that with which Mill experiments here, are quite fundamentally incompatible with the utilitarian schema's own initial starting point in the so-called "felicific calculus" (or calculation of happiness): the utility maximization principle remains workable only so long as happiness is understood as providing a single, quantitative measure of human well-being. Such strictly Benthamite utilitarianisms implicitly endorse the reduction of cultural values to the level of the marketable commodity (for the fact that the commodity is marketable, and saleable, makes it measurable in terms of the universal standard which is money). But if this is the logical terminus of any consistent cultural utilitarianism, it is not one easily arrived at by an individual intellectual, or collective intelligentsia, which remains even half-committed to any notion of traditional cultural value such as is typically sustained by the churches, the education system, and so on. Thus, in practice, the Humean impasse recurs indefinitely. And it does so, we should note, for reasons that are not so much logical as sociological.

The logic of a consistently Benthamite position is impeded by a set of obstructions which are sociological in a double sense: first, by those practical social necessities which inhibit any respectable, middle-class intelligentsia from siding with the pornographer against the pulpit; and second, by the properly theoretical, but not in the philosopher's sense of the term strictly logical, objections which the discipline of sociology itself raises against utilitarianism. The doyen of American sociology, Talcott Parsons, summarized the central sociological case against utilitarianism as early as 1937. Parsons observed that utilitarianism could be considered a type of "action theory", and that, like all such theories, its basic units are the actor; the end towards which the action is oriented; the situation in which the action takes place; and the "normative orientation" of action, that is, the particular mode of relationship between the other elements in the action.[32] The peculiarity of the utilitarian schema, Parsons continued, is that it tends, first, to ignore the relation of ends to each other or, when they are so considered, "to lay emphasis on their diversity and lack of integration";[33] and second, to assume as the normative orientation of the means–end relationship in the unit act, "an overwhelming stress upon one particular type, which may be called the 'rational norm of efficiency'".[34]

In short, utilitarianism proceeds as if people's goals were random, and their ways of knowing the world, and so of identifying those goals, essentially indistinguishable from those of rational-scientific knowledge.[35] But in reality, human goals are not at all random: they are very clearly structured, or patterned. In reality, human actors know the world in ways other than that of positive science: their goals are patterned as much by systems of religious, political, ethical and aesthetic value as by any kind of cognitive knowledge, scientific or otherwise. The theory of possessive individualism is thus revealed as far less obviously grounded in social fact than Macpherson would later suppose. And in classical European sociology, and more especially in the work of Vilfredo Pareto and Emile Durkheim (but also in that of Alfred Marshall, the utilitarian economist), there develops a growing recognition, or so Parsons argued, of the significance for social science of "the conception of a common system of ultimate values as a vital element in concrete social life".[36]

It is precisely such systems of ultimate value, according to Parsons, which organize, integrate and de-randomize the ends of particular individual actors, and which also shape the normative orientations through which the analytically separate elements in the unit act are structurally related to each other. This stress on "ultimate values" is characteristically "cultural", though it is not, in fact, as characteristically sociological as Parsons himself supposed. Parsons's own sense of the importance of truly *common* values is almost certainly open to at least as much criticism as the initial utilitarian conception itself.[37] But Parsons is nonetheless quite right to identify a fundamental incapacity on the part of utilitarian thinkers to understand the significance for action of human values, whether religious, political, ethical or aesthetic. Neither Benthamite indifference nor the Humean subterfuge by which evaluative judgements are misrepresented as acts of cognition are at all adequate. For the economists, perhaps even the political scientists, such sins are merely venial. But for the cultural theorist, they become irreparably mortal.

Utilitarian culture and capitalist civilization

The enduring appeal of utilitarianism owes a great deal more, however, to a happy coincidence between its thematics and those of powerful business interests than it does to whatever inherent intellectual power it may possess. And this has indeed always been so. As Alvin Gouldner observes: "in the eighteenth century, utility emerged as a dominant social standard. What is relevant here is utilitarianism not as a technical philosophy but as a part of the popular, everyday culture of the middle class".[38] Already actually dominant in Britain and in its North American colonies during the 18th century, utilitarian values underlay much of the rhetoric of the French Revolution, and were rapidly transmitted throughout Europe, and thereafter by means of imperialism throughout the world, in the 19th and early 20th centuries. And there can be little doubt that utilitarianism has indeed provided a powerful rationale for the developmental logics of industrial capitalist (and even Soviet state capitalist) civilization. But the immense institutional and intellectual prestige which attaches, for example, to the economics departments of our universities owes almost nothing to that discipline's supposed "scientificity", and almost everything to its effectivity as a form of political and social propaganda. As the German sociologist Max Horkheimer observed, the consonance between "theory" and "fact", in intellectual thought as much as in commonsense, is "conditioned by the fact that the world of objects to be judged is in large measure produced by an activity that is itself determined by the very ideas which help the individual to recognize that world and to grasp it conceptually".[39] Utilitarianism remains chronically incapable of a theory of culture even remotely adequate to the explanation of systems of value. For such a theory we are obliged to look elsewhere.

Utilitarianism will figure in what follows, then, not as an alternative solution to the cultural problems of capitalism, but rather as importantly constitutive of those very problems, as part of the socio-cultural context against which other cultural theories have been obliged to define themselves. This is not to suggest that utilitarianism is unimportant. Quite the contrary: so influential has utilitarian ideology become that it now powerfully shapes the very fabric of our collective common sense. A utilitarian world would be one in which any commodity could be produced for sale, no matter what the costs of its production, so long as demand for that commodity could be proved to exist at a level capable of rewarding those who would produce it. It would be a world in which the ozone layer would be progressively destroyed in the interests of the chemicals industry; in which child prostitution and drug addiction would be rife; in which almost anything and anyone could be bought and sold. It is, of course, the world in which we live, here and now.

In Chapters 2 to 4, I will be concerned to chart the development of four other types of cultural theory, both as general components in the culture of the West and as specific elements in the British national culture. These I will term respectively: culturalism, Marxism, structuralism and feminism. I use the term *culturalism* here to denote an intellectual tradition which deliberately counterposes the value of *culture* to the claims of utility. This is a tradition which typically conceives culture in radically anti-individualist fashion, as an organic whole, and in radically anti-utilitarian fashion, as a repository of values superior to those of material civilization. By *Marxism* I refer, in the first place, to the work of Karl Marx himself, which combined a culturalist sense of the antithesis between culture and civilization with a utilitarian sense of the importance of interests. This led Marx, centrally, to the notion of *ideology*, which he used to explore the articulation of systems of belief with systems of material – and especially class – interest. The intellectual tradition thus established has an obvious affinity to, but is nonetheless not entirely coextensive with, the politics of Marxian socialism. I use the term *structuralism* to refer to an intellectual tradition characterized, in general, by the search for underlying and constraining, patterns and structures, and more particularly for patterns analogous to those which occur in language. On this view cultural artefacts are best understood as elements within systems of *signification*.

Finally, I mean by *feminism* an approach which seeks to uncover the various ways in which human culture has been gendered as either masculine or feminine, and in which that gendering has been connected to the wider social structures of sexual inequality. The key concept in the feminist tradition is that of *patriarchy*, by which feminists describe the systematic oppression of women by men. Culture, ideology and signification are, as it were, rival terms, each indicating a different way of theorizing the same phenomena (in short, our symbolic universe). Utility is a much more portable concept, which refers to all forms of consumption, whether symbolic or not. Patriarchy, by contrast, refers to the unequal distribution of social power between men and women as it affects the whole of human society. Because feminists see patriarchal society as producing a gendered culture, the concept nonetheless becomes centrally relevant to contemporary cultural studies. Theories of patriarchy are thus compatible with notions of utility, culture, ideology and signification, but require of each a radical reformulation in terms of the categories of sexual inequality and sexual difference.

If utilitarianism is almost certainly the normal cultural corollary of capitalist civilization, just as liberal democracy is its normal political form,[40] our four other types of theory are nonetheless themselves equally symptomatic products of that selfsame capitalist civilization. They each develop as the theoretical accompaniment to some deep structural resistance to that commodification of culture which utilitarianism enjoins, a resistance firmly located somewhere within the political, cultural and even economic institutions of capitalism itself.

15

Marxism is an obvious case in point. Whatever its subsequent history as a legitimating ideology for Soviet-style state capitalism, its origins are to be found in that central contradiction between capital and organized labour which lies at the very heart of the Western capitalist system. As the working classes organized themselves industrially into trade unions and politically into socialist and labour parties, so too they began to mount a developing critique of bourgeois culture, a critique which found expression not only in institutions and artefacts, but also in various types of Marxist and quasi-Marxist oppositional cultural theory.

A somewhat analogous relationship pertains between feminism and the women's movement. Feminist opposition to patriarchy, whether or not explicitly conjoined to a critique of capitalism, has typically produced its own set of independent cultural demands and expectations, and with them its own characteristic styles of cultural creation and cultural theory. Moreover, there is a strong sense in which feminist cultural politics have been unavoidably anti-utilitarian or at least non-utilitarian. As we have already noted, utilitarianism typically measures value, or "utility", only in terms of monetary gain: if it sells, then it must be valuable. But the sexual division of labour typical of modern (though perhaps not "postmodern") capitalism consigned women, and more especially middle-class women, to a "private sphere" of domestic labour, that is, to a world of invisible effort in which no money changes hands, and which therefore becomes "without utility". For 19th century feminists in particular it thus became essential to argue for notions of worth other than those provided by the capitalist market.

Culturalist and structuralist versions of cultural theory appear less obviously the products of a specifically capitalist civilization because they are indeed so obviously the creations of a professionalized traditional intelligentsia, to revert to Gramsci's term, and it is characteristic of such intelligentsias to attribute a certain timelessness to their own aspirations and interests. But, as I have already suggested, the traditional intelligentsia is in fact a modern, rather than an archaic or residual, social class:[41] it is brought into being as a result of the combined effects of cultural commodification on the one hand, and state sponsored education on the other. And its intellectual preoccupations are normally very different from those prescribed by utilitarianism. Thus, whatever the utilitarian cultural expectations of business and political leaders, scholarship in the humanities has been much more

16

obviously concerned with problems of belief, and with the various systems of religious, political, ethical and aesthetic value which structure belief, than with the maximization of cultural utility, however defined.

At one level, this antithesis between utilitarian capitalism on the one hand, and the traditional intelligentsia on the other, arises as a direct and unavoidable consequence of the nature of cultural work itself. It is simply in the nature of culture, as also in that of the state, that it remains extremely difficult to organize by means of any thoroughgoing application of the market principles of the capitalist economy. As Mrs Thatcher served to remind us, there is indeed a sense in which a capitalist *society*, as distinct from a capitalist economy, is a contradiction in terms. At another level, however, it might well be argued that this antithesis is itself historically more specific, that it follows a particular trajectory within the more general histories of capitalism and patriarchy.

A relatively far-reaching and controversial debate over such matters engaged much of the intellectual energy of both American and European cultural sociology during the 1970s. Alvin Gouldner, for example, argued that from the early 19th century until the then present day, intellectual anti-utilitarianism had been overwhelmingly Romantic in form: "the long history of Romanticism testifies to the fact that it has not concerned itself with a problem transient or peripheral to the culture".[42] But where earlier Romanticisms had only rejected the promise of industrial society, he continued, the Psychedelic Romanticism of the 1960s "rejects the actually ripened fruits".[43] For Daniel Bell, by contrast, anti-bourgeois intellectualism remained identifiable with modernism, and later post-modernism, and was as such a phenomenon only of "the last 100 years".[44] Moreover, Bell insisted that such modernisms were not so much antithetical to, as a long-term consequence of, utilitarianism itself. On this view, it was Puritanism which had provided early capitalism with its central ideological legitimation, Hobbesian utilitarianism which had powered its economy. As the capitalist economic system developed, however, it rendered Puritanism obsolete, thereby allowing the cultural dominance of this modernism which, simultaneously a culture of self and a highly marketable commodity, was thus the product both of Hobbesian individualism and of corporate capitalism.[45]

Yet a third position was that taken in Jürgen Habermas's *Legitimation*

Crisis, which argued: first, that bourgeois ideologies such as utilitarianism had never been able to provide adequate motivation for individual actors without resort to some more traditional form of religious belief, and that these latter were now becoming decreasingly effective;[46] and second, that bourgeois art and aesthetics, having become autonomous from both economics and politics and having thereby collected together those human needs that cannot be met by either, had thus become "explosive ingredients built into the bourgeois ideology".[47] For Habermas, as for Bell, the cultural contradictions of capitalism had become increasingly explosive over time; for Habermas, as for Gouldner, their source lay in the cultural inadequacies of utilitarianism rather than in the socio-pathology of the intelligentsia. All three were agreed, however, that modern intellectual culture had become, in some deep structural sense, significantly adversarial. As we shall see, both culturalism, of which Gouldner's (19th century) Romanticism is but one particular example, and structuralism and post-structuralism, themselves examples of what Bell means by modernism and postmodernism respectively, constitute extremely important instances of this more general adversarial culture.

It is easy to quibble with particular aspects of each argument: Psychedelic Romanticism had much less in common with its 19th century "precursor" than Gouldner supposed; modernism has been much less consistently anti-bourgeois and utilitarianism much less consistently hedonistic (for utility can mean "use" as well as "happiness') than Bell supposed; and art and aesthetics seem much more easily tamed by the political and economic systems than Habermas supposed. With the benefit of hindsight, it becomes clear also that all three had been radically over-impressed by the immediate impact of the sixties "counter culture", the New Left, and so on, so much so that they each misinterpret this very specific outcome of a very particular crisis of legitimation (occasioned as much as anything by the Vietnam War) as evidence of some long-run secular trend. The greater visibility, perhaps even near-dominance, of utilitarian and quasi-utilitarian thematics in the public culture of the eighties and nineties is anticipated neither by Gouldner nor by Bell nor by Habermas. The intellectual culture of the past decade and a half has in fact been such as to suggest even the possibility of a directly contrary long-run trend, by which intellectual radicalism has become progressively incorporated into and subservient to the driving imperatives of commodification and bureaucratization (each in themselves equally utilitarian trends). Be that as it may, there is nonetheless a considerable body of evidence, much of which has been re-presented and reproduced within cultural theory itself, attesting to the presence of at least certain recurrent anti-utilitarian structural pressures arising from within the traditional intelligentsia intermittently over the past two hundred years.

The possibility, however, of a disjuncture between the intellectual culture of the present and immediate past on the one hand, and that of the prior history of capitalism on the other, broaches the subject matter of the book's sixth and final chapter, that of the debate over *postmodernism* (a term which, as we have seen, Bell himself actually used). Where utilitarianism, culturalism, Marxism, structuralism and feminism each represent a distinctive type of cultural theory, each with its own characteristic core concepts – utility, culture, ideology, signification and patriarchy – postmodernism, by contrast, remains not so much a kind of theory as a particular question posed to each of the other kinds. The question, of course, is that of whether contemporary Western society has undergone a transformation in either its culture or its political economy so far-reaching as to mark the end of modernity as such, and the beginnings of something that might properly be deemed "postmodern". Particular though the question undoubtedly is, it nonetheless radically reproblematizes the whole of contemporary cultural theory, for each of these other theories is, as we have seen, a characteristically *modern* cultural construct. Utilitarianism and culturalism, Marxism and feminism, structuralism and perhaps even post-structuralism might well prove as irrelevant to a genuinely postmodern culture as have been Christian neo-Platonism and neo-Aristotelianism to modern culture itself. The book will conclude, then, with a discussion not of what cultural theory has been to date, but of what it might need to become for the future.

Chapter 2
CULTURALISM

The second of our six main kinds of cultural theory is that which I have chosen to describe by the term *culturalism*. This term is of only recent origin, and it is one which has typically been defined only by way of an antithesis between itself and structuralism. Moreover, it has often been accorded a quite distinctly Marxist inflection. Thus Richard Johnson, for example, sees the new discipline of cultural studies as founded upon a theoretical terrain demarcated between, on the one hand, a kind of Anglo-Marxist culturalism best represented by the work of the historian E. P. Thompson and the literary critic Raymond Williams, and on the other, that type of Francophone structuralist Marxism established by the philosopher, Louis Althusser.[1] Johnson's usage seems to me far too preoccupied with these comparatively recent culturalist and structuralist Marxisms, to the extent that it clearly underestimates the significance for each of their respective non-Marxist precursors. I propose, then, to use the term rather differently: to denote that type of anti-utilitarianism which became incorporated within a largely "literary" tradition of speculation about the relationship between culture and society, variants of which recur within both British and German intellectual life. In both German and British versions, the concept of culture is understood as incorporating a specifically "literary" sense of culture as "art" with an "anthropological" sense of culture as a "way of life". And in each case, the claims of culture are counterposed to those of material civilization. Hence Shelley's famous dictum that: "Poets are the unacknowledged legislators of the world".[2]

My main theoretical concerns here will be with British, rather than German, culturalism, if only because of its much greater influence over the largely British tradition of "contemporary cultural studies". The classic account of the historical evolution of this British culturalist tradition is still Raymond Williams's *Culture and Society 1780–1950*. The central motif in culturalist theory is that of a necessary antithesis between culture and utilitarian civilization. In *Culture and Society*, Williams traces the history of the concept, "culture", as it developed in British intellectual life from Edmund Burke (1729–97) to George Orwell (1903–50). During the nineteenth century, Williams argues, the concept increasingly emerged as "an abstraction and an absolute", merging two distinct responses: "first, the recognition of the practical separation of certain moral and intellectual activities from the driven impetus of the new kind of society; second, the emphasis of these activities, as a court of human appeal, to be set over the process of practical social judgement and yet to offer itself as a mitigating and rallying alternative".[3] The antithesis between culture and civilization, as also that between the authenticity of natural, lived "experience" and the mechanistic imperatives of industrialization, clearly attest to the pain and the trauma of the very first industrial revolution, that which occurred in Britain itself.

This is a tradition which, from Burke through to T. S. Eliot (1885–1965), clearly embraced, in one important register, a radically conservative reaction against capitalist modernity. But in another, and equally important register, it embraces also a radically progressive aspiration to go beyond that modernity: the obvious instances here include William Blake (1757–1827), Shelley (1792–1822), William Morris (1834–96), Orwell of course, but also Williams, whose intellectual career is properly intelligible only as a late continuation of this Anglo-culturalist tradition. Whatever the register, however, culturalism remains irretrievably adversarial in its relations both to capitalist industrialization and to utilitarian intellectual culture. This is a tradition which underpins much of English romantic poetry, but also much of what we often describe as the 19th century English realist novel. It is a tradition which, in the work of Matthew Arnold (1822–88), decisively opted for state sponsorship of education as the mechanism by which culture could be preserved and extended, and as the centre of resistance to the driving imperatives of an increasingly mechanical and materialist civilization. In the late 19th century, and even more so in the 20th, this culturalist discourse finally became institutionalized within the academic discipline we now know as "English".

Matthew Arnold

I do not intend to repeat here Williams's account of the culturalist tradition as a whole, which would be simply impertinent, but rather to concentrate on what seem to me four representative figures: Arnold, Eliot, the literary critic F. R. Leavis (1895–1978), and finally Williams himself. Matthew Arnold is indisputably one of the central figures in the culturalist tradition: professor of Poetry at Oxford, inspector of schools, and assistant commissioner on the Schools Inquiry Commission, he is, both theoretically and practically, perhaps the single most important 19th century progenitor of contemporary English studies. The key text for our purposes is almost certainly *Culture and Anarchy*, first published in 1869, in part by way of response to the extension of the franchise in the Reform Bill of 1867. Arnold's definitions of culture are various: it is sweetness and light, it is the best that has been thought and said, it is essentially disinterested, it is the study of perfection, it is internal to the human mind and general to the whole community, it is a harmony of all the powers that make for the beauty and worth of human nature. But, however defined, culture stands in opposition to mechanical civilization: "culture . . . has a very important function to fulfil for mankind. And this function is particularly important in our modern world, of which the whole civilization is . . . mechanical and external, and tends constantly to become more so".[4]

Culture is thus for Arnold a social force in opposition to material civilization, the equivalent, at the societal level, to his own individual rôle as inspector of schools. As such, it clearly requires embodiment in some social group or another. But, as is well known, Arnold firmly rejected the pretensions to the title of guarantor of culture of each of the three major social classes: the Barbarian aristocracy suffers from a "natural inaccessibility, as children of the established fact, to ideas'; the Philistine middle class is so preoccupied with external civilization that "not only do they not pursue sweetness and light, but . . . even prefer . . . that sort of machinery of business . . . which makes up [their] dismal and illiberal life'; and the working class Populace either aspires to follow the middle class, or is merely degraded, "raw and half-developed . . . half-hidden amidst its poverty and squalor".[5] No class, but rather the "remnant" of the cultured within each class – what today we might perhaps term "an intelligentsia" – sustains the continued development of human culture: "persons who are mainly led, not by their class spirit, but by a general *humane* spirit, by the love of human perfection".[6] This group is by no means necessarily fixed in size. Quite the contrary: it can be expanded through state-sponsored education.

For Arnold, the state becomes, in effect, the institutional corollary of the concept of culture. Hence the title of the book, in which culture is counterposed, not to material civilization, but to *anarchy*. If the preservation and extension of culture is a task which devolves essentially upon the state, then it must follow that any threat of "anarchy and disorder" will be directed as much at culture as at the state itself: "without order there can be no society, and without society there can be no human perfection".[7] And anarchy, Arnold is clear, emanates from the "working class . . . beginning to assert and put into practice an Englishman's right to do what he likes".[8] Arnold's defence of culture is conceived in organicist and anti-individualist terms suggestive of a rejection of middle class utilitarianism closely parallel, as we shall see, to those attempted by both classical sociology and classical Marxism. But the critique of utilitarian culture becomes displaced, through a similarly organicist and anti-individualist conception of the state, into a fear of anarchy, and a corresponding faith in the remnant, much more reminiscent of sociology, and especially of French sociological positivism, than it is of Marxism. The Arnoldian programme becomes, then, a programme of liberal, but not thereby individualist, social reform.

Williams argues that the key weakness in Arnold is his inability to explain how it is that the state might be influenced by the remnant, rather than by the classes, so as to make it possible for it to fulfil the cultural rôle allocated it. In short, Arnold can offer no institutional mechanism by which the remnant might be organized. Thus the case for the ideal state collapses into a defence of an actual state which is in reality far from ideal.[9] There is one obvious reply to this charge, though it is not one of which Arnold could have availed himself. It could be argued that Arnold's remnant is better understood as a social class in its own right, rather than as an aggregate "number of *aliens*",[10] and that it should therefore prove at least as capable of directing the state, at least in particular directions, as are the Barbarians, Philistines and Populace. Neither Arnold nor Williams contemplates this prospect. But had either done so, it might well have provided them with an explanation for the transparently, and increasingly, educative rôle of much of the business of the modern state. A problem remains, however: understood thus – that is, as an intellectual class – the remnant would in all probability be motivated, not by a general humane spirit, but by their own class spirit. Such a class spirit would, of course, prove unusually sympathetic, by comparison with those of the three main classes, to the business of intellectual work. But there is no reason at all to imagine it inspired by the love of human perfection. If Arnold's remnant has indeed proved able to direct state policy towards deliberately "cultural" goals, in exactly the way he envisaged, then this can have been so only because it possessed powers of organization and interest quite specific to itself as a class. And if the remnant is indeed as distinct a social class as this appears to suggest, then a *prima facie* case, at least, exists for the proposition that its motives are likely to be as ulterior as are those of any other major social group.

The rise of English studies

A recognizably Arnoldian discipline of "English" slowly began to emerge in the British Isles during the mid–late 19th century. The origins of English criticism can actually be traced back to the late 17th and early 18th centuries, and to the network of London clubs and coffee houses which sustained Defoe's *Review*, Steele's *Tatler*, and Addison's *Spectator* (founded, respectively, in 1704, 1709 and 1711). But this was very much a general "cultural" criticism, rather than a technical "literary" criticism and, whatever else it might have been, it was certainly not "academic': neither Oxford nor Cambridge taught "English" as a university subject. Following Habermas,[11] Terry Eagleton has argued that such cultural criticisms can be understood as characteristic of the developing liberal "public sphere": "A polite, informed public opinion pits itself against the arbitrary diktats of autocracy; within the translucent space of the public sphere it is supposedly no longer social power, privilege and tradition which confer upon individuals the title to speak and judge, but the degree to which they are constituted as discoursing subjects by sharing in a consensus of universal reason".[12]

This bourgeois public sphere was progressively undermined during the 19th century, Eagleton argues, firstly by the expansion of the literary market and the concomitant rise of an anonymous public, and secondly, by the eruption into the public sphere of social interests opposed to its rational norms, in particular the working class, radical-ism, feminism and religious dissent. Criticism was thus increasingly faced with the choice between, on the one hand, a general cultural humanism which necessarily became increasingly amateur as capital-ist society developed, and, on the other, an expert professionalism which could only achieve intellectual legitimacy at the price of social relevance. The eventual outcome was the institutionalization of criti-cism within the universities.[13]

English had been taught as a subject during the 18th century, but only in the dissenting academies and the Scottish universities (where it was intended to facilitate cultural incorporation into the Anglo-Scottish union). From the 1820s, however, University College Lon-don, and from mid-century the University of Manchester, began to offer similar such courses. And during the late 19th century, a prop-erly Arnoldian discipline began to evolve: chairs of English language and literature were established at Trinity College Dublin, and at the Universities of Glasgow, Edinburgh, Birmingham and Newcastle.[14] But Oxford and Cambridge remained stubbornly resistant. Chris Baldick has argued that the growth of English in higher education was determined by three main factors: the movement for working class education, the movement for women's education, and the mid-cen-tury reorganization of the Indian Civil Service. For both the labour-ing classes and the weaker sex English would provide a liberal edu-cation much less costly than that provided by classics, for the Empire it would provide the means by which the natives might be educated in a civilized culture.[15]

In 1906, Sir Henry Newbolt founded the English Association to promote the teaching of English; in 1917, an English paper was in-troduced into the public schools' common entrance examination. Of the two ancient universities, it was Oxford which first appointed a "lit-erary" professor of English, Sir Walter Raleigh, in 1904, but the sub-ject's future, in the face of determined hostility from both classicists and philologists, remained very uncertain. Cambridge appointed its first professor of English literature, A. W. Verrall, as late as 1911, but in general events proceeded rather more smoothly than at Oxford, and in 1917 an independent English school, with a distinctly literary bias, was finally established. It was the First World War which even-tually enabled English studies to liberate itself from the claims of a conveniently "Teutonic" philology: neither Raleigh nor Verrall's suc-

CORNWALL COLLEGE
LEARNING CENTRE

cessor at Cambridge, Sir Arthur Quiller-Couch, was slow to identify the potentially sinister implications of too enthusiastic an interest in German culture.

English Literature's contribution to post-war reconstruction, the 1921 Newbolt Report on the teaching of English, proposed to establish the study of English language and literature at the centre of a national education in national consciousness. The Newbolt Committee's vision of English Literature as the cement of national unity found enthusiastic echo at Cambridge (Quiller-Couch served as a member of the Committee), but never really gained favour at Oxford, where an older, pluralist, dilettantism held sway.[16] Thus it was Cambridge, rather than Oxford, which would witness both the "revolution in English studies", and the appearance of "Leavisism", a new literary-critical doctrine which would, in turn, decisively shape the character of the profession of English teaching in the years after the Second World War. English Literature had justified itself as a discipline not in terms of the particular class interests of the Arnoldian remnant, but rather the contribution that sweetness and light might make to the construction of a unitary Anglo-British national culture. It was thus inextricably connected to the development of modern English nationalism, and to that of its wider imperial extension, greater British imperial nationalism. In retrospect, it becomes difficult to avoid the speculation that many of those inspired both by Newbolt's Association and by his discipline must have eventually ended their lives in some corner of a foreign field that would be forever "English".

T. S. Eliot

If Arnold is the central 19th century figure in the development of the culturalist tradition, then the equivalent status for the period since the First World War, at least insofar as the general intellectual culture is concerned as distinct from the more specialist rituals of academic professionalism, is almost certainly that of the poet, T. S. Eliot. Eliot was born and brought up in the United States, and became English only by an act of conversion, which came to embrace not only British naturalization but also High Tory politics, High Anglican religion and High Royalist monarchism. A deeply learned man, his prose writings include an intellectually very serious attempt to fashion a specifically

Christian social theory: strongly influenced by Hegelian philosophy, Eliot was familiar with the work in the sociology of religion of Emile Durkheim, the famous French anthropologist, and would later collaborate, in "the Moot", with Karl Mannheim, the distinguished German-Hungarian sociologist.

For Eliot, as for Arnold, culture comes to be understood in essentially totalistic and organicist a fashion: thus, a specifically "literary" culture evolves, not as the creation of an aggregate of individual writers, but rather as that of "the mind of Europe . . . which abandons nothing *en route*".[17] Eliot's most celebrated discussion of the concept of culture, in his *Notes Towards the Definition of Culture* draws on Arnold's insistence on the connectedness of the literary and the non-literary, but expands upon it so as to develop a much more contemporary, anthropological, sense of the term. "By 'culture' ", Eliot writes, "I mean first of all . . . the way of life of a particular people living together in one place. That culture is made visible in their arts, in their social system, in their habits and customs, in their religion".[18] This last reference to religion is especially significant: for Eliot, the culture of a people is necessarily an "incarnation" of its religion. Hence, the gloomy prognosis, outlined at some length in *The Idea of a Christian Society*, that unlimited industrialization might generate a generalized detachment from tradition, and an alienation from religion, and thereby, in effect, the demise of culture.[19]

A culture, in Eliot's sense of the term, is only properly such insofar as it is shared in common by a whole people. But a common culture is not, however, one in which all participate equally: it will be consciously understood only by the cultural élites of the society, but can nonetheless be embodied in the unconscious texture of the everyday lives of the non-élite groups. The model here is a somewhat idealized understanding of medieval Christendom. In principle, Eliot's cultural élite can be much more happily reconciled to the dominant class than could Arnold's remnant to either the Barbarians or the Philistines: "An élite must . . . be attached to *some* class . . . it is likely to be the dominant class that attracts this élite to itself".[20] In principle, culture is not a minority resource to be disseminated through education, but is rather already (more or less consciously) present in the lives of all classes, including both the aristocracy and the bourgeoisie. But if this is so for a "healthy" society, such as Eliot imagined medieval Europe to have been, then it is much less so for the increasingly non-Christian society conjured into being largely as an effect of industrialization.

Like Arnold, Eliot remains deeply critical of modern, mechanical civilization; but unlike Arnold, he actually proceeds to the development of a theory of cultural decline. In a much quoted essay on "The Metaphysical Poets", Eliot compared the early 17th century English poets, Chapman, Donne and Lord Herbert of Cherbury, with the poets of the 19th century, such as Tennyson and Browning. He argues that in the Metaphysicals, and by implication in all previous poetry, there had existed what he terms a "unified sensibility", in which thought and feeling retained an essential unity. During the 17th century, however, and especially in the work of Milton and Dryden, a "dissociation of sensibility" set in from which English culture has never recovered. "The difference is not a simple difference of degree between poets", he writes, "It is something which had happened to the mind of England".[21] Elsewhere, Eliot stresses that this dissociation of sensibility had been "a consequence of the same causes which brought about the Civil War".[22] Their eventual outcome will be capitalist industrialization itself, which will in turn press the logics of dissociation towards their own terrible terminus: "more insidious than any censorship", Eliot argues, "is the steady influence which operates silently in any mass society organized for profit, for the depression of standards of art and culture".[23] For all the obvious theoretical affinities between Eliot and Arnold – an organicist conception of culture, the central antithesis between culture and civilization – such pessimism as this remains quite fundamentally incompatible with Arnold's own reforming zeal. For Eliot's insistence on the priority of religion over culture leaves him much more positively sympathetic to the feudal past, and correspondingly much more fearful of an unlimitedly industrialized future. Eliot's Anglo-Catholicism thus precludes the possibility of a meliorist strategy such as had been readily available to Arnold.

There is an important sense in which Eliot's social theory becomes simply inoperable: if the good society is one modelled as closely as possible on those of the European Middle Ages, then in truth the good society is no longer attainable. For, whatever the deleterious social and cultural consequences of the rise of capitalism (and there can be little doubt that Eliot is here often very acute), industrialization itself appears an essentially irreversible process, at least for so long as the human race continues to abstain from the use of its nuclear weaponry.

Deindustrialization may very well be occurring, and in ways which may very well foreshadow the development of a properly post-industrial society. But any such society will be of necessity post-capitalist, rather than pre-capitalist, in form. That it might bear any resemblance at all to medieval feudalism seems, to say the least, highly improbable. Stripped of its peculiar Christian medievalism, and rendered compatible, if not with secularism, then at least with Nonconformist Protestantism, Eliot's social theory might easily have proved much less pessimistic in its general import. It is precisely such a transformation in the culturalist paradigm, requiring a partial rehabilitation, at least, of Arnold's earlier reformism, that we find in the work of Dr Leavis of Cambridge.

F. R. Leavis

Leavis was perhaps the best known of all Eliot's academic champions during the interwar period. The journal *Scrutiny*, and the group around it — Leavis himself, his wife Q. D. Leavis, Denys Thompson, L. C. Knights — forged an elaborate literary-critical doctrine, in many respects indebted to Eliot, but much less specifically Christian, and quite definitely more Protestant than Catholic, which would eventually provide the central rationale for the profession of English teaching. For the moment, however, let us confine our attentions to the immediately theoretical content of the Leavisite programme. Leavis and the Leavisites inherited from Eliot a number of their characteristic themes, especially a clearly organicist conception of culture, and a correspondingly pessimistic understanding of recent historical process as cultural decline. But, during the 1930s, "the Marxizing decade",[24] as Leavis recalled it, these became synthesized with a developing critique of communist Marxism, then enjoying an unusual, and entirely temporary, influence over Anglophone literary-critical circles.

In some important respects, Leavis's "practical criticism" played a similar rôle, in emphasizing the importance of the text as against the remorseless contextualism of much Marxist criticism, to that of the New Criticism of John Crowe Ransom in the United States. But Leavis shared little of Ransom's hostility to historical explanation *per se*. And precisely because he did share in Eliot's fundamentally holistic, semi-Hegelian notion of culture, and perhaps, too, because he recognized the strength of part, at least, of the Marxist case against individualism, Leavis's thought came to take on a distinctly "sociological" cast. Leavis's socio-historical preoccupations led him, further, to a quite deliberately this-worldly strategy for cultural renovation, much more reminiscent of Marxism at its most intellectually militant than of Eliot's pained withdrawal from the world.

Leavis's own organicism is at its most apparent in his sense of literature itself "as essentially something more than an accumulation of separate works: it has an organic form, or constitutes an organic order in relation to which the individual writer has his [sic] significance".[25] The centre of Leavis's intellectual effort consists in an attempt to map out the tradition of the English novel on the one hand, the tradition of English poetry on the other, each imagined in exactly such organicist terms, and imagined, moreover, as bearing important moral truths – in particular, as bearers of the value of "life", by which Leavis means, in short, non-determined, spontaneous creativity.[26] For Leavis, as for Eliot, literary and non-literary culture are thus inextricably connected: in a healthy culture, there is "behind the literature, a social culture and an art of living".[27] And for Leavis, again as for Eliot, such cultural health must entail some kind of unity of sophisticated and popular cultures. But nonetheless Leavis privileges élite culture, or "minority culture" to use his own phrase, much more so than did Eliot. The essential value of a common culture for Leavis devolves upon its capacity to sustain a culturally superior minority: "In their keeping . . . is the language, the changing idiom, upon which fine living depends, and without which distinction of spirit is thwarted and incoherent. By 'culture' I mean the use of such a language".[28]

This stress on language is distinctively Leavisite: it explains the peculiar significance for Leavis of *literary* culture (the equivalent rôle in Eliot is very obviously that played by religion); and also the power of his insistence on the need for a close reading of literary texts. It is in the language itself, in its most literary moments of articulation, that the truths of life are most clearly formed. Such a view runs directly contrary to that characteristically structuralist view of the linguistic sign as radically arbitrary, to which we shall turn in Chapter 4. The contemporary intellectual climate allows little credence today to those, such as Leavis, who have sought to establish non-contingent patterns of relationship between the linguistic sign and its non-linguistic referent. Structuralism typically dismisses even onomatopoeia as a matter

of entirely arbitrary, linguistic convention. It is thus fashionably easy
to scoff at Leavis's preference in poetry for words which "seem to do
what they say".[29] But if language is not entirely arbitrary, if there is
indeed a substantial reality beyond "the prison house of language",[30]
then a Leavisite linguistics might well appear rather less inherently im-
plausible than it so obviously does at present. The ultimate alternative to some version or another of linguistic referentiality is that kind
of theoretical vertigo which linguistic scepticism occasions amongst
much of the French and American literary intelligentsia. We shall
return to this matter in the chapters that follow.

Like Eliot, Leavis also subscribed to a theory of cultural decline.
In his version, however, the problem arises quite specifically as a result of industrialization, and not, therefore, as a result of whatever it
was that caused the Civil War (a set of causes which must include the
Protestant Reformation). Pre-industrial England constitutes for Leavis
the exemplar of an "organic community", and it is only in communities such as this that a cultural unity between the sophisticated and
the popular remains possible. But industrialization, and the techniques
of mass production that unavoidably accompany it, together generate a "technologico-Benthamite" civilization, the defining characteristics of which are cultural levelling and standardization. Hence the
remarkably bleak conclusion to *New Bearings in English Poetry*: "the finer
values are ceasing to be a matter of even conventional concern for any
except the minority . . . Elsewhere below, a process of standardization, mass production and levelling down goes forward . . . So that
poetry, in the future, if there is poetry, seems likely to matter even less
in the world".[31]

Such pessimism very obviously echoes that of Eliot, though the
weight accorded to material factors is, perhaps, more reminiscent of
1930s Marxism. And yet Leavis remains a distinctly Protestant thinker,
neither an Anglo-Catholic content to mourn the passing of the Middle Ages, nor a fatalistic Marxist content to await the arrival of the
socialist utopia. Thus Leavis: "enormously . . . as material conditions
count, there is a certain measure of spiritual autonomy in human af-
fairs . . . human intelligence, choice and will do really and effectively
operate".[32] It is through the discipline of English, through the University English School, and through the English teachers that it will
train, that such intelligence, choice and will are eventually to become
operative. And so Leavis recovers for the culturalist tradition both the

general cultural evangelism and the more specifically pedagogical strategic orientation first broached by Arnold.

As with Arnold and Eliot, so too with Leavis, a common culture, that of the pre-industrial organic community, and its continuing echo in the legacy of the English language, are pitted against modern industrial civilization, in both its capitalist and its communist forms.[33] Here, though, there can be no compromise with the existing class structure, such as Eliot was clearly prepared on occasion to countenance. Rather, the literary intelligentsia was to be mobilized around *Scrutiny*, and against the developing mass society. In itself, this almost certainly represents a much more plausible programme of action than any in either Arnold or Eliot. But nonetheless, *Scrutiny* no longer exists; and even Cambridge itself never adopted Leavis's proposal for a model English school. What Leavis recognized, in a way that Arnold could not, was the capacity for collective self-organization latent within the intellectual class. He failed, however, to confront its obvious likely corollary: that the intelligentsia as a whole – the cultured minority, and not simply Bloomsbury and the *Times Literary Supplement*, both of which Leavis detested – might prove as incapable of Arnoldian "disinterestedness" as is the establishment itself. In that failure is surely to be found the source of much of the bitterness and rancour which so soured Leavis's later years.

Leavisism as a professional ideology

It was Leavisism, and the peculiar claims advanced by the Leavisites on behalf of the discipline of English, which provided Perry Anderson with one of the keys to his extremely influential reading of the structure of the English national intellectual culture. His argument is by now an old one, but nonetheless one which warrants repetition. Britain alone of the major European countries, he observed, produced neither a classical sociology nor an indigenous national Marxism. The intellectual culture thus constituted lacked any "totalizing" conceptual system, and remained indelibly marked by this absence at its very centre. Anderson adds, however, that in anthropology, the study of *other* societies, and above all in literary criticism, such totalizing thought did develop: "in a culture which everywhere repressed the notion of totality, and the idea of critical reason, literary criticism represented a refuge".[34] Indeed it did, though we need to stress the full extent to which it was Cambridge rather than Oxford English which came to provide that refuge. "It was not by chance", Anderson writes, "that the most significant work of socialist theory of the fifties, Raymond Williams's *Long Revolution*, should have emerged out of literary criticism".[35] From Cambridge literary criticism, one should surely add.

Anderson's analysis has been importantly supplemented by Francis Mulhern's *The Moment of "Scrutiny"*. Let me draw attention, in particular, to Mulhern's characterization of Leavisism as: "a quintessentially *petit bourgeois* revolt, directed against a cultural order that it could not fundamentally alter or replace . . . It was, accordingly, a *moralistic* revolt from within the given culture: bearer not of an alternative order but of the insistence that the existing order should live by its word".[36] Leavisism's ultimate fate, its simultaneous success and failure during the 1950s, arose precisely from this "petit bourgeois" character. In the years immediately following the 1944 Education Act, the existing order did finally begin to live by its word. Thus, Mulhern argues, the very success of *Scrutiny's* cultural project increasingly rendered obsolete its organised intellectual militancy, so that subsequent English criticism became dominated by a kind of tame "Leavisism", a Leavisism increasingly shorn both of the intellectual combativity and of the interdisciplinary competence that had characterized *Scrutiny* itself. The hegemony of this tame Leavisism remained effectively unchallenged until the late 1960s and the 1970s, when the emergence of various structuralisms finally precipitated, in England as elsewhere, a "crisis in English studies".

English criticism had its origins in the liberal public sphere of the late 17th and early 18th centuries; the disintegration of that public sphere resulted, in the late 19th century and, more importantly, in the 20th century, in the institutionalization of a new academic criticism within the university; Leavisism, the guilty conscience of this academicism, represents, as Eagleton says, "nothing less than an attempt to reinvent the classical public sphere, at a time when its material conditions had definitively passed".[37] The impossibility of any such project explains not only the obsessive, almost paranoid, quality of much of Leavis's own writing, but also both Leavisism's gradual decline into an increasingly inoffensive aestheticism, and its ultimate demise in the face of later structuralisms as guiltless in their academicism as they were self-consciously "guilty" in their choice of reading strategies.

For our current purpose, however, that of developing an understanding of Leavisism's powerful professional appeal to the discipline of English, let us call attention to four especially salient features of the Leavisite system: its organicist aesthetic, its historicism, its radicalism and its nationalism. Consider each in turn. Leavis's aesthetic, which sought to derive the organic properties of "great" literature from the organicism of human social life itself, enabled a relatively precise definition and demarcation of the subject's intellectual and institutional boundaries. English literature, E. A. Freeman had argued in 1887, could not become an examination subject because all such "chatter about Shelley" is essentially a matter of personal taste.[38] But if criteria of literary value can be found to which students and teachers can, or at least should, subscribe, and which have greater validity than other criteria available to the untrained reader, then students can indeed be examined for their ability to "discriminate" and "criticize". This, then, was Leavisism's central achievement: to ground an examinable pedagogy on an aesthetic which sharply distinguished between literature, which is valuable, and fiction, which is not.

It was Leavis's own peculiar apocalyptic historicism, which had sought to characterize the previous three hundred years of English history in terms of the process of disintegration and decline consequent upon industrialization, that came to provide the profession of English with its very particular sense of moral purpose and intellectual mission. If "creative intelligence and corrective purpose"[39] can indeed reverse the cultural logic of industrialization, as Leavis envisaged, then English literature can be transformed into a vital resource in the struggle to free the minds of the young from the pernicious influence of both popular fiction and commercial advertising. Thus the discipline emerges, perhaps in unconscious echo of the Hegelian *Geist* (Spirit), as simultaneously both knowledge of and solution to the historical trauma of industrialization.

Leavis's historicism actually led to a rejection of the immediately cognate discipline of history (and also of sociology) as inadequately concerned with problems of value. Hence his characteristically militant, characteristically radical, understanding of the special nature of English studies. Of course, Leavisism was never unambiguously radical in the conventional sense of being on the political "left". But if Leavis's culturalism, or for that matter Eliot's, is a conservatism, then it is a conservatism of a very different kind to those now common in

British politics. British Conservatism, in the party political sense of the term, is merely another variant of utilitarianism, of what Leavis himself contemptuously described as "technologico-Benthamism".[40] And Eliot and Leavis were not, in this sense, conservatives at all, but rather reactionaries, in revolt against precisely that capitalist civilization which contemporary Conservatism so tenaciously defends. Thus inspired, English literature became not simply one intellectual discipline amongst others, but rather a rallying point for the defence of humane values, "a centre of consciousness (and conscience) for our civilization".[41] Leavisite English aspired, then, in Mulhern's phrase, to create "an intellectual formation of a type virtually unknown in and deeply alien to English bourgeois culture: an 'intelligentsia' in the classic sense of the term, a body of intellectuals dissociated from every established social interest".[42]

For all its distinctly unEnglish intellectual sectarianism, Leavisism also came to embody a particular form of English nationalism. As Perry Anderson observed, "prejudice and bafflement were predictable products" of Leavis's disorientation in the face of foreign literature.[43] This Leavisite nationalism is evident, for example, in the peculiar centrality attached to the notion of a national literary canon. It is evident too in Leavis's own peculiar theory of language, with its improbable affirmation of the non-arbitrary nature of the (English) sign. For Leavis, as we have seen, English is a language, unlike either Latin or Greek, in which "words seem to do what they say'; hence, the famous dismissal of Milton's Latinized English as exhibiting a "feeling *for* words rather than a capacity for feeling *through* words".[44] The result is a nationalistic preoccupation with the superior virtues, if not of the contemporary English, then of their peasant ancestors and of the language bequeathed them by those ancestors. In England, at least, such nationalism continued powerfully to underwrite the emotional and intellectual appeal of Leavisite English. As Martin Green would insist, Leavis remained "intensely and integrally British. Not Europeanized, not of the intelligentsia, not of the upper classes, not of Bloomsbury . . . Alone in all Cambridge his voice has echoes of the best things in my parents' England".[45]

Left culturalism

Such essentially conservative "Britishness" had much less appeal, however, to those of a more radical political persuasion. Distanced from Leavisite English by its seemingly endemic political conservatism and cultural élitism, the more independently-minded left-wing British intellectuals of the 1950s began to forge their own "third way", between Leavisism on the one hand and Marxian socialism on the other, both in practical politics and in cultural theory. The politics eventually became that of the "New Left"; the theory what would be represented in structuralist retrospect as "culturalism", but is surely much more accurately described as "left culturalism". As a political movement the early New Left was to prove fairly short-lived. Its more permanent achievement, however, was the establishment in 1960 of the *New Left Review*, almost certainly the central journal of radical thought in Britain. The founding theoretical moment of left culturalism can be located fairly precisely in the early writings of three "key" figures: E. P. Thompson (1924–1993), Richard Hoggart and Raymond Williams (1921–1988). The first issue of the *New Left Review* included a discussion between Williams and Hoggart on the theme of working class culture;[46] and both Thompson and Williams served on the journal's editorial board.

Something of what would become "left culturalism" had first been explored in Thompson's *William Morris*,[47] a deeply appreciative study of a writer hitherto marginal to the canonical wisdoms of both left and right. If Thompson here reclaimed Morris for socialism, then he simultaneously discovered in Morris much of the strength of the earlier Romantic critique of utilitarianism. Thompson's best-known work, *The Making of the English Working Class*, would later quite explicitly compare working-class resistance to utilitarianism with the tradition of Romantic anti-utilitarianism. The "heroic culture" of the early English working class, Thompson argued, had "nourished, for fifty years, and with incomparable fortitude, the Liberty Tree".[48] "After William Blake," he concludes, "no mind was at home in both cultures, nor had the genius to interpret the two traditions to each other. In the failure of the two traditions to come to a point of junction, something was lost. How much we cannot be sure, for we are among the losers".[49]

Less directly political in intent, Hoggart's *The Uses of Literacy* nonetheless marks the point at which post-Leavisite culturalism decisively shifted emphasis away from "literature" and towards "culture". Hoggart combined an ethnographic account of Yorkshire working-class culture with a Leavisite practical criticism of mass media texts. His central theme was that of the damage done to the older, inter-war working-class culture by the newer mass arts, newspapers, books, magazines, and so on: "The old forms of class culture are in danger of being replaced by a poorer kind of classless . . . culture . . . and this is to be regretted".[50] Much like Leavis, Hoggart was in effect arguing a theory of cultural decline. But for Hoggart it was working-class culture, rather than that of the "sensitive minority", which needed to be valorized, if only so as, in turn, to be elegized. Hoggart's achievement was thus to divest Leavisism of much of its cultural élitism, if not perhaps of its nostalgia, Thompson's to divest British socialism of its Marxian economic determinism, and to make explicit what had previously only ever been an implicit, and barely acknowledged, Romanticism.

Whatever their respective achievements, the full analytical range of this left culturalism would only become apparent in the work of Raymond Williams. Williams had been a student of Leavis at Cambridge and would himself eventually become professor of drama at the same university. I have already observed that Williams's work can most profitably be examined as part of the Anglo-culturalist tradition. Much available commentary on Williams chooses to regard him rather differently, however, that is very much as a Marxist writer. There can be no doubt that, in the 1970s, Williams did indeed effect some sort of an accommodation between his own left culturalism and a neo-Gramscian version of Western Marxism: he coined the term "cultural materialism" to describe the resultant synthesis. But this is a relatively late development in his career, and one, moreover, which still needs to be situated in relation to the more conventionally culturalist writings of the 1950s and 1960s. This is not to suggest that even the early work of Williams remains in any sense unaffected by Marxism. Quite the contrary: it is best understood, it seems to me, in terms of a doubly ambivalent relationship, to Leavisism on the one hand, and to orthodox communist Marxism on the other, a relationship which entailed a simultaneous partial acceptance and rejection of each. From *Scrutiny*, Williams inherited Leavis's organicism – his stress on the importance both of the text and of "life", and on the importance of culture itself – but rejected its cultural élitism. From communist Marxism, he accepted a powerfully socialistic critique of the political and economic establishment, but rejected the economic determinism of the so-called base/superstructure model with which communists had attempted to explain cultural phenomena. We shall have occasion to explore some, at least, of the detail of Communist cultural theory in the chapter that follows. But for now let us consider Williams's own position in some little detail itself.

Williams's originality in relation to the culturalist tradition, as he had encountered it in the work of Eliot and Leavis, is to effect a dramatic reversal of socio-cultural evaluation, such that a distinctly working-class cultural achievement comes to be valorized positively rather than negatively. Doubtless, this reversal has its deepest roots in the facts of Williams's own biography: a Welshman of Welsh descent, his father was a railwayman, a trade unionist and a supporter of the Labour Party. But its theoretical consequences are at their most apparent, first, in Williams's further expansion of Eliot's anthropological conception of culture, and second, in his substitution of a theory of (actual and potential) cultural progress for that of cultural decline.

Quite centrally, Williams insists that "culture is ordinary", and, more famously: "a culture is not only a body of intellectual and imaginative work; it is also and essentially a whole way of life".[51] In principle this is little different from Eliot. But in the practical application of that principle, Williams so expands its range as to include within "culture" the "collective democratic institution", by which he means, primarily, the trade union, the co-operative, and the working class political party.[52] Thus redefined, the notion of a single common culture becomes supplemented, and importantly qualified, by that of a plurality of class cultures: "The basis of a distinction between bourgeois and working-class culture . . . is to be sought in the whole way of life . . . The crucial distinction is between alternative ideas of the nature of social relationships".[53] For Williams, the antithesis of middle-class individualism is no longer the minority culture of the intelligentsia, but rather proletarian solidarity. If the common culture is not yet properly common, then, it follows also that the literary tradition must be seen not so much as the unfolding of a group mind, but as the outcome, in part at least, of a set of interested selections made necessarily in the present: "selection will be governed by many kinds of special interest, including class interests . . . The traditional culture of a society will always tend to correspond to its *contemporary* system of interests and values".[54]

Despite such qualification, the ideal of a common culture remains of quite fundamental importance to Williams. A common culture may not yet properly exist, but it is nonetheless desirable, and moreover, it provides for Williams, as for Eliot and Leavis, the essential theoretical ground from which to mount an organicist critique of utilitarian individualism. A common culture, Williams argues, could never be truly established on the basis of that kind of vicarious participation which Eliot had all too readily sanctioned: "The distinction of a culture in common is that . . . selection is freely and commonly made and remade. The tending is a common process, based on common decision".[55] In a characteristically radical move, Williams thus relocates the common culture from the historical past to the not too distant future. And insofar as any of the elements of such a culture can indeed be found in the present, then they occur primarily within the culture of the working class itself: "In its definition of the common interest as true self-interest, in its finding of individual verification primarily in the community, the idea of solidarity is potentially the real basis of society".[56] Where Eliot and Leavis diagnosed cultural decline, Williams, by contrast, discerns a "long revolution" leading towards, rather than away from, the eventual realization of a presumably socialistic, common culture.

There is, however, an important second sense in which Williams makes use of the concept of a common culture. For, even as he insisted on the importance of class cultures, Williams was careful also to note the extent to which such distinctions of class are complicated, especially in the field of intellectual and imaginative work, by "the common elements resting on a common language".[57] For Williams, any direct reduction of art to class, such as is canvassed in certain "leftist" versions of Marxism, remains entirely unacceptable. In studying literature, and other cultural artefacts, Williams develops the key concept of "structure of feeling". "In one sense", he writes, "this structure of feeling is the culture of a period: it is the particular living result of all the elements in the general organization".[58] He continues: "in this respect . . . the arts of a period . . . are of major importance . . . here . . . the actual living sense, the deep community that makes the communication possible, is naturally drawn upon".[59] So, for example, the English novel from Dickens to Lawrence becomes, for Williams, one medium amongst many by which people seek to master and absorb new experience, through the articulation of a structure of feeling, the key problem of which is that of the "knowable community".[60]

Such deep community must, of course, transcend class; and yet it remains irredeemably marked by class. For the early – culturalist – Raymond Williams this remained a circle which stubbornly refused to be squared. Only in the later encounter with western Marxism did it finally become possible for him to explain, to his own satisfaction at least, how it is that structures of feeling can be common to different classes, and yet nonetheless represent the interests of some particular class. We shall return to this matter in the next chapter. For the present, let us simply note the way in which the working class, and with it socialism, perform a functionally equivalent rôle for Williams to that of Leavis's English School and Arnold's remnant, as a social force capable of effective resistance to utilitarian civilization. In Williams's work, as in that of Morris or Orwell, we are confronted by a determined effort to remould the Anglo-culturalist tradition so as to render it compatible with the politics of socialism. But in general the socialist movement has preferred to derive its theoretical resources from much more orthodoxly Marxist quarters. It is to Marxism, then, and initially to the work of Marx himself, that we will proceed in Chapter 3. But let us add two further observations to this account of the development of Anglo-culturalism: first, we need to recall the quite decisive contribution of such left culturalisms to the development of British cultural studies; second, we should note the deep complicity between culturalism and yet another "ism", that of nationalism.

Left culturalism and British cultural studies

Excluded from "English" by Leavisism, "the popular" became the subject matter of the new proto-discipline of "cultural studies" largely at the instigation of Williams and Hoggart themselves. In 1962, Hoggart was appointed Professor of Modern English Literature at Birmingham University. Two years later he became Director of the new Centre for Contemporary Cultural Studies. For Hoggart, Williams's "interesting work" was to be one source of intellectual inspiration for the Centre.[61] Williams reciprocated, judging this "an excellent pioneering example"[62] of institutional innovation. Moreover, Williams's own work sketched out much of the subject matter of the new discipline. In two books on the media, *Communications* and *Television: Technology and Cultural Form*,[63] he was able to develop a critique of existing mass media institutions and texts that avoided the disabling cultural élitism of Leavisite criticism. Both books sought to identify the institutional forms that could sustain a properly democratic communications system. Thus the new televisual technologies were, in Williams's opinion, "the contemporary tools of the long revolution towards an educated and participatory democracy".[64]

When Hoggart left Birmingham in 1968, he was succeeded by Stuart Hall, then still very much under the influence of the left culturalist argument. Hall established a house journal for the Centre, *Working Papers in Cultural Studies*, and later a joint publishing venture with Hutchinson. Though both Hall himself and the Centre generally were to prove increasingly susceptible to structuralist and later post-structuralist developments in cultural theory, the culturalist position remained nonetheless more or less in play. This is particularly evident in the Centre's work on youth subcultures, where an ethnographic focus inspired by *The Uses of Literacy* is combined with an emphasis on generation and class deriving in part from Williams, so as to produce accounts of subcultural resistance to the dominant culture.[65] Though some of this work has been essentially structuralist and post-structuralist in theoretical inspiration,[66] strongly culturalist themes remain present, for example, in the work of Paul Willis.[67] Indeed, Willis's more recent work can be read as a determined celebration of the empirical as against the theoretical, agency as against structure, "common culture" as against élite culture.[68] Elsewhere, an equally developed culturalism persists into the work, for example, of the sociologist, Jeremy Seabrook.[69]

Nationalism and culture

From Herder onward, German culturalism has displayed a recurrent disposition to connect cultural specificity and uniqueness with the native language, and with notions of nationality or race.[70] In Hegel's *Philosophy of History*, it is, characteristically, the nation that is the medium through which the World Spirit is consciously realised.[71] For the Anglo-culturalists also the ideal organic community had more often than not been imagined as that of the nation. This is clearly so for Eliot and Leavis. Hence the manner in which the Leavisites constructed English studies as an almost quintessentially nationalist discourse. Less clear, and perhaps thereby all the more suggestive of the depth of this complicity, is Williams's own later sympathy, not so much for British, still less for English, but for Welsh nationalism. If radicalisms have typically forsworn allegiance to politically dominant cultural nationalism, preferring rather to lay stress on cultural difference both within and from the dominant nation, then they have nonetheless proved much less reluctant to endorse such subordinate nationalisms as the Welsh or Scottish.

Nationalism, we should note, is not so much an effect of nationality as its cause. As the social philosopher, Ernest Gellner, observed: "Nationalism is not the awakening of nations to self consciousness: it invents nations where they do not exist".[72] Nations are thus not so much matters of natural "fact" as forms of collective imagining. That there is some deep connection between the developing social rôle of the modern intelligentsia and the creation of such imaginings has become something of a commonplace. If it is now no longer fashionable to hold German idealist philosophy entirely responsible for the subsequent history of nationalism, as Elie Kedourie once argued,[73] then this is so only because attention has shifted, in Gellner's own work and in that of Tom Nairn for example,[74] away from formal, philosophical systems of thought and toward the needs and aspirations of intelligentsias, understood as particular, historically specific, social groupings.

Benedict Anderson's *Imagined Communities* considerably advanced this line of argument through its focus on the specific nexus connecting intellectuals to the printing industries. A nation, wrote Anderson, "is an imagined political community . . . imagined as both inherently limited and sovereign".[75] Nations are imagined in a very particular way, moreover, that is, as passing through an homogeneous empty time in which simultaneity is indicated only by temporal coincidence in terms of clock and calendar. This is a distinctly modern type of imagination, Anderson observes, the technical preconditions for which are provided by the novel and the newspaper. Print capitalism has thus been central to the rise of nationalism: the capitalist publishing industry, driven by a restless search for markets, assembled the multiplicity of pre-modern vernaculars into a much smaller number of print communities each of which prefigured a modern nation.

Anderson himself identified four main waves of nationalism: first, early American nationalism in which language *per se* was irrelevant, but in which printer-journalists, producing self-consciously "provincial" as opposed to "metropolitan" newspapers, powerfully shaped the development of national consciousness; secondly, European popular nationalisms centred on middle-class reading coalitions, which mobilized the popular masses in opposition to the polyvernacular dynastic state; thirdly, the official nationalism of those polyvernacular dynasties that sought, through "Russification" or "Anglicization", to impose a nationalism from above; and lastly, those anti-imperialist nationalisms in which an intelligentsia educated within the confines of the colonial educational system came to imagine and later constitute the colony itself as a nation.[76]

Insofar as the former Soviet Union and the continuing United Kingdom can each be construed as successors to the 19th century polyvernacular dynastic state, then Ukrainian and Welsh nationalisms can be understood as contemporary variants of 19th century European popular nationalism. The more obviously communitarian and solidaristic aspects of such radical nationalisms sit fairly comfortably with equivalently communitarian and solidaristic elements in left culturalist theory. As Raymond Williams himself told a 1977 Plaid Cymru summer school, a "truly prospective", as distinct from "merely retrospective", radical nationalist politics might produce "the kind of complex liberation which genuine community . . . could be".[77] Williams knew, of course, that the building of nation-states had been "intrinsically a ruling-class operation";[78] he knew too that, as late as the 1930s, Welsh nationalism had been "on the cultural Right . . . Wales was offered . . . as the last noble fragment of a classical and catholic world".[79] His own Welshness, however, was of a very different kind, democratic and emancipatory, self-declaredly that of a "Welsh European". Whatever its emancipatory intent, however, radical nationalism seems open to two fundamental objections: first, that in a world becoming increasingly internationalized and culturally cosmopolitan it still articulates a by now demonstrably "retrospective", rather than "prospective", structure of feeling; and secondly, that it threatens to repress cultural identities other than its own. The latter charge becomes particularly telling, moreover, when linked to feminist critiques of solidarism: Welsh community was sustained, after all, both in reality and very often also as a normative ideal, by an obvi-

ously patriarchal sexual division of labour. But a parallel argument
might well be mounted on either socialist or "multicultural" grounds.

The first of these two objections bears very directly on the subject
matter of those recent debates over "postmodernism" to which we will
turn in Chapter 6. To anticipate the argument a little, we need only
note here that many commentators have attributed a peculiarly
transnational character both to socio-economic postmodernity and
to cultural postmodernism. Such transnational cultural forms can be
represented as in some ways peculiarly American and, no doubt, this
internationalization has been massively facilitated by the brief American imperium that endured for much of the second half of the twentieth century. But the resultant politico-economic and cultural con-
figurations are no longer in any meaningful sense specifically American. Wherever the origins of science fiction and jazz, rock and the
Hollywood movie, these have become internationally available cultural forms, part of the common cultural heritage of the species.
Postmodernity thus threatens to reduced to redundancy all cultural
nationalisms, including the American. We already read Latin American novels and watch Italian soccer onTV; we already live in a world
in which Welsh people will happily queue to watch a Scottish actor
perform in an American movie based on the bestselling novel by an
Italian semiotician. The problem for cultural theory and for cultural
studies is to render this actually existing transnational postmodernity
comprehensible, and thereby hopefully changeable. Neither traditional English studies nor radical nationalist cultural criticism seem
fully appropriate to the task.

Williams's own later work did in fact engage with arguments of this
kind. His *Towards 2000*, for example, displayed a very strong sense of
the internationalization of the contemporary world order. To the "official community" of nation-states such as "the Yookay", he sought to
counterpose an internationalism that would nonetheless be compatible with the "lived and formed identities" of the "minority peoples",
not only the Welsh, but also the Scots, Irish and West Indian, and even
the English "regions".[80] The particularities of the Welsh and the com-
plexities of a "paranational" world system thus became simultaneously
more pressing than the peculiarities of a Britain understood as English, an England understood as "the South", and a South understood
as its ruling and intermediate classes. For Williams, then, cultural
internationalization threatens to subvert the false totalities of the ex-

isting nation-state rather than the subnationalisms of more local proto-communities. No doubt, he has a point: insofar as the cultural boundaries of Greater British nationalism have indeed been prised open, then the Yookay has increasingly been exposed to the foreignness within as well as to that without, to Wales as well as to California.

But the second objection remains. If Wales were to become an independent nation-state, limited and sovereign, then what would there be to prevent its nationalism from becoming any the less presumptuously exclusionary than those of other nation-states? In any already independent nation-state in peacetime the nationalist political imagination is normally directed not against possible external enemies, but against various internal enemies, and in particular against those non-national imaginations which most threaten to subvert the seamless web of national unity. There might well be a necessary and unavoidable conflict, then, between a nationalist imagination centred on the category of nation and, for example, a feminist imagination centred on that of gender; between nationalism and the kinds of socialist imagination centred on class; between nationalism and the "multicultural" imaginings of non-national or sub-national ethnic groups.

The latter case is especially complicated, given that the not-yet independent nation is easily imaginable as itself a subordinate ethnicity. There is a certain confusion in Williams's own position here. While Wales, Scotland and Ireland are in fact already imagined as nations and as would-be nation-states, and although even the English regions are in principle imaginable as such, the West Indian community in Britain, by contrast, remains simply unimaginable as a nation-state, though not, of course, as part of a wider non-British nation. Though the Welsh or the Quebecois might well still choose between nationalism and multiculturalism, only the latter remains at all available to the Afro-Carribean and Bengali communities in Britain or to the Greek and Italian communities in Canada or Australia. For these last, multiculturalism seems likely to remain radically incompatible with any but the most tentative of cultural nationalisms.

Meaghan Morris, the Australian feminist cultural critic, has argued that cultural nationalisms and especially those which have a "strong indigenous-Maoist streak . . . seem to impose a discourse on identity – not just national or cultural identity . . . but also the call for a programme in which speakers identify themselves, take a position in a struggle".[81] Morris's remarks seem pertinent not only to Australian radical nationalism, but to all culturalisms. It is possible, however, to construe this peculiar "solidarity effect", as I will term it, much more positively than did Morris, at least insofar as the solidarity thus invoked is indeed emancipatory in its practical political and cultural implications. And this has very often been the case for those solidarities by which subordinated communities of class, gender, race or ethnicity have sought to organize their collective lives. Solidarity, community and culture need not always prove bogus; they might very well render social life meaningful, creative and, indeed, genuinely co-operative. The imagined community of the nation-state remains a very special case, however, precisely because it seems unimaginable except as superordinate to and sovereign over all other imaginable communities: the nation-state is not simply a community, but also a state, and states are by definition sovereign.

Arguing in defence of Irish cultural nationalism, Terry Eagleton has borrowed from Williams an analogy between class and nation[82] that points to the need to go, not so much around nationality as "all the way through it and out the other side". "To wish class or nation away, to seek to live sheer irreducible difference*now*", Eagleton continues, "is to play straight into the hands of the oppressor".[83] In this specific instance of a people constituted as Irish and Catholic by centuries of Anglo-Scottish and Protestant oppression, and of a state still not yet fully independent, a nation imaginable and imagined as whole but not yet so, it becomes difficult to dissent from Eagleton's judgement. The whole process of nation-state building is here so obviously already under way, and yet so obviously already stalled, as to make of nationality an almost unavoidable politico-cultural referent. Much the same could be said of Palestine. But in fully sovereign "post-colonial" states such as Australia or Canada, the practical import of such cultural nationalisms already appears both much less radical and much less unavoidable. And even if the Irish or the Palestinians are indeed doomed to go through nationalism and out the other side, then this surely need not mean that all imaginable nations must follow suit. Given the presence of a sufficiently persuasive and materially interested local intelligentsia, almost any geographically defined social group can be imagined as a nation, and any nation as a nation-state. The practical political and cultural questions then become immediately concrete: what real emancipatory potential would it yield were the peoples of Yorkshire or Lancashire, for example, to begin to imagine themselves in ways analogous to those of Serbia or Croatia? Very little, one cannot help but feel: the invariable consequence of "going through" nationality has been not its supersession but rather its installation into a position of monopolistic cultural privilege, typically the central site and source of a more or less conservative cultural hegemony.

The left culturalist challenge to literary studies has been consistently overshadowed in recent years and, as it were, out-radicalized by new theoretical perspectives associated, in turn, with Western Marxism, second wave feminism, structuralism and post-structuralism. Moreover, each of these has very often affected a certain self-conscious theoretical cosmopolitanism, essentially both anti-empirical and anti-nationalist in character. It is to these other intellectual radicalisms that we turn in the chapters that follow. But this is not to suggest that the theoretical and practical questions typically posed by culturalisms of the left and of the right were somehow either resolved or transcended. Quite the contrary. The matters at issue in these older debates over community and culture, class and nation, have repeatedly returned to haunt both literary and cultural studies. The pretensions to theoretical and practical adequacy variously advanced for Marxism and feminism, structuralism and post-structuralism, will thus be adjudicated, in part at least, precisely by the decision as to how well they each propose new answers these older culturalist questions.

Chapter 3
MARXISM

Marxism as an intellectual tradition owes more to the work of a single thinker, Karl Marx (1818–83), and more also to a mass political movement, the international socialist movement, than does either utilitarianism or culturalism. The socialist movement has its origins in early 19th century Europe, in particular in England and France. It took as its central project the abolition of capitalist private property, and its supersession by some form or another of social ownership. Developing alongside the infant labour movement, it gave voice to working-class anger at the newly developing system of industrial capitalism.

Marx himself was neither English nor French nor working class, but rather a German radical intellectual trained in Hegelian philosophy. In Chapter 2 we were concerned mainly with the development of British culturalism. But at this point we do need to remind ourselves of the presence of a similarly culturalist tradition within German thought. In Germany, however, culturalism led in significantly different directions from those mapped out in Britain. In the work of the philosopher G. W. F. Hegel (1770–1831), a powerful synthesis was effected between culturalist romanticism and the rationalism of the 18th century French Enlightenment (which had derived its individualism, in part, from British utilitarianism). For Hegel, an appreciation of the cultural specificity of each age could be subsumed within a wider understanding of historical development as possessing an overall rationality and direction. As we have already had occasion to remark, Hegelian philosophy exercised some real fascination for Eliot. But in Germany itself, Hegel's "historicism" opened up the intellectual space from within which there emerged: much of the modern discipline of history; Marx's own Marxism, or "historical materialism", as he termed it; and finally, that set of responses to Marx, both positive and negative, which provided the founding moment and much of the continuing momentum behind German sociology.

Political repression drove Marx himself into exile, at first to Paris and then to London, where he would live for most of his adult life. A committed socialist excluded from the academic career to which he had originally aspired, he sought to fashion a self-consciously progressive social theory that would be of political value to the working-class movement. His own academic training nonetheless profoundly affected the shape of this theory. What emerged was a synthesis between Hegelian philosophy and British utilitarian political economy, which combined a culturalist sense of the antithesis between culture and utilitarian capitalist civilization with a utilitarian sense of the importance of material interest, and incorporated each into an overall Hegelian understanding of history as process. Marx is thus led to a dual stress, first on the logics of capitalist development, and second on the notion of ideology, by which he seeks to denote the nexus between belief and interest. Both themes become central not only to Marx's own Marxism but also to that of the international socialist movement in the late 19th and early 20th centuries, and later to that of the international communist movement.

In Germany itself, Marxian socialism attained to a much greater political and intellectual influence than in Britain: the major socialist party, the SPD, which grew to become the largest German political party in the years before the First World War, had formally adopted a version of Marxism as its official social theory. Socialist intellectuals such as Karl Kautsky (1854–1938), Eduard Bernstein (1850–1932) and Rosa Luxemburg (1871–1919) were employed by the party itself, and were thus able to achieve public prominence in German intellectual life from outside the university. This very visible presence of Marxist ideas in late 19th and early 20th century Germany came to command the attention of many liberal academics working within the universities. Classical German sociology was born out of this academic engagement with the legacy of Marx: as Albert Salomon famously observed, Max Weber, the German "bourgeois Marx", became a sociologist "in a long and intense debate with the ghost of Marx"! This debate, in turn, decisively shaped the entire subsequent history of German sociology; and also of what is often termed "western Marxism", a phrase coined originally by the French philosopher, Maurice Merleau-Ponty, to describe that tradition of critical Marxism which developed in Western Europe, and especially in Germany itself, in more or less deliberate opposition to official, Soviet, "scientific" Marxism.[2]

Classical Marxism

It is, of course, quite impossible to do anything like justice to a theoretical legacy as rich and as complex as this in the short space available to us here. What does remain possible, however, is a relatively
schematic account of what I take to be adequately representative instances of the major kinds of Marxian, and quasi-Marxian, cultural
theory. Our obvious starting point must needs be the work of Marx
himself, and also that of his close friend and collaborator, Frederick
Engels (1820–95). We might begin by noting that Marx was a near
contemporary of Matthew Arnold, and that many of the categories
of his political economy, in particular, were derived from, but also
counterposed against, that same English utilitarian tradition which
Arnold had rejected in the name of culture. It should come as little
surprise, then, to discover in Marx one element, at least, that runs
closely parallel to Arnold: the notion of an antithesis between cultural
value on the one hand, and modern capitalist civilization on the other.

This antithesis is present, above all, in Marx's theory of alienation.
It is in the *Economic and Philosophical Manuscripts* of 1844 that Marx first
explores this notion. He does so by way of a conceptual dichotomy
between actually existing alienated labour, in which labour power is
transformed into a commodity and the worker reduced to a mere
thing, and an ideal of non-alienated labour incorporated in the notion of "species-being".[3] By the latter term Marx means, quite simply, the humanness of humanity, constituted, above all in his view, by
our capacity for conscious, collective, creative production: human
beings alone of all the animal species are by nature social, conscious
and creative, he insists.[4] Interestingly, Marx's attempts to concretize
this notion of unalienated labour almost invariably involve instances
drawn from art and intellectual culture. Thus Marx: "Animals produce only according to the standards and needs of the species to which
they belong, while man is capable of producing according to the standards of every species . . . hence man also produces in accordance with
the laws of beauty".[5]

It is, moreover, one of the central features of capitalist civilization,
according to Marx, that all such labour should become progressively
commodified, and hence alienated. "The bourgeoisie has stripped of
its halo every occupation hitherto honoured and looked up to with
reverent awe", he writes: "It has converted the physician, the lawyer,

the priest, the poet, the man [*sic*] of science, into its paid wage-labourers".[6] In volume I of what is widely regarded as Marx's masterpiece, *Capital*, we find a further development of this understanding of alienation in the concept of "commodity fetishism", a perhaps unfortunate term by which he chose to refer to that process by which human relations come to take on the appearance in a market economy of relations between things (that is, between commodities). Capitalist culture is thus a fetishized culture in which "a definite social relation between men [*sic*] . . . assumes, in their eyes, the fantastic form of a relation between things".[7]

For Marx, modern civilization is one founded essentially on commodified, alienated labour, as distinct from that kind of free, unalienated labour which finds only occasional expression in residually uncommodifiable instances of intellectual work. Thus the culturalist antithesis between culture and civilization becomes transposed into that between culture as unalienated labour and capitalist civilization as commodification. Furthermore, for Marx, as for Arnold, this fetishized culture "tends constantly to become more so". The crucial difference between them, however, consists in Marx's stress on production as distinct from Arnold's on cultural consumption. And it is precisely this difference that propels Marx away from any possible pedagogical solution to the cultural crises of capitalism – for any such solution can only ever aspire to a reform of the habits of consumption (or "taste") – and towards the alternative of a revolutionary transformation in the system of production itself.

The single most important idea in Marx, insofar as cultural theory has been concerned, is nonetheless not that of alienation but rather that of ideology, an entirely original notion (though not in itself an original term) with no counterpart in Arnold, designed so as to express the inner connectedness of culture and economy (or class). In its most general form, Marx's theory of ideology maintains simply that: "Life is not determined by consciousness, but consciousness by life".[8] But this gives way, by turn, to two much more specific theses: firstly, that the ideas of the ruling class are the ruling ideas; and secondly, the famous, perhaps even notorious, base/superstructure model. The first thesis is that argued in *The German Ideology* itself: "The ideas of the ruling class are in every epoch the ruling ideas: i.e. the class which is the ruling *material* force of society, is at the same time its ruling *intellectual* force".[9] Culturally dominant ideas thus become, for Marx, the ideal expression of the dominant material relations, produced in the interests of the ruling class, and by that class's own specialist ideologists. Though the ruling ideas may be dominant, they are not thereby uncontested. Rather, rival classes produce rival ideas in the struggle for social leadership, and historically these become increasingly more abstract and universal in form: "For each new class . . . is compelled . . . to represent its interest as the common interest of all the members of society . . . it has to give its ideas the form of universality, and represent them as the only rational, universally valid ones".[10] Like the class struggle itself, this struggle for intellectual and cultural mastery will come to an end only in the future classless society to be ushered into being by the proletarian revolution.

The base/superstructure model, by contrast, appears initially in the 1859 "Preface" to *A Contribution to the Critique of Political Economy*. So succinct is Marx's own formulation that it is as well to quote it at length: "The totality of . . . relations of production constitutes the economic structure of society, the real foundation, on which arises a legal and political superstructure and to which correspond definite forms of social consciousness. The mode of production of material life conditions the general process of social, political and intellectual life".[11] Marx adds, in an important qualification, that a distinction should always be made "between the material transformation of the economic conditions of production, which can be determined with the precision of natural science, and the legal, political, religious, artistic or philosophic – in short, ideological forms in which men [*sic*] become conscious of this conflict and fight it out".[12]

There is no necessary incompatibility between the two arguments. Neither directly denies the sense of an antithesis between cultural creativity as a positive value and the commodity fetishism of capitalist civilization. But both insist that culture is also always ideology, that is, that it is conditioned by material reality. The first, it is true, lays much greater stress on the significance of class, as distinct from that of economy. But this is partly a matter of semantics: the "relations of production" referred to in the 1859 "Preface" are, for Marx, invariably relations of class. The second, it is true, makes use of a peculiar analogy with construction (foundation/superstructure), and combines this with a powerfully evocative reference to the precision of natural science, so as to suggest a process of mechanical causation, where the economy is the cause and culture the effect. But much of that suggestion is nonetheless denied both by the carefully qualifying verbs – rises/corre-spond/conditions, but *not* causes, nor even determines, in the sense of causation as distinct from that of cognition – and by the clear implica-tion that cultural transformation, unlike material transformation, *can-not* be determined (that is, known) with the precision of natural science.

But if there is no necessary incompatibility in the sense of the two theses themselves, there certainly has been an incompatibility between the rival systems of subsequent interpretation which have attached to each. In general, "scientific" Marxisms such as those of both the pre-1914 socialist movement and the post-1917 communist movement, tended to opt for a version of the base/superstructure model that drifts towards a theory of mechanical causation; and "critical" Marxisms, whether German, Italian or French, for a version of the ruling ideas thesis which theorizes the relation between economy and culture in terms of the category of totality, rather than that of cause/effect. The difference can be described as that between models of, respectively, mechanical and expressive causality.[13] We will turn to examine each of these instances in the history of Marxism very shortly.

But first let us raise one last question about Marx's Marxism, that of its own epistemological status, as either science or ideology. There is no doubt that Marx imagined his work to be in some significant sense scientific.[14] On the other hand, he understood it also as politi-cal, as a form through which the socialist movement would become conscious of itself in the class struggle. As such it is a superstructure, and presumably, therefore, subject to those self-same processes of material conditioning that operate on all other superstructures, proc-esses which might well be interpreted as denying to Marxism any extra-social objectivity such as is often implied by the term science. In short, Marxism's pretensions to scientificity might run contrary to its claims to political efficacy. For Marx himself this does not appear to have been a problem. Subsequent Marxisms have found it much less easy, however, to reconcile the two notions. Marxism has often appeared in the guise of an objective science, dispensed normally by a proletarian, or supposedly proletarian, political party; sometimes as proletarian consciousness, or ideology, whether that of party or un-ion; and sometimes as the critical consciousness of oppositional intel-lectuals. But the sense of Marxism as science and that as ideology have rarely been combined so effectively, and so apparently unproblematic-ally, as in Marx.

Second and Third International Marxism

To proceed from Marx's own Marxism to the scientific Marxism of the Socialist and Communist Internationals, is to proceed to a normally strongly determinist version of the base/superstructure model. The key instances here are those provided by, respectively, Georgei Plekhanov (1856–1918) and A. A. Zhdanov (1896–1948). Plekhanov's *Art and Social Life*, first published in 1912, is perhaps the single best known example of the type of cultural theory which emanated from the pre-1914 international socialist movement. Its authorship in Russian, rather than in German, the more influential language within the movement as a whole, also secured the relatively easy incorporation of many of its themes into later communist Marxism. It is, then, a peculiarly significant text. For Plekhanov, culture is the outcome of an interaction between biology and material history.[15] But insofar as art in particular is concerned, as distinct from culture in general, Plekhanov conceives this material history as operating in a very peculiar way. In effect, Plekhanov comes to think of artistic form as a kind of superstructure, and artistic content as its material base: "the value of a work of art is determined, in the last analysis by its content".[16] Content can be imagined thus only because it becomes equated with the realistic representation of material history, where the term realism denotes not simply a set of literary conventions designed so as to create the illusion of an accurate depiction of some extra-textual reality, but rather a genuinely accurate depiction of a genuinely extra-textual reality. Such accuracy provides the measure of literary value: "when a work distorts reality, it is a failure".[17]

This valorization of "realism" echoes Engels (though not, I think, Marx). But what in Engels is mere personal preference here emerges as a realist aesthetic, in which bourgeois "modernism" (cubism, for example) is judged decadent.[18] This analogy between base/superstructure and content/form is, of course, bizarrely contrived, since by any reasonable definition both form and content are quite obviously equally superstructural. Moreover, whether we accept the analogy or not, any deterministic formulation of the base/superstructure thesis must necessarily preclude the need for a prescriptive aesthetic. If the base *does* indeed determine the superstructure, then the insistence that it *should* do so remains clearly redundant. And, in any case, the very notion of art as a mode of cognition, significantly analogous to scientific knowledge, remains radically untenable: the most realistic of novels are nonetheless fiction, not history, their realism a matter of literary convention, not cognitive adequacy.

Whatever its transparent theoretical demerits, Plekhanov's embryo aesthetic at least possessed neither legislative intent nor power. Once elevated to the level of official Soviet government policy, the theory of socialist realism, or Zhdanovism as it became known, was possessed of each. At the 1934 Soviet Writers' Congress, Zhdanov, then Secretary to the Central Committee of the Communist Party of the Soviet Union, had announced that, of all the world's literatures only the Soviet could have become "so rich in ideas, so advanced and revolutionary". It had become so, he insisted, because its authors "correctly and truthfully depict the life of our Soviet country".[19] Elsewhere, by contrast, "bourgeois literature . . . is no longer able to create great works of art . . . Characteristic of the decadence and decay of bourgeois culture are the orgies of mysticism and superstition, the passion for pornography".[20] For Zhdanov, as for Plekhanov, literary modernism is thus essentially a form of cultural decadence. For Zhdanov, as not for Plekhanov, the legislative means were available for the suppression of all such decadence, both from the Soviet Union itself and from the ranks of the foreign Communist Parties.

There is an important sense in which these theories of realism represent the reassertion within Marxism of a type of utilitarianism that had only ever lain dormant in Marx's own work. The connection between culture and interest, from which Marx had forged the concept of ideology, is, in fact, partly reminiscent of Bentham. For Marx, this connection is a hidden secret, to be exposed and demystified. It was that, too, for socialists and communists, in their struggles against bourgeois ideology. But in their advocacy of socialist realism, a much more properly Benthamite conception of a desirable and desired connection between value and utility is observable. It is this connection which explains not only the genuine appeal to socialist and communist militants of literary and artistic realism, but also the much more ulterior motivation of Zhdanovism proper.

That Western radicalisms, whether socialist, communist or, more recently, feminist, should have on occasion come enthusiastically to endorse the techniques of literary realism is in itself neither surprising nor suspicious. To require of their own writers that their art be of some directly political use, by virtue of its potential to expose the injustices either of capitalism or of patriarchy, is simply to insist on the political possibilities of political art. That working-class radicalism should often have been accompanied by an antipathy towards high modernist art forms is similarly unsurprising: there is a wealth of available empirical, sociological evidence to suggest that popular aesthetic taste is "based on the affirmation of continuity between art and life" and "a deep-rooted demand for participation",[21] neither of which are especially compatible with highly formalist types of literary or artistic experimentation. What is surprising is that such preferences should have ever become codified into a prescriptive aesthetic which sought to deny not only the political, but also the artistic, legitimacy of alternative cultural strategies. This development occurred only as a result of the intervention into the international communist movement of the Soviet government, and bespoke the power of that government's own more sinister intentions and aspirations.

What the Soviet authorities demanded, and imperatively so, was also an art that would be of directly political use. But it was to be of use to the new post-revolutionary ruling class, to be supportive rather than subversive, conservative rather than radical. The hint is there in Zhdanov himself: "Comrade Stalin has called our writers engineers of human souls. What does this mean? . . . it means knowing life so as to be able to depict it truthfully . . . not . . . in a dead, scholastic way, not simply as 'objective reality', but to depict reality in its revolutionary development . . . the truthfulness and historical concreteness of the artistic portrayal should be combined with the ideological remoulding and education of the toiling people".[22] Where Western socialist realisms sought to expose the inequities of Western capitalism, Soviet socialist realism found itself commanded to disguise those of Soviet-style state capitalism.

For so long as it existed, the international communist movement yoked together a collection of Western working-class political parties on the one hand, a group of modernising state capitalist dictatorships on the other. In cultural theory, as in almost all else, this improbable alliance was secured only at the price of a systematic linguistic ambiguity that bordered on duplicity. Western and Eastern communisms spoke the same language, and meant almost entirely different things.[23] No doubt Trotsky was right to describe Soviet socialist realism thus: "The official art of the Soviet Union – and there is no other over there – resembles totalitarian justice, that is to say, it is based on lies and deceit".[24] The same cannot be said of Western socialist realist writers such as Upton Sinclair, Frank Hardy or, for that matter, Raymond Williams.[25]

British communist Marxism

During the 1930s, almost exactly contemporaneously with the early development of the *Scrutiny* group, communist Marxism came to exercise a considerable albeit temporary influence over significant sections of the British literary intelligentsia. Key figures here included: C. Day Lewis, W. H. Auden, Stephen Spender, Christopher Caudwell, Edward Upward, Ralph Fox and Alick West. Communist Marxism had inherited the base/superstructure formula from Marx and a strong preference for literary "realism" from Engels. To these, it had added an immediate diagnosis of contemporary capitalist society as crisis-ridden and of contemporary bourgeois culture as decadent. And, in the more specific case of British communism, all of this was compounded by a quasi-Romantic sense of the social mission of the creative writer. For socialist intellectuals, the communist experience came to represent a deeply ambiguous legacy. On the one hand, the normally authoritarian doctrines and disciplines of the Party were frequently directed at those questions of cultural policy that most concerned the radical intelligentsia itself. On the other, the depth and extent of Party organization permitted the creation of a whole series of alternative cultural institutions capable of sustaining an often very vital oppositional culture.

In Britain, as elsewhere, the Communist Party subscribed to a series of more or less Zhdanovite variants of the theory of socialist realism. Christopher Caudwell was by far the most influential of the British communist cultural theorists. His *Illusion and Reality* was first published in 1937, only a few months after he had been killed in action with the International Brigade during the Spanish Civil War. For Caudwell, as for communist Marxism generally, the literary superstructures remained essentially an effect of the developing material base. "What is the basis of literary art?", he wrote, "What is the inner contradiction which produces its own onward movement? Evidently it can only be a special form of the contradiction which produces the whole movement of society".[26] Literature is thus essentially a by-product of economic activity: "Poetry is clotted social history, the emotional sweat of man's struggle with Nature".[27] Perhaps the book's most striking feature is its attempt at a general historical sociology of literature, defining different kinds of poetry as the "expression" of one or another stage in the development of the mode of production. Cultural modernity was thus "the superstructure of the bourgeois revolution in production", and modern poetry notoriously "*capitalist* poetry".[28]

Like Plekhanov, Caudwell thought of culture as having an essentially adaptive function: "The poem adapts the heart to a new purpose, without changing the eternal desires of men's hearts".[29] In Caudwell's view, these eternal desires are fixed by the human "genotype", that is, "the more or less common set of instincts in each man".[30] And for Caudwell, as for Plekhanov, a socio-functional explanation for the existence of art leads easily to a valorization of realist cultural forms. Art, he wrote, "remoulds external reality nearer to the likeness of the genotype's instincts . . . Art becomes more socially and biologically valuable and greater art the more that remoulding is comprehensive and true to the nature of reality".[31] During the "epoch of imperialism", which in Caudwell's view had then only recently come to an end, such bourgeois modernisms as surrealism had attempted "entirely to separate the world of art from that of society".[32] The result had been "the pathos of art . . . torn by insoluble conflicts and perplexed by all kinds of unreal phantasies".[33] Hence, the concluding address to the bourgeois artist, made unselfconsciously in the name of "the conscious proletariat": "You must choose between class art which is unconscious of its causality and is therefore to that extent false and unfree, and proletarian art which is becoming conscious of its causality and will therefore emerge as the truly free art of communism".[34]

Doubtless, there is much in Caudwell that is idiosyncratic, indeed original: his psychologism for instance. But both the general structure of communist Marxism and the more specifically Romantic, as distinct from utilitarian, conception of the rôle of the militant artist-intellectual recur throughout the British communist cultural criticism of the 1930s. Alick West, for example, could move readily from the quasi-sociological proposition that the "source of value in the work of literature is . . . social energy and activity"[35] to the quasi-Romantic prescription that "the criticism of our lives, by the test of whether we are helping to forward the most creative movement in our society, is the only effective foundation of the criticism of literature".[36] A similarly sociological moment informs Ralph Fox's understanding of art as a "means by which man grapples with and assimilates reality";[37] a similarly Romantic moment his later call to arms: "we must strain our inventive and creative faculties to the utmost . . . let us go into the fight together encouraged by the thought that the fate of our language and the struggles to develop it, have . . . always been . . . closely bound up with the struggles of our country for national salvation".[38]

In each case, determinist sociology and Romantic polemic are held in dynamic tension only by a near-apocalyptic understanding of the supposed "general crisis of capitalism", in many respects startlingly reminiscent of Leavis's own. For it was the very urgency of the perceived crisis, the same urgency that compelled both Caudwell and Fox to volunteer for Spain, that conjured up the peculiar necessity of this voluntarism. But when Western capitalism settled into its long post-war boom, all of this began to seem hopelessly antiquated. As Raymond Williams was to recall of his own brief association with British communism: "It may have seemed a natural response [to Leavisism] to retort that the point was not how to read a poem, but how to write one that meant something in the socio-political crisis of the time. But when the productive mood which was our way of re-plying by not replying faded away after the War, and we had to engage in literary criticism or history proper, we found we were left with nothing".[39] As cultural theory, socialist realism remains radically inadequate: predicated on a fundamental epistemological confusion between fiction and history, it led to a type of cultural criticism that was often both authoritarian and philistine. Much more readily defensible, however, was the communist insistence, first, that the political effects of art are perfectly proper matters of concern for the politically motivated artist; and secondly, that realistic literary technique might very well have a distinctly subversive such effect, by virtue precisely of its capacity to expose to public view previously hidden aspects of contemporary social reality.

German sociology

Western Marxism very obviously developed by way of reaction against communist Marxism. But it derived much of its initial theoretical inspiration, at least, from an earlier encounter between German classical sociology and Second (that is, Socialist) International Marxism. The founding text of the Western Marxist tradition is widely agreed to be Georg Lukács's *History and Class Consciousness*, first published in 1923, a work clearly indebted to its author's own one-time mentor, Max Weber (1864–1920). Before we proceed to an account of Western Marxism, a brief detour through German sociology therefore becomes necessary. Weber himself is undoubtedly the key figure in the development of German sociology. A direct contemporary of Kautsky, his work was informed by a very immediate response to Second International Marxism. It is common in the anglophone literature to link Weber together with Emile Durkheim as the "founding fathers" of sociology, and to contrast the classical sociology thereby constructed with the classical Marxism of Marx and Engels. In my view, this exaggerates the affinities between Weber and Durkheim, and also overlooks the extent to which Marx and Weber can both be situated within a specifically German tradition of debate about culture and society. Weber's stress on the causal efficacy of culture, it seems to me, is better seen as an important corrective to an over-emphasis on material factors in SPD Marxism than as embodying any outright rejection of Marx's Marxism *per se*. This is certainly the position which Weber himself took in 1905: "it is, of course, not my aim to substitute for a one-sided materialistic an equally one-sided spiritualistic causal interpretation of culture and of history".[40]

Western Marxism would learn three things from Weber: that ideas matter a great deal more than Kautsky and Plekhanov had imagined, and significantly more than had Marx; that the capitalist system remains subject to a developmental logic of rationalization; and that social order depends substantially on political legitimacy. The first such lesson is asserted most effectively in *The Protestant Ethic and the Spirit of Capitalism*. Weber clearly accepted, and indeed became fascinated by, the type of correlation between social stratification and cultural belief that Marx had analysed in terms of ideology. Between Marx (or, at least, Engels) and Weber there is no real disagreement as to the correlation between Calvinism and capitalism. What Weber insists on, however, is the view that Protestant beliefs played an active, energising, rôle in the social process by which capitalism came into being. Thus *The Protestant Ethic* is designed to demonstrate the extent to which "religious forces have taken part in the qualitative formation and the quantitative expansion"[41] of the spirit of capitalism.

The rationalization thesis is central to Weber's account both of modernity and of modernization: capitalism is above all a system of rational economic calculation; bureaucracy is the distinctly modern form of rational organization; Protestantism is a system of religious belief peculiarly conducive to a radical rationalization of individual ethical conduct; and even occidental music and its system of notation is distinctively and characteristically rationalized.[42] In some respects this notion runs parallel to Marx's theory of alienation, and especially so in its negative moment, as in the characterization of modernity as an iron cage of reason.[43] It is sometimes suggested that Weber's rationalization thesis implies a much more benign vision of capitalism than that in Marx. I doubt that this is so, for Weber feared the negative moment in rationalization, just as Marx had acknowledged the positive in capitalism.

Paradoxically, the fundamental difference between Marx and Weber is, as Giddens recognizes, over whether history itself has a rationality: Marx, following Hegel, though that it had; Weber, following Kant, that it had not.[44] Thus Weber's position might very well be described, in Gouldner's phrase, as a "nightmare Marxism",[45] a Marxism with pessimism substituted for optimism. Hence Weber's suspicion that socialism, far from providing a solution to the problems of bureaucratization, might only exacerbate them.[46] This understanding of the modern world as an iron cage of disenchantment, we should note, is yet another instance of the culturalist antithesis between culture and civilization, or, to use Weber's own terms, between *Wertrationalität* and *Zweckrationalität*.[47]

Weber's theory of legitimation is only one especially important particular instance of his general stress on the social effectivity of belief. Despite the recognition, in *The German Ideology*, of the significance of ruling ideas, both Marx himself and most immediately subsequent Marxists had tended to explain social order, insofar as it could be said to exist at all, as a consequence either of the mode of production or of the state. Weber, by contrast, stressed legitimate authority, that is, a type of imperative control based on the acceptance by subordinates of the right of superordinates to give orders.[48] Weber sketches out an ideal typology of three main kinds of legitimation, but by far the most significant for modernity is the rational/legal type, which rests "on a belief in the 'legality' of patterns of normative rules and the right of those elevated to authority under such rules to issue commands".[49] In effect, this is little more than a restatement of the "ruling ideas" version of Marx's theory of ideology, but with the extremely important qualification that such ideas are conceived not simply as ruling, but as ruling effectively. Insofar as legitimate authority does exist, it is uncontested. Moreover, there is for Weber no necessary succession of different types of class rule, and hence of ruling ideas, as there had been for Marx. In principle, at least, a legitimate authority might last indefinitely.

Western Marxism

To proceed, finally, to Western Marxism proper, let us begin by noting the quite remarkable extent to which culture itself has provided this sub-variant of the Marxist tradition with its central preoccupation. As Perry Anderson observes: "Western Marxism as a whole . . . came to concentrate overwhelmingly on study of *superstructures* . . . It was culture that held the central focus of its attention".[50] Western Marxism is an intellectual tradition the characteristic thematics of which have been human agency, subjective consciousness, and hence also culture. This is true of Georg Lukács (1885–1917), the Hungarian born but German speaking and German educated philosopher; of his Franco-Rumanian disciple, the sociologist of literature, Lucien Goldmann (1913–70); and of Lukács's heirs in the Budapest School, notably Agnes Heller and Ferenc Fehér. It is true of each of the major members and associates of the Frankfurt School, Theodor Adorno (1903–69), Max Horkheimer (1895–1973), Walter Benjamin (1892–1940), Herbert Marcuse (1898–1979), and, more recently, Jürgen Habermas. It is true also of the French existential Marxist, Jean-Paul Sartre (1905–80), and of the Italian revolutionary leader, Antonio Gramsci (1891–1937). Even the structural Marxism of the French philosopher, Louis Althusser (1918–90), and the school inspired by him, takes ideology as its central focus, though without the connotations of agency or consciousness elsewhere associated with it.

At its point of origin in the early 1920s, in the earlier work of Lukács, in Karl Korsch (1886–1961), and in the young Gramsci, this stress on agency and consciousness served so as to underwrite a leftist rejection of the political fatalism implicit in Second International economic determinism, in favour of the immediate possibilities of revolution. As Gramsci observed of the Bolshevik Revolution of 1917, it was a revolution against *Capital*.[51] But as that moment of revolutionary optimism failed, as Lukács came to terms with Stalinism, as Gramsci struggled to produce the *Prison Notebooks* in an Italian fascist prison, as the Frankfurt School retreated into an increasingly academic exile from politics, and thence to the literal exile of escape to the United States, then so the emphasis shifted towards an analysis of the system-supportive nature of cultural legitimations.

Where scientific socialism had theorized the relationships between culture and society in terms of the base/superstructure model, critical Western Marxism, by contrast, sought to understand both base and superstructure as particular moments within a contradictory totality. Thus, for Lukács, the revolutionary principle in Marx, as in Hegel, is that of the dialectic, "the concept of totality, the subordination of every part to the whole unity of history and thought".[52] For the Lukács of *History and Class Consciousness*, this notion of totality provides the positive pole against which is developed the central, critical concept of reification. Here Lukács expands upon the discussion of commodity fetishism in *Capital*, reading it in the light both of Hegel, and of Weber's rationalization thesis (but not that of the as yet still unpublished *Economic and Philosophical Manuscripts*), so as to develop what is, in effect, a version of the theory of alienation.[53] By reification Lukács means the process by which human relations come to be understood as relations between things, an important instance of which is, of course, commodity fetishism. But Lukács generalizes the notion so as to insist that capitalism is itself a system of reification. Human reality is thus necessarily detotalized under capitalism, both by commodity fetishism and by the various reified forms of consciousness, the most important of which is, in fact, science.[54]

For the young Lukács, such reified thought could be overcome only by the proletariat's coming to consciousness of itself as the identical subject and object of history.[55] There can be little doubt that, in the early 1920s, Lukács had viewed the prospects for such a development as fairly imminent: the "imputed" class consciousness[56] embodied in Marxism was to become actualized in the empirical consciousness of a working class organised and led by the revolutionary Communist Party. But, as Lukács recoiled from both Nazism and Stalinism, this revolutionary optimism gave way to an increasing reliance on the realist novel as the principal totalizing instance in our culture.[57]

Lukács's later socialist realist writings are complicit, both politically and theoretically, with Zhdanovism. Yet there is evidence to suggest that he arrived at a theory of realism both independently of, and prior to, the Comintern. And Lukács's position is never simply Zhdanovite: for him the model for socialist realism is provided by the great bourgeois realists, Tolstoy, Balzac, and Thomas Mann, not Zhdanov's "revolutionary romantic" propaganda.[58] Hence the political audacity with which Lukács was to nominate Solzhenitsyn as of central significance to contemporary socialist realism.[59] But hence, too, the vigour with which Lukács prosecuted his own case against literary modernism: "modernism leads not only to the destruction of traditional literary forms", he wrote, "it leads to the destruction of literature as such".[60]

History and Class Consciousness exercised a considerable fascination for the Frankfurt School (as it did also for Karl Mannheim). From Lukács the School inherited a stress on the notion of totality, a rejection of both science and scientific socialism as partial and detotalizing, and a sense of the truth value of theory as related to its social rôle, initially as theoretical companion to the working class, always as in itself emancipatory. They inherited also Lukács's quasi-Weberian notion of reification. For Adorno and Horkheimer, capitalism is a fully rationalized system of domination, a system whose inherent logic tends towards fascism. Fascism is thus a culmination of the dehumanized and positivistic, science and society unleashed by the Enlightenment: "Enlightenment behaves toward things as a dictator toward men [*sic*]. He knows them in so far as he can manipulate them".[61] The mass media − the culture industry, as they termed it − became central targets for this critique. Art involves a necessary confrontation with already established traditional styles, they argue, "inferior" work the practice of mere imitation: "In the culture industry . . . imitation finally becomes absolute. Having ceased to be anything but style, it reveals the latter's secret: obedience to social hierarchy".[62] The working class, which had appeared to the young Lukács as a prospective identical subject and object of history, is thus transformed into a passive "mass", the object of systematic manipulation by the media.

For almost all the writers associated with the Frankfurt School, modernist art and music came to represent key sites of resistance to domination. In Benjamin, the connections are deliberately forged between the cultural avant-garde on the one hand, and the new popular media on the other, pitting the emancipatory potential of each against the bourgeois myth of the autonomous work of art.[63] Adorno shared many of Benjamin's concerns, but viewed his antipathy to traditional art and his corresponding enthusiasm for mass culture as essentially one-sided.[64] Adorno, it is true, is neither simply a high modernist nor simply hostile to mass culture. But it is very clear that modernism appears to him as an adversarial culture of quite fundamental importance, and that he can therefore have no sympathy at all for the later Lukács's nostalgia for realism.[65]

The dispute between Lukácsian anti-modernism, Benjamin's enthusiastic popular modernism, and Adorno's tortured and tortuously pro-modernist dialectic, is perhaps the single most intellectually intriguing incident in the history of Western Marxism. For all the acrimony with which it was conducted, especially as between Lukács and Adorno, it should be obvious that the entire debate rests upon the shared assumption of an antithesis between culture (whether realist or modernist) and mechanical (rationalized, reified and detotalized) civilization. But where Marx had linked that antithesis to the critique of ideology, and had aspired to its transcendence in the proletarian revolution, both the later Lukács and Adorno remain content with its reproduction in essentially unamended culturalist form. Benjamin alone of the three, like that other enthusiastic popular modernist, Leon Trotsky,[66] had continued to aspire to a revolutionary politics that would be at once proletarian and avant-garde. Their respective fates, Trotsky's assassination by the Soviet secret service, and Benjamin's suicide after an unsuccessful attempt to escape into Spain from Nazi-occupied France, both in 1940, tell us much about the ultimate destiny of Western Marxism.

While Perry Anderson is clearly mistaken to suggest that Western Marxism was *born* from a moment of failure (quite the contrary – it was born from a moment of high revolutionary optimism), it is nonetheless certainly true that it came eventually to be characterized by "a common and latent *pessimism*".[67] Hence the preoccupation with the ways in which culture as ideology (reified thought/the culture industry) functions so as to legitimate the capitalist system, and hence too the growing scepticism as to the possibilities for successful working-class opposition. This shift from an initial celebration of the emancipatory potential of culture as human self activity, to a subsequent recognition of the debilitating and disabling power of culture as ideology, marks the historical trajectory of western Marxist thought from the early 1920s to the 1960s. But it recurs also within particular intellectual careers, as for example, in Goldmann's progress from a sociology of the world vision, which stressed the intellectual creativity of social classes and groups, to a sociology of the novel, which sought to establish a rigorous homology between the development of a literary form and that of the commodity market.[68] It even recurs within particular texts. Witness Sartre's *Critique of Dialectical Reason*, which begins from an initial determination to vindicate the rationality of praxis, by demonstrating that human history can be understood entirely in terms of human projects, or "totalizations'; but proceeds to a substantive emphasis on the ways in which real popular revolutions, confronted by scarcity, collapse into "seriality".[69]

Such pessimism is, of course, typically Weberian. Paradoxically, it is Gramsci, perhaps the western Marxist thinker least influenced by Weber, who was to produce by far the most theoretically persuasive, and indeed influential, Marxist theory of legitimation. As is well known, Gramsci substituted, for the more orthodoxly Marxist base/superstructure model, a civil society/political society model, which derived both from Hegel and from Marx, certainly, but which had nonetheless hitherto commanded relatively little attention amongst Marxists. Political society here refers to the coercive elements within the wider social totality, civil society the non-coercive. Where most Marxists had previously stressed politico-economic coercion, and where Weber had stressed legitimation, Gramsci chose to point in the direction of both, and towards their inextricable interconnection in the maintenance of social stability. Hence the famous formula: "State = political society + civil society, in other words hegemony protected by the armour of coercion".[70] The term hegemony here refers to something very similar to Weber's legitimate authority, to the permeation throughout the whole of society of a system of values and beliefs supportive of the existing ruling class. This is, in effect, a value consensus, and one very often embodied in common sense, but one constructed, however, in the interests of the ruling class.

"The intellectuals", Gramsci argues, "are the dominant group's 'deputies' exercising the subaltern functions of social hegemony and political government".[71] They are not in themselves an autonomous and independent social class, but are, rather, the "functionaries" of the superstructures. Gramsci distinguished between "organic" intellectuals on the one hand, that is, the type of intellectual which each major social class creates for itself so as to "give it homogeneity and an awareness of its own function";[72] and "traditional" intellectuals on the other, that is, "categories of intellectuals already in existence . . . which seem to represent . . . historical continuity".[73] Intellectuals of the latter type, most importantly the clergy but also administrators, scholars and scientists, theorists and philosophers, affect a certain autonomy from the dominant social classes, but it is an autonomy which proves ultimately illusory. For Gramsci himself, the central political problem was that of the creation of a layer of organic working-class intellectuals capable of leading their class in the battle for counter-hegemony. But in his own work, and even more so in that of subsequent Gramscians, the substantive focus very easily slides towards the explanation of an apparently impregnable bourgeois hegemony. If hegemony is never in principle either uncontested or indefinite, it can quite often come to appear both.

It was this Gramscian theory of hegemony which seemed to the later Raymond Williams "one of the major turning points in Marxist cultural theory".[74] And it may very well be that Williams's reading of Gramsci (as one organic working-class intellectual reading another?) has been by far the more successful in reconstructing the original authorial intention. But for all that, by far the most influential reading, in the 1970s at least, became that proposed by Althusserianism. Althusser's distinctive contribution was to reread Marx's Marxism as if it were a structuralism. For Althusser, Marxism was a science, sharply distinguished from, and counterposed to, ideology, both by its own defining "knowledge function" and by the "epistemological break" with which it had been founded.[75] This science is characterized above all, according to Althusser, by a new mode of explanation, in which structural causality is substituted for both mechanical and expressive models of causation. Here, culture is neither superstructural effect nor an expression of the truth of the social whole. It is, rather, a relatively autonomous structure, with its own specific effectivity, situated within a structure of structures, each level of which is subject to "*determination of the elements of a structure . . . by the effectivity of that structure . . .* [and] *determination of a subordinate structure by a dominant structure*".[76]

In a much quoted essay on "Ideology and Ideological State Apparatuses", Althusser proceeded to argue: that ideology is necessarily embedded in institutions, or "ideological state apparatuses" as he termed them; that its central social function is that of the reproduction of structured social inequality, or more specifically the "relations of production"; that it functions by constituting biological individuals as social "subjects"; and that it thereby represents the imaginary relation of individuals to their real conditions of existence.[77] This is very obviously a reworking of Gramsci's theory of hegemony, but one which represses the notion of agency in favour of a kind quasi-structuralism. And since art, though not itself ideology according to Althusser, nonetheless alludes to ideology,[78] it becomes possible to read culture "ideologically". Althusser himself had developed a theory of symptomatic reading which sought to reconstruct the "problematic" of the text,[79] that is, the structure of determinate absences and presences which occasion it. For Althusser the object of this symptomatic reading had been Marx's "scientific" discoveries. But for Althusserian cultural criticism, as represented most importantly by Pierre Macherey,[80] such readings were to be directed at the texts of ideology. Althusserianism thus aspired to demystify the artistic or literary text by exposing ideology itself as its real object. It was an approach which would exercise a considerable fascination not only for socialists, but also for very many feminists throughout much of the 1970s and early 1980s.

The New Left: from structural Marxism to cultural materialism

Just as Zhdanovism was imported into Britain by the Communist Party, so Western Marxism crossed the English Channel largely at the behest of the British New Left of the 1960s and 1970s. Peter Sedgwick has distinguished between an "Old New Left", which formed from the political crises of 1956, and a "New New Left", whose central political experience became the May '68 Events in Paris, the Vietnam Solidarity Campaign, the Prague Spring and the revolt on the campuses.[81] Raymond Williams and E. P. Thompson had belonged to the earlier formation, Perry Anderson, Tom Nairn and Terry Eagleton to the later. The shift between the two formations had been marked by a distinctly acrimonious transfer of the editorship of the *New Left Review* from Stuart Hall to Anderson during 1962. Where the Old New Left had attempted to preserve the particularities of the British national experience from Communist "internationalism", the New New Left spurned the "peculiarities of the English" in favour of an uncompromisingly internationalist sympathy for the Vietnamese Revolution. Where the Old New Left had counterposed "experience" and "culture" to Communist dogmatism, the New New Left discovered in Western Marxism a type of "Theory" that would function as an antidote to the alleged empiricism both of English bourgeois culture and of the British Labour Party.

Much in the Western Marxist tradition had been unavailable in English translation until well into the 1960s. Indeed, substantial translations of Lukács's *History and Class Consciousness* and Gramsci's *Prison Notebooks*, perhaps the tradition's two "key" texts, only appeared as late as 1971. For the New New Left the lure of "Theory" reached its apogee, however, not so much with either of these humanist Marxisms as with Althusserian structural Marxism: the reconstructed *New Left Review* adopted as its central theoretical project the translation and importation into Britain of a version of Western Marxism selectively "weighted" towards Althusserianism.[82] This interest in continental Marxism can be represented as a simple disengagement from the analysis of British society and culture, and from the practicalities of British politics, that had concerned the Old New Left. But such an interpretation captures a part only of the truth. For, in a series of extremely ambitious essays, Anderson and his colleagues, and in particular Tom Nairn, had propounded a distinctly original account of British history, which in turn came to provide an essentially practical political rationale for their developing interest in Western Marxism.

According to Anderson and Nairn, the English revolution of the 17th century remained essentially uncompleted, its central political legacy a class compromise between the aristocracy and the bourgeoisie rather than a fully-formed bourgeois polity, its central cultural legacy a deeply conservative combination of traditionalism and empiricism. Out of this class compromise, they argued, there had arisen in England a peculiarly archaic state form, a peculiarly supine bourgeoisie, a peculiarly subordinate proletariat, and a peculiarly philistine intelligentsia.[83] Anderson, Nairn and their collaborators saw the importation into Britain of Western Marxism as a device by which to break the politico-intellectual log-jam they had detected. This analysis has been subsequently amended by Nairn's work on nationalism and by his practical political involvement with Scottish nationalism;[84] by

Anderson's own reassessment of the traditions of English socialism;[85] and by Nairn's recognition that, in the period up to the Second World War at least, pre-bourgeois "backwardness" was not so much a peculiarity of the English as a more general property of European political culture.[86] But its more general features have persisted. And, insofar as Anderson has subsequently acknowledged the presence of a relatively resilient intellectual radicalism within contemporary Britain,[87] then this is explained precisely in terms of its cultural novelty, thus in effect providing further testimony to the success of the *New Left Review*'s own practical project rather than to any deficiencies in its earlier analyses.

In the specific field of literary and cultural studies the most significant of the *New Left Review* Althusserians was almost certainly Terry Eagleton. Eagleton's *Criticism and Ideology*, published by New Left Books in 1976, combined a full-blown Althusserianism with a trenchant critique of Williams's earlier culturalism. The Althusserianism consisted in a highly formalist elaboration of "the major constituents of a Marxist theory of literature", centring around the twin concepts of "mode of production" and "ideology";[88] and in the proposal for a structuralist "science of the text", taking as its theoretical object the ways in which literature "produces", in the sense of performs, ideology.[89] The critique of Williams found the latter guilty, by turn, of an "idealist epistemology, organicist aesthetics and corporatist sociology", all three of which have their roots in "Romantic populism".[90] The defining characteristic of that Romanticism, as of the very notion of "culture" itself, is, for Eagleton, a radical "over-subjectivizing" of the social formation, in which structure is reduced to experience.[91] For Eagleton, meanings are not culture, but ideology; and "structure of feeling" only an essentially inadequate conceptualization of ideology, which actually misreads structure as mere pattern.[92]

We may perhaps concede something to the power of Eagleton's critique of Williams's earlier culturalism. But it was surely his own position, rather than Williams's, that was the more "idealist and academicist".[93] Eagleton's quintessentially Althusserian insistence on the determining power of ideology over the human subject is, as Thompson might say, "*exactly* what has commonly been designated, in the Marxist tradition, as idealism".[94] It led almost unavoidably to an enormous condescension toward popular activity, whether political or cultural. The equally Althusserian defence of the notion of aesthetic value, coupled as it was with both a substantive acceptance of the content of the literary canon and a passing sneer at the "abstract egalitarianism" of cultural studies,[95] is similarly academicist. As Howard Felperin would later unkindly observe: "you can take the boy out of Cambridge, but you cannot take Cambridge out of the boy".[96]

For many on the Old New Left, this new generation remained incorrigibly alien. For E. P. Thompson, settling old and not so old scores in the "Foreword" to his *The Poverty of Theory*, the ten years after 1968 had been "a time for reason to sulk in its tent", a time when: "Every pharisee was being more revolutionary than the next; some of them have made such hideous faces that they are likely to be stuck like that for life".[97] *The Poverty of Theory* was itself an anti-Althusserian polemic and Eagleton one of its more incidental targets.[98] But whilst Thompson continued to beat "the bounds of '1956'",[99] Williams followed a rather different route. That Williams's political and intellectual sympathies, from 1968 on, lay with the second generation of New Left intellectuals became increasingly apparent. He shared much of the *New Left Review*'s interest in Western Marxism. Indeed, in the "Introduction" to *Marxism and Literature* he would recall that "I felt the excitement of contact with . . . new Marxist work . . . As all this came in, during the sixties and early seventies . . . an argument that had drifted into deadlock . . . in the late thirties and forties, was being vigorously and significantly reopened".[100] The end result would be a shift in Williams's own position, away from the earlier "left culturalism" and toward what he would himself term "cultural materialism".

Cultural materialism, Williams explained in a short essay itself first published in the *New Left Review*, "is a theory of culture as a (social and material) productive process and of specific practices, of 'arts', as social uses of material means of production".[101] The theory is elaborated upon at some length in *Marxism and Literature*, and in more accessible fashion in the slightly later *Culture*.[102] *Marxism and Literature* has been hailed by Graeme Turner as an "extraordinary theoretical 'coming out'", in which "Williams finally admits the usefulness of Marxism".[103] But this seems to me to overestimate radically the extent of Williams's conversion to "Marxism". Much more appropriate is Alan O' Connor's emphasis on "a *fundamental* theoretical continuity" with Williams's earlier work, "although there were shifts and changes".[104]

In Williams's earlier, left culturalist writings, the "deep community" that is culture simultaneously transcends class and is yet irredeemably marked by it. For all the eloquence with which this position is argued, it remains quite fundamentally incoherent: the competing claims of commonality and difference, culturalism and Marxism, form a circle which stubbornly refuses to be squared. But in the later, cultural materialist phase of his work, it finally became possible for Williams to explain, to his own satisfaction at least, how it could be that structures of feeling are common to different classes, and yet nonetheless represent the interests of some particular class. It was Gramsci's theory of hegemony which finally delivered to Williams that resolution of culturalist and Marxist thematics hitherto denied him. For Williams, Gramsci's central achievement is contained in the articulation of a culturalist sense of the wholeness of culture with a more typically Marxist sense of the interestedness of ideology. Thus hegemony is "in the strongest sense a 'culture', but a culture which has to be seen as the lived dominance and subordination of particular classes".[105] Understood thus, culture is neither "superstructural", as the term had normally been defined in the Marxist tradition, nor "ideological", in the more generally Marxist or more specifically Althusserian definition. On the contrary, "cultural tradition and practice . . . are among the basic processes", which need to be seen "as they are . . . without the characteristic straining to fit them . . . to other and determining . . . economic and political relationships".[106]

For Williams, as for Gramsci, the counter-hegemonic moment remains especially significant. Dissenting from the implied consensualism of Althusserian theories of ideology, Williams is insistent that: "*no dominant culture ever in reality includes or exhausts all human practice, human energy, and human intention*".[107] Hence, his attempt to expand upon Gramsci's initial distinction between organic and traditional intellectuals, so as to identify "dominant", "residual" and "emergent" cultural elements.[108] By "residual" Williams means those elements, external to the dominant culture, which nonetheless continue to be lived and practised as an active part of the present "on the basis of the residue . . . of some previous social and cultural institution or formation".[109] Unlike the merely archaic, the residual may be oppositional or, at least, alternative in character. Thus Williams distinguishes organized religion and the idea of rural community, which are each predominantly residual, from monarchy, which is simply archaic. But it is the properly "emergent", that is, those genuinely new meanings and values, practices, relationships and kinds of relationship, which are substantially alternative or oppositional to the dominant culture,[110] that most interest him. The primary source of an emergent culture is likely to be the formation of a new social class. But there is also a second source of emergence peculiarly pertinent to the analysis of artistic and intellectual movements: "alternative perceptions of others, in immediate relationships; new perceptions and practices of the material world".[111] And at this second level, the situation is often much less clear than in that of an emergent social class: "No analysis is more difficult than that which, faced by new forms, has to try to determine whether these are new forms of the dominant or are genuinely emergent".[112]

In *Marxism and Literature*, Williams offers an unusually interesting formulation of this problem, which significantly redefines his earlier notion of "structure of feeling". An emergent culture, he argues, unlike either the dominant or the residual, requires not only distinct kinds of immediate cultural practice, but also and crucially "new forms or adaptations of forms". Such innovation at the level of form, he continues, "is in effect a *pre-emergence*, active and pressing but not yet fully articulated, rather than the evident emergence which could be more confidently named".[113] Structures of feeling, writes Williams, in a strikingly arresting formulation, "can be defined as social experiences *in solution*, as distinct from other social semantic formations which have been *precipitated* and are more evidently and more immediately available . . . The effective formations of most actual art relate to already manifest social formations, dominant or residual, and it is primarily to emergent formations . . . that the structure of feeling, *as solution*, relates".[114] Structures of feeling thus represent not so much the general culture of a period as its more specifically counter-hegemonic elements.

Williams's cultural materialism also signalled a renewed critique of the base/superstructure formula. This was no simple return to culturalism, however, but an entirely new argument seeking to convict Marxism of an *insufficiently*, rather than excessively, materialist understanding of "the superstructures". What the base/superstructure formula fails to acknowledge, Williams charges, is precisely the materiality of the superstructures themselves. Hence, his judgement that: "The concept of 'superstructure' was . . . not a reduction but an evasion".[115] The way forward, he insists, is "to look at our actual productive activities without assuming in advance that only some of them are material".[117] If Williams retains a concept of determination, then, it is a concept of multiple determination, more akin to the culturalist sense of a whole way of life than to the Marxist notion of a determining base and a determined superstructure. But that whole way of life is now both thoroughly material and thoroughly marked by the impress of power and domination, in all its particular aspects. What for Leavis had been a "Literature", a canon of exemplary creative works expressive of the national tradition, and what for Marxism had been an ideological superstructure of the economic system, becomes in Williams's cultural materialism a distinctive subset of socially specific, materially determinate, forms and practices.

Comparison between Eagleton's *Criticism and Ideology* and Williams's *Marxism and Literature* shows nicely how structural Marxism and cultural materialism offered alternative, and in some ways opposed, ways out of the theoretical deadlock between culturalism and Marxism. The analytical logic of Althusserianism pointed towards a perennial search for the impress of ideology concealed within the deep structures of the text. Though the enabling rhetoric was both radical and contextual, the substantive focus remained the business as usual of literary-critical canonical exegesis. By contrast, the analytical logic of cultural materialism pointed towards a necessary decentring both of texts into the contexts of their production, reproduction and consumption, and of Literature into culture, literary studies into cultural studies. If Williams's rhetoric was a great deal less "revolutionary" than Althusser's, the substantive case at issue was surely very much more so. Certainly, this was to prove Eagleton's own eventual assessment: "Williams . . . refused to be distracted by the wilder flights of Althusserian . . . theory and was still there, ready and waiting for us, when some of us younger theorists, sadder and wiser, finally re-emerged from one or two cul-de-sacs to rejoin him where we had left off"[117].

From the early to mid 1980s onwards, cultural materialism seems to have attracted an increasing audience both amongst erstwhile Althusserian recidivists, including Eagleton himself, and amongst younger scholars such as those associated with the journal *News From Nowhere* and "Oxford English Limited". The introduction to a 1985 collection of *New Essays in Cultural Materialism* cites as instances of such work: Terry Lovell, Janet Wolff, Alan Sinfield and the Terry Eagleton of *Literary Theory*.[118] Both Lovell and Wolff have continued to combine a broadly cultural materialist theoretical position with distinctly feminist politics.[119] As for Eagleton, "the notion of cultural materialism", he would later write, "is . . . of considerable value . . . it extends and completes Marx's own struggle against idealism, carrying it forcefully into that realm ('culture') always most ideologically resistant to materialist redefinition".[120] Sinfield's later work certainly does take issue with the alleged universalism of Williams's "left-culturalism", but it does so, nonetheless, precisely on the grounds of a whole set of cultural materialist categories: cultural production, the distinction between dominant, residual and emergent practices, "middle class dissidence", and so on.[121] One could continue with other more recent examples: Christopher Hampton's *The Ideology of the Text*, for example, or Sinfield's own *Faultlines*.[122]

Closer to Williams's own later work, however, are the kind of cultural and media studies associated with Nicholas Garnham, James Curran, and the journal *Media, Culture and Society*. As its editors have since explained, *Media, Culture and Society* "was in large measure conceived as a counter-argument" to Althusserian and post-Althusserian structural Marxism.[123] Its distinctive contribution, they continue, was a stress, first, on the ways in which culture is produced, and secondly, on media and communication policy viewed, not from a technical or administrative vantage point, but from that of a "critical intelligentsia", serving a "democratic public interest".[124] The *Media, Culture and Society* approach has on occasion been represented as little more than a return to economistic Marxism.[125] But this is a misrepresentation of a developing position that owes at least as much to cultural materialism as to historical materialism. It would be absurd to suggest that every single article in every single issue of the journal is somehow directly inspired by Williams. But its continuing project clearly derives direct theoretical inspiration from that stress on cultural production which distinguished *Marxism and Literature* and *Culture*; and its substantive focus is very much that defined by Williams in his earlier *Communications* and *Television: Technology and Cultural Form*.[126] It is in such studies of the institutional production of culture that the central theoretical legacy of what was once "Marxism" still remains powerfully present in British cultural studies.

CORNWALL COLLEGE
LEARNING CENTRE

Chapter 4
STRUCTURALISM

The culturalist tradition shares with the Marxist at least two major theoretical presuppositions: first, the analytical postulate of a necessary, and quite fundamental, contradiction between cultural value on the one hand, and the developmental logic of utilitarian capitalist civilization on the other; and secondly, the prescriptive imperative to locate some social institution, or social grouping, sufficiently powerful as to sustain the former against the latter. Culturalist hopes have been variously invested in the state, the church, the literary intelligentsia and the labour movement; Marxist aspirations in theory much more uniformly in the working class, but in practice also in the state, as for communist Marxism, and in the intelligentsia (and very often more especially the literary intelligentsia) for Western Marxism. *Structuralism* accepts neither analytical postulate nor prescriptive imperative. For the former, it substitutes a dichotomy between appearance and essence, in which essence is revealed only in structure; for the latter, a scientistic epistemology which typically denies both the need for prescriptive practice and the possibility of meaningful group action.

There are many different versions of structuralism, of course, both in general and as applied to literature and culture in particular. But, for our purposes, and very broadly, structuralism might well be defined as an approach to the study of human culture, centred on the search for constraining patterns, or structures, which claims that individual phenomena have meaning only by virtue of their relation to other phenomena as elements within a systematic structure. More specifically, certain kinds of structuralism – those denoted very often by the terms semiology and semiotics – can be identified with the much more precise claim that the methods of structural linguistics can be successfully generalized so as to apply to all aspects of human culture.[1] Structuralism secured entry into British intellectual life initially during the late 1960s and the 1970s. But in France – and structuralism has been an overwhelmingly francophone affair – it has a much longer history. Indeed, a perfectly plausible case can be mounted for Auguste Comte (1778–1857) as a central precursor of the structuralist tradition.[2] Much less controversially, however, that title belongs, first, to the French anthropologist, Emile Durkheim (1858–1917), and secondly, to Ferdinand de Saussure (1857–1913), the French-speaking Swiss linguist. Durkheim's work on "primitive" religion and Saussure's on language directly anticipate the subsequent histories of the two academic disciplines most directly implicated in structuralism: anthropology and semiology.

Durkheim and Saussure: anthropology and semiology

Durkheim made no strong claim for the special significance of linguistics, although, interestingly, he did nominate language as an important instance of the archetypal "social fact".[3] But his general social theory is, nonetheless, quite significantly proto-structuralist. Durkheim's last major work, *The Elementary Forms of the Religious Life*, first published in 1915, takes as its theoretical objects first knowledge, and secondly religion. In his treatment of the former, Durkheim explicitly rejects both the empiricist view that what we know is given by experience, and the rationalist, or apriorist, that the categories of knowledge are somehow immanent within the human mind. Rather, he argues, such categories are constituted by and through systems of thought that are themselves socially variable: "A concept is not my concept; I hold it in common with other men [*sic*]".[4] The "collective consciousness is . . . a synthesis *sui generis* of particular consciousness . . . ", he writes, "this synthesis has the effect of disengaging a whole world of sentiments, ideas and images which, once born, obey laws all of their own".[5] The collective consciousness is thus absolutely central to social order: it is only through it that society is able to control, indeed construct, the individual human personalities which inhabit it.

This understanding of systems of thought as ultimately determining is very obviously quasi-structuralist, though the language in which it is expressed, that of consciousness, most certainly is not. In his more specific treatment of religious belief, Durkheim introduces a further structuralist trope, or metaphor, that of the binary opposition. The "real characteristic of religious phenomena", he argues, "is that they always suppose a bipartite division of the whole universe . . . into two classes which embrace all that exists, but which radically exclude each other".[6] These two classes are, famously, those of the sacred and the profane. What matters, for Durkheim, is not the specific content of either, but rather the relation between each and the other. Sacred things are thus "*things set apart and forbidden*",[7]whatever they may be, and defined only in relation to the profane, that is, to things not set apart and not forbidden.

Saussure's *Course in General Linguistics* was first published in 1916, only a year after *The Elementary Forms*. Its central thesis, strikingly reminiscent of Durkheim, is that every language is in itself an entirely discrete system, the units of which can be identified only in terms of their relationships to each other, and not by reference to any other linguistic or extra-linguistic system. Saussure distinguishes between *langue*, the social and systemic rules of language, and *parole*, the individual and particular instance of speech, or utterance. Only the former, he insists, can properly be the object of scientific study, for it alone is social rather than individual, essential rather than accidental. "Language is not a function of the speaker", argues Saussure, "it is a product that is passively assimilated by the individual . . . Speaking . . . is an individual act. It is wilful and intellectual".[8] This distinction between institution and event is of central importance to almost all subsequent structuralisms, for it is the institution – the structure – which comes to constitute the defining preoccupation of structuralist analysis.

Just as Durkheim had insisted on the essential arbitrariness of the specific content both of sacredness and of profanity, so too Saussure insists that "*the linguistic sign is arbitrary*".[9] For Saussure, language is a system of signs; and a sign is the union of signifier – or symbol – and signified – the idea or concept, as distinct from the thing, which is symbolized. Thus: "The linguistic sign unites, not a thing and a name, but a concept and a sound-image".[10] This suppression of the referent, or "thing", frees the signifier both from the referent itself and from the signified. Language is thus entirely a matter of social convention, in which the signifier and the signified, and the relations between them, are all radically arbitrary. Each element in the language is definable only in terms of its relation to other elements in the system of signs. And, just as Durkheim had defined the sacred and the profane in terms of their difference from each other, so too Saussure insists that "in language there are only differences *without positive terms* . . . language has neither ideas nor sounds that existed before the linguistic system, but only conceptual and phonic differences that have issued from the system".[11]

Saussure also posits a very sharp distinction between so-called synchronic analysis, of the structure of a given language at a given point in time, and diachronic analysis, of the way in which language changes over time. Given that every language operates at any given time as an independent system, historical analysis is thus, for Saussure, necessarily synchronically irrelevant: "Since changes never affect the system as a whole . . . they can be studied only outside the system".[12] In this respect, as in so many others, Saussure is the archetypical proto-structuralist thinker. For, where Durkheim had continued to adhere to a residual evolutionism,[13] Saussure, by contrast, initiates an in principle methodological antipathy to historicist modes of explanation, which has proved characteristic of almost all subsequent structuralisms and post-structuralisms.

Saussure's single most daring theoretical move, however, was surely to foreshadow the eventual creation of a semiology proper, that is, of a general science of signification: "Language is a system of signs that express ideas, and is therefore comparable to a system of writing, the alphabet of deaf mutes, symbolic rites, polite formulas, military signals, etc . . . *A science that studies the life of signs within society is conceivable* . . . I shall call it *semiology*".[14] A general science of signs, using methods similar to those of Saussure's own structural linguistics, would thus prove applicable to all meaningful human actions or productions, since insofar as human behaviour is meaningful, it is indeed signifying. Thus construed, semiology aspires to direct our attention toward the basis in social convention of much of human life, and toward the systems of rules, relations and structures which order it. For Saussure, as for Durkheim, and for modern structuralism, what is at issue is not the relation between culture on the one hand, and some other extra-cultural structure of social power on the other, but, rather, the social power of discourse, the power of the system of signs itself.

Structuralism: a general model

Structuralism, we have already observed, has been at its most theoretically influential in the disciplines of anthropology and semiology.

Durkheim himself had tended to think of his field as "sociology", a French word coined originally by Comte. But both his own most important work and much of the later intellectual effort of the French Durkheimian school were directed towards what is customarily regarded as "anthropology" in the anglophone world. The obvious instances here include Durkheim's nephew, Marcel Mauss (1872–1950), and Lucien Lévy-Bruhl (1857–1939). But the key figure is nonetheless that of Claude Lévi-Strauss, whose anthropological researches are indebted not only to Durkheim but also to Saussure. Hence the way in which a communication model, a linguistic model in fact, is substituted for the more strictly Durkheimian notion of a collective consciousness in his *Structural Anthropology*.[15] During the late 1950s and the early 1960s, this continuing tradition of post-Durkheimian anthropology comes to coincide with a positively Saussurean revival of semiology, initiated in the first place by Roland Barthes (1915–80), and with the translation into French of a series of texts from the Russian Formalist school of literary criticism, which had briefly flourished in the early 1920s, so as to generate, finally, the theoretical moment of French high structuralism. This is, above all, the moment of Barthes himself and of Michel Foucault (1926–84), but tangentially also that of Althusser and the Althusserian Marxists.

Before we proceed to a more detailed exposition of certain particular structuralisms, let us attempt a brief sketch of what I take to be the five major characteristics of structuralism in general: its positivism; its anti-historicism; its adherence to a (possible) politics of demystification; its theoreticism; and its anti-humanism. As to the first of these, it should be obvious that, from Durkheim and Saussure onwards, the structuralist tradition has exhibited both a habitual aspiration to scientificity and, normally, a correspondingly positive valorization of science, such as can be described either pejoratively as scientistic, or more neutrally as positivist. This understanding of itself as a science, in the strong sense of the term, sharply distinguishes structuralism from both culturalism and "critical" (that is, non-Althusserian) Western Marxism, although somewhat analogously positivist themes clearly saturate the more orthodox versions of scientific socialism, and are indeed present in the later Marx himself.

Anti-historicism is a much more distinctively defining feature of structuralism. Both Marxism (in all but its Althusserian variant) and culturalism translate their antipathy to utilitarian capitalist civilization into a historicist insistence that this type of civilization is only one amongst many, so as to be able thereby to invoke either the past or an ideal future against the present. By contrast, structuralisms typically inhabit a never-ending theoretical present. The only important exception to this observation is Durkheim, whose residual evolutionism we have already noted. But so structuralist is his conception both of primitive "mechanical solidarity" and of complex "organic solidarity", that Durkheim cannot actually account for the shift from the one to the other, except by a badly disguised resort to the demographic fact of population growth, which entails, on his own definition, a theoretically illegitimate appeal to the non-social, in this case, the biological.[16] So structuralist are Durkheim's fundamental preoccupations that this account of the dynamics of modernization becomes, in effect, theoretically incoherent, an accusation that could be levelled neither at Marx nor Weber, Eliot nor Leavis. And after Durkheim, even this residual evolutionism disappears from structuralism.

Structuralism's anti-historicism leads it to take as given whatever present it may choose to study, in a fashion quite alien both to culturalism and to non-Althusserian Marxism. This certainly makes possible a non-adversarial posture *vis à vis* contemporary civilization; it does not, however, require it. A stress on structures as deeper levels of reality, submerged beneath, but nonetheless shaping, the realm of the empirically obvious, can very easily allow for a politics of demystification, in which the structuralist analyst is understood as penetrating through to some secretly hidden truth. For so long as this hidden reality is seen as somehow confounding the truth claims of the more obvious realities, then for so long can such a stance remain compatible with an adversarial intellectual politics. Even then all that eventuates is a peculiarly enfeebled, and essentially academic, version of intellectual radicalism, in which the world is not so much changed, as contemplated differently. And again, while structuralism is certainly compatible with such radicalism, it does not require it. Hence the rather peculiar way in which the major French structuralist thinkers have proved able to shift their political opinions, generally from left to right, without any corresponding amendment to their respective theoretical positions. For structuralism, as neither for culturalism nor for Marxism, the nexus between politics and theory appears irretrievably contingent.

This combination of positivism and what we might well term "synchronism" with a commitment to the demystification of experiential reality, propels the entire structuralist enterprise in a radically theoreticist direction. A science of stasis, marked from birth by an inveterate anti-empiricism, becomes almost unavoidably preoccupied with highly abstract theoretical, or formal, models. Hence the near ubiquity of the binary opposition as a characteristically structuralist trope. Theoretical anti-humanism arises from essentially the same source: if neither change nor process nor even the particular empirical instance are matters of real concern, then the intentions or actions of human subjects, whether individual or collective, can easily be disposed of as irrelevant to the structural properties of systems. In this way, structuralism notoriously "decentres" the subject.

Before finally proceeding to an account of French high structuralism, let us briefly recall the theoretical legacy of Russian Formalism. The Formalists were directly influenced by Saussurean linguistics. The Petrograd Society for the Study of Poetic Language, founded by Victor Shklovsky in 1916, and the Moscow Linguistic Club, founded a year earlier by Roman Jakobson (1896–1982), had each aspired to establish the study of literature on properly scientific and systematic foundations. Suppressed by the Soviet government in 1930, the exiled Jakobson continued the work of the Formalist School through the Prague Linguistic Circle, from whence it was transmitted to France, notably by Tzvetan Todorov, the Franco-Bulgarian literary theorist, who first published a selection of Formalist writings in French translation in Paris in 1965.[17]

The Formalists aspired to understand literature as a system, just as Saussure had language. Literary science, Jakobson argued, should study not the supposedly empirical facts of literature, but rather "literariness", that is, whatever it is that endows literature with its own distinctively systemic properties. Literariness, the Formalists concluded, was that process by which literary texts defamiliarize, or make strange, both previous literature and also the world itself.[18] The central focus for their work thus became those formal literary devices by means of which such defamiliarization is achieved. It should be obvious, however, that that which defamiliarizes can itself become familiar, and thereby cease to be literary, in Formalist terms at least. Literariness is not, then, essentially a property of the text, nor even of the particular devices that the text might deploy, but of the literary system itself, of what later structuralists would term the relations of intertextuality between texts. The literary text is thus to the system of texts as *parole* is to *langue*, a singular element within a system of arbitrary conventions, the meaning of which is explicable neither referentially nor historically, but only synchronically. In yet another, much more explicitly Saussurean, version of literariness, Jakobson proposed a six factor model of the speech event in which the poetic function of language is defined as attached to the linguistic message itself, as distinct from the addresser, addressee, context, contact and code, to each of which is attached a different linguistic function.[19] In short, language fulfils a poetic, or literary, function to the extent that it becomes self-conscious of itself as language. Both variants of literariness, it should be noted, provide an implicit theoretical legitimation for literary modernism, as no doubt they were so intended to do.

High Structuralism

Roland Barthes, we have said, is the single most important, representative figure of French high structuralism, an immensely prolific writer, literary critic, sociologist and semiologist, structuralist and post-structuralist, whose bizarre death – he was run over by a laundry truck – was as untimely as it was improbable. Barthes's most famous work, *Mythologies*, was first published in 1957. Strongly influenced by Saussure, it sought to analyse semiologically a whole range of contemporary myths, from wrestling to advertising, from striptease to Romans in the cinema. Here Barthes aspires to "read" washing powder advertisements, for example, as languages, that is, as signifying systems with their own distinctive grammars. The book includes a long essay, entitled "Myth Today", which attempts to sketch out the theoretical corollaries of the often very entertaining, almost journalistic, and invariably insightful, particular analyses which occupy the bulk of the text.

In "Myth Today", Barthes defines myth as a second order semiological system, in which the signs of language, that is, both signifiers and signifieds, function as the signifiers of myth, signifying other mythical signifieds.[20] By myth, Barthes means something very close to a Weberian legitimation. In bourgeois society, he argues, myth is "depoliticized speech", which "has the task of giving an historical intention a natural justification, and making contingency appear eternal".[21] By so naturalizing the historically contingent, myth proves fundamentally supportive of the social *status quo*. Hence Barthes's famous observation that: "Statistically, myth is on the right".[22] At this point in his intellectual career Barthes himself was still, of course, on the left. Indeed, the essay provides an excellent example of the way in which structuralism as demystification can be linked to an adversarial intellectual stance. In *Mythologies*, as in the later *Elements of Semiology* and *The Fashion System*, first published in 1964 and 1967 respectively,[23] Barthes's semiology strays furthest from the realm of the literary, and into fashion, food, furniture and cars. His central theoretical preoccupation was, nonetheless, that provided by writing.

At his most structuralist, and at his most influential, during the late 1960s and early 1970s, Barthes's work proceeded along three main lines: first, to the development of a set of highly formal analyses of the structures of narrative; secondly, to the definition of a quasi-Formalist notion of literariness; and finally, to the famous announcement of the death of the author. Barthes's narratology is striking both for its manifest scientism, and for its clear indebtedness to themes originally initiated by Shklovsky and Jakobson. His treatment of literariness is similarly inspired. Writing and language are not instrumental, Barthes maintains, but function in their own right and for themselves. Thus, as Barthes put it in his contribution to a 1966 international symposium on structuralism, the verb to write is an apparently intransitive verb: the writer doesn't write something, but rather just writes.[24] Despite the originality of the formulation, there is an obvious parallel between this stress on the near-intransitivity of writing and Jakobson's on the self-consciousness of the poetic function. And, as with Jakobson, so too with Barthes, this understanding of literariness is necessarily aligned to an endorsement of modernist, that is, non-realist, aesthetics. Hence Barthes's enthusiasm for the attempt by "modern literature . . . to substitute the instance of discourse for the instance of reality (or of the referent), which has been, and still is, a mythical 'alibi' dominating the idea of literature".[25] For Barthes, as for Jakobson, an apparently descriptive aesthetic rapidly acquires prescriptive capacity.

Barthes's much quoted essay on the death of the author insists that literary texts be understood in terms of intertextuality rather than of supposed authorial intentions. The essay itself is very obviously intended as a polemic against the more traditionally humanist view of the writer as author (literally, the source) of literary meaning. Formally,

Barthes does in fact recognize in the reader a point at which intertextual meaning can finally become focused: the reader, he writes, is the *"someone* who holds together in a single field all the traces by which the written text is constituted". But this reader is nonetheless "without history, biography, psychology".[26] That is, it is not an empirically concrete reader which concerns Barthes, but rather, the structural rôle of the reader, to borrow a phrase of Umberto Eco.[27] Barthes's structuralism is here concerned, not with the intrinsic properties of the text, but with the conventions that render it intelligible to the reader. This intelligibility is, however, a function of the discourse itself, rather than of any individual reader's capacities and interests. This entire argument, which became extremely influential both in France and elsewhere, is informed throughout by a rigorous theoretical anti-humanism, which is in no way belied by its merely rhetorical conclusion that "the birth of the reader must be at the cost of the death of the Author".[28]

Where Barthes happily announced himself a structuralist, Foucault repeatedly denied any such theoretical affinities and predilections.[29] In the most specifically Saussurean of senses, we might very well endorse such protestations. But, in a more general sense, Foucault's earlier work is indeed structuralist. His first truly influential books, *Madness and Civilization* and *The Birth of the Clinic*, were published in French in 1961 and 1963.[30] In both, Foucault was concerned to establish the systematic, and in its own terms perfectly valid, nature of the dominant understandings of madness and of illness of the 17th and early 18th centuries; and to contrast these with the new, equally systematic, and equally internally valid, conceptions which emerged, very rapidly, in the late 18th century. For Foucault, the later conceptions are merely different, not better. What matters is not the epistemological problem of truth, but rather what we might term the sociological problem of the fit between new ways of knowing and new institutional practices.

This earlier institutional emphasis is temporarily superseded by a much more deliberate focus on discourse as such, both in *The Order of Things*, first published in 1966 as *Les Mots et les Choses*, and in *The Archaeology of Knowledge*, first published in 1969.[31] Here Foucault defines the objects of his inquiry as discursive formations, or *epistemes*, that is, systematic conceptual frameworks which define their own truth criteria, according to which particular knowledge problems are to be resolved, and which are embedded in and imply particular institutional arrangements. The central focus falls, unsurprisingly, on a contrast between the classical *episteme*, which governed knowledge in the 17th and in the early 18th century, and the modern *episteme*, which develops from the late 18th century, and which is only now coming to be challenged by a putatively postmodern, in fact structuralist, *episteme*.

The structuralism of this entire project should be readily apparent. Despite Foucault's profession as historian, his work remained radically anti-historicist, unable either to judge between *epistemes*, or to explain the shift from one to another (hence the characteristically structuralist sense of change as discontinuity). Moreover, Foucault pursues a typically structuralist strategy of demystification towards, for example, modern medicine and modern psychiatry. And his approach is, of course, theoretically anti-humanist. Thus, the strength of the new sciences of psychoanalysis and structural anthropology consists in their ability "to do without the concept of man . . . they dissolve man".[32] One very interesting essay of Foucault's quite specifically takes up Barthes's theme of the death of the author, and seeks to explain authorship by its various institutional uses.[33] Finally, we should add, Foucault's earlier writings are also deeply positivist in inspiration. Given Foucault's very obvious animus towards modern science, his persistent attempt to demystify and relativize "scientific knowledge", this might well appear the strangest of observations. And yet, this vast archaeology – a history of previous *epistemes*, no less – is unthinkable except as a knowledge of an object produced by a subject external to it, which is precisely the positivist, and structuralist, position.

At the end of *The Archaeology of Knowledge*, Foucault confesses, uncomfortably, that his discourse "is avoiding the ground on which it could find support".[34] The embarrassment is distinctive, but not the problem. For Durkheim and Lévi-Strauss, Saussure and Barthes, as for Foucault, the central repressed problem had been throughout that of how to guarantee the scientificity of a knowledge that was itself, according to the logics of their own argument, either social or intra-discursive. No solution to this problem seems possible from within structuralism itself. Hence the move by both Barthes and Foucault, during the 1970s, toward different versions of post-structuralism. Hence, too, the meteoric rise to intellectual pre-eminence, during the same period, of Jacques Derrida.

Post-structuralism

If structuralism proper displays a recurrent aspiration to scientificity, then post-structuralism clearly betrays that aspiration by its equally recurrent insistence that meaning can never be pinned down, not even by structuralism itself. The three major variants of French post-structuralism are those represented by: first, that type of literary "deconstruction", practised by the later Barthes, and more especially by Derrida; secondly, Foucault's later writings on the theme of the knowledge/power relation; and thirdly, Lacanian psychoanalysis. Given that the latter has proven influential mainly by virtue of its partial incorporation into recent feminist theory, I propose to postpone consideration of Lacan's work until the chapter that follows. Derrida, and the later Barthes and Foucault, have proved much more independently influential, however, especially in the field of literary and cultural studies. Wherein, then, lies the theoretical novelty of this post-structuralist departure?

For Barthes himself, the key moment of transition from structuralism to post-structuralism, occurs with *S/Z*, his study of Balzac's short story, *Sarrasine*. In what appears initially as conventionally structuralist narratology, Barthes breaks up the text into 561 lexias, or units of reading, and analyses them, exhaustively, in terms of five main codes. He also distinguishes between readerly and writerly texts, respectively those which position the reader as passive consumer, and those which demand that the reader actively participate as co-author of the text.[35] This distinction provides, once again, for a valorization of modernist aesthetics, if not in this case of a modernist text. But if *Sarrasine* is a writerly text, as Barthes argues, then it follows that it can have no single meaning: "to decide on a hierarchy of codes . . . is *impertinent* . . . it overwhelms the articulation of the writing by a single voice".[36] Barthes's five codes are thus self-confessedly arbitrary, and the story itself thus has no determinate meaning, but is rather both plural and diffuse.

The distinction between readerly and writerly texts is later reformulated as that between *plaisir* and *jouissance*, that is, between pleasure and ecstasy, or "bliss", in the slightly later *The Pleasure of the Text* (1973). Here Barthes advances the, in itself perfectly sensible, proposition that reading is pleasurable, and pleasurable, moreover, in a strongly erotic and corporeal sense. Barthes is still too much of a structuralist to contemplate a return to the reading subject; but the reading body, "my body of bliss",[37] is somehow a very different matter. The text of *jouissance*, in effect the modernist text, is thus the incomplete text, just as the body is less erotic when completely naked than "where the garment gapes".[38] It should be obvious that this is Barthes at play. But it is play in a double sense, both as eroticism and also as indeterminacy, as that play of meanings which will fascinate, not only Barthes himself, but also Derrida.

Derrida's 1966 paper, "Structure, Sign, and Play in the Discourse of the Human Sciences",[39] very clearly anticipates many of the characteristic themes and preoccupations of the later Barthes. Derrida himself is the post-structuralist thinker*par excellence*, with no properly structuralist past, a more profound thinker than Barthes, a philosopher rather than a critic, to borrow a distinction of which neither approved. Insofar as the developing discourse of post-structuralism has been concerned, the key theoretical option emerged increasingly, during the late 1970s and the 1980s, as that between Foucault and Derrida, rather than between Foucault and Barthes. Derrida's three major works, *Writing and Difference, Speech and Phenomena*and *Of Grammatology*, all first published in 1967, thus mark the founding moment of French post-structuralism.

Derrida rejects the "logocentric" notion of language as "voice", that is, as the expression of intentional human meaning, and insists that its true nature is more clearly revealed in writing than in speech. Just as for Saussure *langue* is more permanent and durable than *parole*, so for Derrida writing outlives and outlasts its supposed authors. But Derrida takes the argument a stage further. Where Saussure had privileged sign over referent, Derrida privileges signifier over signified, so much so, in fact, that writing consists, not of signs, but of signifiers alone. Thus for Derrida, the meaning of meaning is an indefinite referral of signifier to signifier "which gives signified meaning no respite . . . so that it always signifies again".[40] Linguistic meaning thereby entails an "infinite equivocality". Derrida inherits also the Saussurean notion of language as founded on difference, but coins the neologism, *différance*, to stress the double meaning of the French verb, *différer*, as both to differ and to defer or delay.[41] Thus difference is also deferral, for the moment at least, of other, alternative meanings. That characteristically Derridean device, the pun, is deployed precisely so as to enable a remorseless worrying away at the other possible meanings of words.

For Derrida, this theory of language leads to deconstruction, as a particular way of reading texts. What is entailed in deconstruction is a deliberate pushing of textual meaning to its limits, intended so as to discover the blindspots within the text – the ways in which it fails to say what it means to say. This might well appear little more than a peculiarly obtuse form of literary criticism – and so it has been interpreted by the Yale School of American "Derrideans". But for Derrida himself, deconstruction is as much a philosophy and a politics as a type of literary criticism. For Derrida "what one calls . . . real life"[42] is itself a text, and it can, therefore, be deconstructed. It should be obvious that Derrida's work clearly anticipates, and perhaps initiates, many of the preoccupations of the later Barthes. But despite the undoubtedly "ludic" element in his work, as in the punning, for example, Derrida's own position is much more theoretically serious, much less self-indulgently hedonistic. For Derrida's insistence on the indeterminate openness of meaning is deliberately subversive of all authoritarianisms, whether epistemological, ethical or political, and of the fear of change that often inspires such authoritarianism. Hence Derrida's concluding invocation, at Johns Hopkins University, of "the as yet unnamable which is proclaiming itself and which can do so . . . only under the species of the nonspecies, in the formless, mute, infant, and terrifying form of monstrosity".[43] A Derridean politics would be, above all, a politics of demystification through relativization.

In Foucault's late work, as in Derrida, we also find a repudiation of the older structuralist aspiration to scientificity. Here, however, post-structuralism moves in a very different direction. Indeed, one might even add an opposed direction: certainly, Foucault himself remained deeply dismissive of Derrida's "little pedagogy".[44] The later Foucault relativizes discourse, not by any radical reconstruction of the notion of signification itself, but rather by the attempt to substitute relations of power for relations of meaning. "I believe one's point of reference should not be to the great model of language . . . and signs", argues Foucault, "but to that of war and battle. The history which bears and determines us has the form of a war rather than that of a language".[45] The term coined to describe this later approach is "genealogy", as distinct from "archaeology". And the key text which announces the shift is *Discipline and Punish* (1975), a study of the birth of the modern prison.[46] For Foucault himself, there is little novelty in a focus on the interconnectedness of discursive and institutional practices as such.

But the real theoretical innovation here consists, first, in a new sense of this connectedness as necessarily *internal* to discourse; and secondly, in a growing awareness of the human body itself as the central object of control in such institutions as the modern prison, but also as the source of possible resistance to that control. This new recognition of the significance of human corporeality runs interestingly parallel to that of Barthes's *The Pleasure of the Text*.

For the later, but not the very late,[47] Foucault, power in modern society has become essentially ubiquitous. Thus he speaks of its "capillary form of existence . . . the point where power reaches into the very grain of individuals, touches their bodies and inserts itself into their actions and attitudes, their discourses, learning processes and everyday lives".[48] But this very ubiquity of power renders it open and indeterminate: "it induces pleasure, forms knowledge, produces discourse. It needs to be considered as a productive network which runs through the whole social body".[49] There is, then, no single structure of power, but rather a play of powers. Foucault's work is thus not an "objective" account of discourse, positioned outside it, but rather a strategic, or tactical, intervention into that play. The deeper affinity between Foucault and Derrida, despite their apparent mutual animosity, resides around this persistent scepticism *vis à vis* discourse, a scepticism which seeks to identify the possibilities within discourse which discourse itself seeks to repress. Both thus adopt an adversarial stance toward dominant discourse in their respective practice of what one might term disruptively immanent critique, the hallmark, I suspect, of a peculiarly post-structuralist politics of demystification. But this is demystification through relativization, rather than through the kind of absolutist scientism which underpinned classical structuralism; its central achievement and aspiration not the discovery of hidden truths, but of marginalized inconsistencies.

For Derrida, and for the later Barthes and Foucault, knowledge is social, and its scientificity cannot therefore be guaranteed. This is no longer a problem, however, it is merely, pragmatically, the way things are. Perry Anderson describes the emergence of post-structuralism thus: "Structure therewith capsizes into its antithesis, and poststructuralism proper is born, or what can be defined as subjectivism without a subject".[50] This latter phrase strikes me as very suggestive of the way in which post-structuralism brings into play all the indeterminacy of phenomenological culturalisms, but without any corresponding sense of the practical creative efficacy of the human subject. For post-structuralism persists in structuralism's rigorous anti-humanism: Foucault's genealogy, as much as Barthes's early semiology, requires a "form of history which can account for the constitution of knowledges . . . without having to make reference to a subject".[51] Indeed, for all the *éclat* with which the transition from structuralism to post-structuralism has invariably been announced, the latter clearly exhibits a remarkable fidelity to all but one of the five major structuralist *motifs* we identified above: positivism seems the sole casualty of this bloodless revolution in thought.

The fundamental continuity between structuralism and post-structuralism is, nonetheless, not so much logical as sociological. Where Marxism aspired to mobilise the working class, and culturalism – at its most successful at any rate – the intelligentsia, against the logics of capitalist industrialization, both structuralism and post-structuralism subscribe to a very different, and much more modest, sense of the intellectual's proper political function. In an observation actually directed at Sartre (or at least to intellectuals of a Sartrean kind), but which could just as easily be directed toward Leavis, Foucault writes thus:

> For a long period, the . . . intellectual spoke and was acknowledged the right of speaking in the capacity of master of truth and justice . . . To be an intellectual meant something like being the consciousness/conscience of us all . . . Some years have passed since the intellectual was called upon to play this rôle. A new mode of the "connection between theory and practice" has been established. Intellectuals have got used to working, not in the modality of the "universal", the "exemplary", the "just-and-true-for-all", but within specific sectors, at the precise points where their own conditions of life or work situate them . . . This is what I would call the "specific" intellectual as opposed to the "universal" intellectual.[52]

Foucault himself affects a genuine enthusiasm for the likely political rôle of this "specific" intelligentsia. But he is far too acute an observer not to notice its probable limitations: that its struggles will be merely conjunctural, that it may well be open to manipulation, that it will lack both global strategy and wider support.[53] What Foucault does fail to register, however, is the possibility that an increasingly professionalized intelligentsia, such as that which he describes, might not actually constitute an oppositional force at all, but might rather find itself progressively reconciled to its position of particular privilege within the social structures of late capitalism.

Structuralism, post-structuralism
and British cultural studies

In the United States, structuralism secured entry into the national intellectual life mainly through the liberal academy rather than through its more radical opponents: Jonathan Culler's *Structuralist Poetics* won a large audience within the American intelligentsia for an appropriately depoliticized version of structuralist theory as early as 1975.[54] Similarly, the institutionally dominant North American response to post-structuralism was to prove that of the Yale School's singular appropriation both of Derrida himself and of Derridean deconstruction. In this reading, which acquired both the shape of a collective enterprise and the apparent stamp of Derrida's personal approval with the publication of *Deconstruction and Criticism*,[55] deconstruction became yet another depoliticized literary formalism.

Anthony Easthope insists that British post-structuralism, by contrast, remained heavily indebted to Althusserian Marxism.[56] There is an element of exaggeration here: Marxism was by no means so obviously the "parent discourse" of British post-structuralism, nor the latter so obviously committed "to political purposes", as Easthope supposes.[57] Terence Hawkes's *Structuralism and Semiotics*, a widely used textbook published in 1977 as one of the first titles in Methuen's influential "New Accents" series, inaugurated a much less overtly politicized variant of structuralism.[58] Though Hawkes's later work[59] has had much post-structuralist fun with the "Bardbiz" of the Shakespearean canon, and much of it to some real political effect, there is nothing very obviously "Marxist" about all this. Moreover, Hawkes himself was by no means a marginal figure in British semiotics: Professor of English at the University of Cardiff, general editor of the "New Accents" series, and later editor of the journal *Textual Practice*, he has probably exercised at least as much influence over literary post-structuralism as has Terry Eagleton, for example. Still less Marxist and much less political has been the work in cultural studies of Hawkes's one-time colleague at Cardiff, John Fiske.[60]

Easthope's general characterization still stands, nevertheless: from the mid 1960s onwards, a heady combination of Western Marxist and structuralist or post-structuralist continental European "Theory" did indeed come into direct and often explosive conflict with an already dominant culturalism, both in literary studies itself and in the newly forming proto-discipline of cultural studies. In the latter case the conflict was more or less effectively orchestrated and managed by Stuart Hall. But whereas cultural studies had itself been the effect of a prior rupture within culturalism, mainstream literary studies was still very much the domain of a more or less unreconstructed Leavisism. The incursion of Theory, sometimes radical and always foreign, into the erstwhile conservative heart of the national intellectual culture thus precipitated what Peter Widdowson rightly termed a "crisis in English studies".[61] The crisis was acted out in the "Sociology of Literature" conferences organized annually from 1976 to 1984 by Francis Barker and his colleagues at Essex University; in the journal *Literature and History*, edited from 1975 to 1988 by Widdowson and others at Thames Polytechnic; and in *Screen*, the journal of the Society for Education in Film and Television (SEFT).

If the disintegration of traditional culturalism had begun with the rupture from which cultural studies had emerged, then it proceeded thereafter through three reasonably well defined stages. In the first, during the early to mid 1970s, the radical critique was overwhelmingly Marxist in character, its own internal debates in effect a confrontation between culturalist and structuralist Marxisms. This was very much the moment of Anderson's *New Left Review* and of the Birmingham Centre under Hall. In the second, during the very late 1970s and early 1980s, left culturalism evolved into cultural materialism at much the same time as Althusserian structuralism imploded on itself, leaving behind a legacy of Derridean, Foucauldian and Lacanian post-structuralisms. This was the theoretical moment of *Screen* and the political moment of a kind of radical feminism often determinedly post-structuralist in its theoretical predilections. In the third, during the late 1980s and the early 1990s, the debate shifted focus away from such abstract questions of "Theory" and towards a much more substantive engagement with the problem of postmodernism. The "'theory wars' of the 1970s and 1980s",[62] as Easthope, after Kreiswirth, nicely terms them, were thus concluded, not so much in the victory of any one protagonist as in a sudden diminution of theoretical interest, itself a consequence of a previous process of prolonged theoretical attrition.

During the 1970s Stuart Hall, like Raymond Williams, had moved from an essentially left-Leavisite culturalism toward a kind of "Gramscianism": the "concept of 'hegemony'", Hall would recall in 1980, "has played a seminal rôle in Cultural Studies".[63] Hall, however, was much more responsive than Williams to the appeal both of structuralism and of post-structuralism. His essay on "Encoding and Decoding in Television Discourse", which drew heavily on French and Italian semiotic theory, had first been published as a Centre Stencilled Paper as early as 1973.[64] By 1980, when Hall produced his own seminal sketch of the current state of the theoretical art in cultural studies,[65] Williams and Thompson's "culturalism" was no longer the obvious starting point for the would-be discipline, but rather only one of two competing paradigms, each with its attendant strengths and weaknesses; and, for all its professed evenhandedness, Hall's own position had already become effectively anti-culturalist.

The difference between Hall's and Williams's readings of Gramsci takes us to what was very probably the theoretical heart of the matter at issue between cultural materialism and structuralism: whether to understand hegemony as culture or as structure, and what relative weight to attach to the hegemonic and the counter-hegemonic respectively. If hegemony is a culture, then it is materially produced by the practice of conscious agents, and may be countered by alternative, counter-hegemonic, practices; if hegemony is a structure of ideology, then it will determine the subjectivity of its subjects in ways which radically diminish the prospects for counter-hegemonic practice, except in the characterizically attenuated form of a plurality of post-structuralist resistant readings. Hegemony as culture is a matter of material production, reproduction and consumption; hegemony as structure a matter for textual decoding. Where Williams's interpretation of Gramsci provided the theoretical basis for cultural materialism, Hall's interpretation became progressively assimilated to a developing structuralist and post-structuralist paradigm. Hence Hall's eventual view of Gramsci as anticipating "many of the actual advances in theorizing" brought about by "structuralism, discourse and linguistic theory or psychoanalysis".[66] As the decade proceeded, post-structuralist thematics, particularly those deriving from Foucault, were to become much more obviously present both in Hall's own work[67] and in cultural studies more generally.

The "crisis in English studies" had proceeded along roughly similar lines. Easthope distinguishes two main currents in what he terms British "post-structuralist" literary theory:[68] first, the kind of textual "deconstruction", pursued by Colin MacCabe and Catherine Belsey, which sought to analyse the ways in which the text makes available to the reader certain definable subject positions; and second, the kind of "institutional" analysis, pursued by the later Eagleton and by Tony Bennett, which sought to problematize the institutional conditions of the production of textual meaning. The latter is what Easthope means by "left deconstruction".[69] These are what Felperin refers to as "textualist" and "contextualist" versions of post-structuralism, which he associates, respectively, with the work of Derrida and Foucault?[70] Felperin's formulation certainly seems appropriate to the American intellectual context: textualist deconstruction such as that of the Yale School has been by and large Derridean; contextualist deconstruction such as that of Frank Lentricchia[71] by and large Foucauldian. But, as Easthope rightly stresses, MacCabe and Belsey worked with a style of deconstruction that derived as much from Althusser, by way of *Screen*, as from Derrida.[72]

From 1971 onwards, *Screen* became the effective intellectual centre initially for "cultural" Althusserianism, later for textualist post-structuralism. Its influence extended well beyond the specialist area of film studies and, through MacCabe and Stephen Heath, even into Cambridge English. Both MacCabe and Heath were interested in the ways in which different kinds of text differently position their readers. Substantively, this led to a sustained assault on literary and cinematic "realism". Echoing Barthes's distinction between readerly and writerly texts, and invoking Brecht against Lukács, MacCabe and Heath insisted on the essential conservatism of such formal realisms.[73] The texts of mass culture and high culture alike were thus exposed as instances of a single underlying structure that functioned to secure mass subservience to the dominant ideological discourse. The original Althusserian *Screen* position laid stress on the ways in which the text positions the reader. But this was soon superseded by a more properly deconstructionist sense of a multiplicity of possible readerly responses. Thus, both Barker's *The Tremulous Private Body*[74] and Belsey's *The Subject of Tragedy*[75] each construct the literary-historical past as, to all intents and purposes, a narrative effect of the present.

In retrospect, Easthope seems to me mistaken to link Eagleton and Bennett as parallel instances of "left deconstruction". For, where

Eagleton's version of "institutional" analysis derived essentially from Williams, Bennett's own would move in a progressively Foucauldian direction. No doubt there are, as Dollimore has stressed, certain very clear affinities between British cultural materialism and North American Foucauldian "new historicism".[76] But their near conflation by Easthope seems unwarranted.[77] Bennett himself had worked with Stuart Hall at the Open University and convened U203, "Popular Culture", an interdisciplinary undergraduate course which in 1982 had attracted over a thousand students.[78] As Easthope notes, U203 was "the most ambitious, serious and comprehensive intervention in cultural studies in Britain".[79] In 1987 Bennett became the first Director of the Institute for Cultural Policy Studies at Griffith University in Brisbane, Australia. Both Bennett himself and his Australian and British co-workers clearly envisaged cultural policy studies as a quite distinctive politico-cultural project. Their shift toward cultural policy was never simply pragmatic. Rather, it evolved from out of a distinctively Foucauldian vision of the political rôle of the intellectual.

The underlying theoretical rationale behind this commitment to cultural policy studies is most clearly argued in Bennett's *Outside Literature*.[80] In a reversal of Williams's intellectual journey towards Marxism, Bennett here sets out to exorcise the ghosts of his own misspent Marxist youth.[81] Bennett argues that recent Marxist and quasi-Marxist criticism has aimed to secure a political relevance for itself "by going back to being . . . a set of interpretive procedures oriented towards the transformation of the consciousness of individual subjects".[82] This was, of course, the traditional function of the "universal intellectual". For Bennett, by contrast, the Foucauldian notion of the "specific intellectual" demands "more specific and localized assessments of the effects of practices of textual commentary conducted in the light of the institutionally circumscribed fields of their social deployment".[83] Rather than denounce the world, Bennett will reform the university and as much else of the culture industries as seems practically reformable. For Bennett, then, a "specific intelligentsia" can only effectively prosecute an essentially technocratic micro-politics. Cultural policy studies will thus stand in relation to cultural studies much as Fabian social engineering once did to sociology. Bennett aspires, in short, to examine "the truth/power symbiosis which characterizes particular regions of social management – with a view not only to undoing that symbiosis but also . . . installing a new one in its place".[84]

The politics of difference:
post-structuralism, post-colonialism and multiculturalism

If a post-structuralist semiotics no longer assumes an epistemology of truth, and can thereby no longer guarantee a science of demystification, it does not therefore follow that it need necessarily become "apolitical". As we have seen, it can readily lead to a micro-politics of the kind advocated by Bennett. Moreover, the more general post-structuralist insistence on the indeterminate openness of meaning threatens to subvert the pretensions to textual authority of all authoritarianisms, be they epistemological, ethical or political. The result can be a politics of demystification through relativization, its central achievement and aspiration the discovery not of hidden truths, but of marginalized inconsistencies within dominant discourses. Such preoccupations have proved especially pertinent to the emergence of new "psycho-semiotic" feminisms, and to recent debates over multiculturalism and post-colonialism. A detailed discussion of post-structuralist feminism must await the chapter that follows. But let us here briefly examine some of the issues involved in the debates over "post-colonialism" and "multiculturalism".

Both post-colonial and multi-cultural theories share in the characteristically post-structuralist ambition to "decentre" the dominant – white, metropolitan, European – culture. The central "post-colonialist" argument, as advanced in Ashcroft, Griffiths and Tiffin's *The Empire Writes Back*,[85] for example, or in the more recent collection of essays edited by Adam and Tiffin,[86] is that post-colonial culture entails a revolt of the margin against the metropolis, the periphery against the centre, by which all experience becomes "uncentred, pluralistic and nefarious".[87] The post-colonial can thus be characterized by a supposedly "inevitable tendency towards subversion".[88] Somewhat analogously, multicultural theory very often invokes ethnic "difference" as in itself a discursively and politically subversive category. Sneja Gunew, for example, has argued that multiculturalism can "deconstruct" the dominant unitary national narratives, that it can become "a strategy which interrogates hegemonic unities", and that it might thereby establish the "basis for constructing 'signifying breakthroughs', the preconditions for a revolutionary, non-repetitive, history".[89]

Post-colonial and multicultural theory derive from a common empirical datum, that of the collapse of European imperialism, and of the British Empire in particular: the result in the former colonies was societies that could meaningfully be described as post-colonial, in the former metropolis and in the affluent colonies of settlement societies that might eventually hope to become multicultural. In both cases, the argument commenced not so much with a celebration of subordinate identity as with a critique of the rhetoric of cultural dominance. The origins of much recent post-colonial theory can be traced to Edward Said's *Orientalism*, a deeply scholarly account not of "the Orient" itself, but of the ways in which British and French scholarship had constructed the Orient as "Other". For Said Orientalism was a "discourse" in the Foucauldian sense of the term: "an enormously systematic discipline by which European culture was able to manage – and even produce – the Orient . . . during the post-Enlightenment period".[90] British cultural studies began to explore the multiculturalism of its own society through a somewhat analogous critique of the ways in which white racism had come to constitute blackness as "Other". Thus Stuart Hall and a number of his colleagues from the Birmingham Centre co-authored a highly acclaimed "cultural studies" account of "mugging", which showed how media constructions of black criminality had conferred popular legitimacy on state authoritarianism.[91]

At the level of practical politics, such critiques of white racist misrepresentation might well suggest the need for a counter-assertion of some authentically black identity. That move is precluded by the logic of post-structuralism, however, for if whiteness and blackness are each constituted within and through discourse, then there can be no extra-discursively "real" black or post-colonial identity, to which a multicultural or post-colonial cultural politics might appeal for validation. As Gayatri Spivak has astutely observed: "when the connection between desire and subject is taken as irrelevant . . . the subject-effect that surreptitiously emerges is much like the generalized ideological subject of the theorist . . . It is certainly not the desiring subject as Other".[92] For Spivak, as a self-declared "post-colonial intellectual", it is essential to ask whether the subaltern "Other" can speak. And yet she is also a "deconstructionist", the translator into English of Derrida's *Of Grammatology*, "a model product", in Colin MacCabe's words, "of an Indian undergraduate and an American graduate education – probably the most scholarly combination on this planet".[93]

Paying her dues simultaneously to both the post-structuralist academy and post-colonialist politics, Spivak suggested to her colleagues in the *Subaltern Studies* group: *"strategically* adhering to the essentialist notion of consciousness, that would fall prey to an anti-humanist critique, within a historiographic practice that draws many of its strengths from that very critique".[94] Which means, in short, that whatever deconstruction's theoretical purchase when directed at European, white, male, bourgeois humanism, post-colonial theorists must nonetheless proceed *as if* humanism were still valid, *as if* the subject had still not been decentred, *as if* deconstruction had failed, if ever they are adequately to represent insurgent, or "subaltern", consciousness itself. As Spivak continues: "the Subaltern Studies group . . . must remain committed to the subaltern as the subject of history. As they chose this strategy, they reveal the limits of the critique of humanism as produced in the West".[95]

This resort to a kind "strategic" humanism is neither so shocking nor so original as Spivak believes. It is reminiscent, at one level, of Derrida's own decision to exempt Marxism from deconstructive critique and of his deliberate refusal to join in the "anti-Marxist concert" of the post-1968 period in France.[96] At another, it even rehearses something of Thompson's older socialist humanist argument against structuralism, an argument which Spivak herself cursorily dismisses as "trivializing".[97] For what made Thompson's humanism distinctively socialist was precisely its own sense of the strategic importance of a kind of class essentialism: this was in fact one of the important matters at issue between Thompson and Williams in the debate over *The Long Revolution*.[98] The *necessity* for this resort to strategic essentialism – not only in Spivak, but also in Derrida and in the feminist theorist, Elaine Showalter[99] – surely casts doubt on the entire anti-humanist theoretical enterprise. For what use is a theory which requires for its effective application that we pretend not to believe in it?

Post-colonial theory was initially very much the creation of "Third World" intellectuals working in literary studies within "First World" universities. Edward Said is Palestinian and Gayatri Spivak Indian, and both teach in English and comparative literature at Columbia University. One could easily add to the list: Homi Bhabha is an Indian in English at the University of Sussex, Dipesh Chakrabarty an Indian in critical theory at the University of Melbourne.[100] The resultant combination of Third Worldist cultural politics and French post-structuralist high theory has become an important, perhaps even characteristic, feature of the contemporary First World radical academy. Aijaz Ahmad, himself an Indian academic, has recently argued very persuasively against this entire position as tending to substitute textualism for activism and nation for class.[101] Moreover, in Ahmad's view, much of the intellectual legitimacy attaching to post-colonial theory actually derives from its fundamental complicity with the structures of social privilege enjoyed by both First and Third World intellectuals and by Third World ruling classes. "The East", he wrily observes, "seems to have become, yet again, a *career* – even for the 'Oriental' this time, and within the Occident too."[102]

Any commentary on these debates from a First World source is open, by a roughly similar logic, to the accusation of its own complicity in the profits of imperialism. But let me here hazard the observation that such textualist politics as post-structuralism enjoins do generally function much as Ahmad argues: so as to defer activism and to bestow the spurious illusion of political radicalism on what is in fact an almost entirely conventional academic activity. Doubtless, the possibilities for activism are peculiarly circumscribed for a Palestinian exile in New York. Doubtless, professors of literature are professionally obliged to a preoccupation with problems of textuality, and doubtless Edward Said or Gayatri Spivak are as entitled to their profession as is Aijaz Ahmad to his. Doubtless, Said's more popular writings[103] attest to a more activist political intention than Ahmad appears to allow. But whatever these particular qualifications, the more general logic of post-structuralism does indeed seem to lead in the direction to which Ahmad points. As Terry Eagleton has recently observed: "Post-structuralism is among other things a kind of theoretical hangover from the failed uprising of '68 . . . blending the euphoric libertarianism of that moment with the stoical melancholia of its aftermath".[104]

That this is so becomes particularly apparent from some of the more recent appropriations of post-colonial theory by First World intellectuals. These have increasingly been premised on the dubious assumption that the settler societies of America and Australasia and the formerly colonized societies of Africa and Asia can meaningfully be assimilated to each other as in some sense analogously post-colonial. Moreover, the category of the post-colonial has typically been expanded to include not simply the post-independence period, but all writing "affected by the imperial process from the moment of colonization to the present day".[105] A paradoxical effect of this argument is to obliterate rather than celebrate difference: both that between pre-independence and post-independence periods; and, more importantly, that between the colonizers and the colonized. For, of course, the colonies of white settlement are not post-colonial in any sense other than that posited by a strict periodization between pre-independence and post-independence. In every other respect, they are instances of a continuing colonization, in which the descendents of the original colonists remain dominant over the colonized indigenous peoples.

Whatever the merits of the kinds of analysis pioneered by Said, these accounts of how European colonial discourse constructed the non-European as "Other" cannot plausibly be applied either to Australia or to Canada, still less to the United States. To the contrary, the colonies of European settlement were typically imagined precisely as overseas extensions of Europe itself, as "Self" rather than "Other", as "New Britannias", in the phrase of an Australian poet.[106]Post-colonial literature – defined both as exclusive of non-English language writing and as inclusive of settler writing – has thus increasingly come to represent little more than a fashionable refurbishment of what used to be called "Commonwealth literature". And, as Salman Rushdie rightly insisted: "'Commonwealth literature' should not exist. If it did not, we could appreciate writers for what they are, whether in English or not; we could discuss literature in terms of its real groupings, which may well be national, which may well be linguistic, but which may also be international, and based on imaginative affinities".[107]

To be fair, the New Zealand post-colonial theorist, Simon During, does concede a distinction between the post-colonialism of the post-colonized and that of the post-colonizer.[108] But no such distinction registers in Ashcroft, Griffiths and Tiffin, for whom the logic of their own argument compels the inclusion of the United States within the category post-colonial.[109] The implication, that American culture is somehow subversively peripheral to a European centre, seems almost wilfully perverse, given that many of the dominant cultural forms of our time – science fiction, jazz, rock, the Hollywood movie, some important television sub-genres – are characteristically American in origin. It can be sustained only at the price of a systematic indifference to such "popular" cultural forms and a corollary insistence on the special value of "Literature". For it is only in the very peculiar and increasingly socially marginal instance of high literary studies that such notions of American marginality retain an even residual credibility. Elsewhere, American centrality is surely almost self-evidently obvious. There is, then, a certain irony in the way post-colonial theory proclaims its own antipathy to the Anglocentrism of traditional English studies, whilst simultaneously rejoicing in notions of Literature clearly reminiscent of Leavisite culturalism.

If the idea of an alternative commonality provided a left culturalist rationale both for radical nationalism and for multiculturalism, then the category of difference performs a similar function in post-structuralism. But in each case the practical politico-cultural dilemma arises of how exactly to reconcile a post-colonial identity, the external difference of which is predicated upon its own internal unity, to a multicultural diversity that will threaten all national cultural unities, including even the post-colonial. In Simon During's opinion, "today, in writing in a First World colony . . . one ought to be nationalistic" and "nationalism in post-colonial nations has virtues that perhaps it lacks elsewhere".[110] This is especially so, he continues, in those settler societies where "nationalism is not used *against* large minority racial/tribal groups".[111] By contrast, Sneja Gunew insists that multiculturalism must seek to "confound those who believe that the land speaks . . . literary nationalism".[112] Ironically, Gunew is here writing against an Australian radical nationalism that is exactly the kind of "virtuous" post-colonial nationalism During seeks to celebrate.

No doubt nationalism "has different effects and meanings in a peripheral nation than in a world power".[113] But these differences may matter much less for those whose own difference is lived in and against the peripheral nation – women, subordinate social classes, ethnic minorities, indigenous peoples – than for the post-colonial national intelligentsia itself. Post-colonial theory is thus repeatedly hoist by its own post-structuralist petard. Ahmad's critique of Said and Rushdie clearly implies as much. And Said himself concedes something of the same, when he writes that "the national bourgeoisies . . . have often replaced the colonial force with a new class-based and ultimately exploitative force; instead of liberation after decolonization one simply gets the old colonial structures replicated in new national terms".[114]

Post-structuralism and postmodernism

Post-structuralism has often been represented as in some sense peculiarly "postmodern". And there is indeed a certain "fit" between post-structuralist theoretical relativism and the kind of social and cultural pluralism which many commentators find distinctive of our contemporary postmodern condition. The institutionalized claims to authoritative cultural judgement characteristic of culturalism were typically predicated on the prior assumption of white, Western, middle-class masculinity. There is no theoretical space at all for the Islamic, the female, the proletarian, even "the scientific", in Leavis's famous claim that culture is necessarily singular: "We have no other; there is only one, and there can be no substitute".[115] By contrast, a contemporary post-structuralist feminist philosopher can argue that: "Feminist antihumanism . . . implies the dismantling of a constricting commonness and the open celebration of specificity".[116]

This assimilation of postmodernism to post-structuralism has become almost routine amongst both protagonists and antagonists of each. And yet the two are by no means synonymous. As Scott Lash rightly insists, there is no necessary parallel between post-structuralism and postmodernism, nor between critical theory and anti-postmodernism.[117] Much of the debate over postmodernity has in fact been conducted within an explicitly historicist theoretical framework which derives at least as much from the Central European, German-speaking variant of Western Marxism, or its emigré American sub-variant, as from any kind of post-structuralism. This is true, for example, of Daniel Bell, Jürgen Habermas, Peter Bürger, Andreas Huyssen, Fredric Jameson, and of Agnes Heller and Ferenc Fehér.[118] It is also true, by way of a strange kind of negative reaction formation, of Jean Baudrillard and Jean-François Lyotard, both of whom are ex-Marxists.[119] In Britain, much of the debate has been carried forward by writers associated with the journal *Theory, Culture and Society*, which has taken as its main theoretical reference points not the combination of French post-structuralism with literary theory, but that of German culturalism with sociology.[120] Indeed, the major post-structuralist thinkers have been almost entirely absent from this debate, and much more so than have those feminists whose supposed absence has excited much (implicitly androcentric) comment.[121]

In general, French post-structuralism has been far too preoccupied with the high modernist canon to accord any serious attention to a contemporary culture that has acquired an increasingly postmodern complexion: Barthes's writerly texts are modernist rather than postmodernist in character; and insofar as Foucault's archaeology is able to envisage a "post-modern" *episteme*, it is that inaugurated by high structuralism itself.[122] As Alex Callinicos notes with perverse approval, it is not at all clear that the major post-structuralist thinkers do endorse the idea of the postmodern.[123] That this is indeed so is part of the failure of post-structuralism, however. Andreas Huyssen has suggestively argued that "rather than offering a *theory of postmodernity* and developing an analysis of contemporary culture, French theory provides us primarily with an *archaeology of modernity*, a theory of modernism at the stage of its exhaustion".[124] But if post-structuralism is thus in no sense a theory of postmodernity, there is another interesting sense in which, as Huyssen also recognizes, it is nonetheless itself an important instance of postmodernism: "the gesture of poststructuralism, to the extent that it abandons all pretense to a critique that would go beyond language games . . . seems to seal the fate of the modernist project which . . . always upheld a vision of a redemption of modern life through culture. That such visions are no longer possible to sustain may be at the heart of the postmodern condition".[125]

There can be little doubt that the transition from structuralism to post-structuralism has entailed a certain retreat both from "macropolitics" of the kind once familiar both to the left and to the right, and from the historical "grand narratives" which often accompanied such politics. Indeed, the attempt to undermine the epistemological and political status of historical knowledge has been characteristic of the entire post-structuralist enterprise. In this respect, post-structuralism remains deeply complicit in what Fredric Jameson terms the more generally postmodernist sensibility of a "society bereft of all historicity".[126] Structuralism was itself a profoundly anti-historicist doctrine; post-structuralism further radicalized this anti-historicism by deconstructing even the notion of structure itself. In its place we find: first, a rejection of the truth both of science and of theory, in favour of the infinitely plural pleasures of a textuality possessed of no determinate relation either to the linguistic signified or to any extra-linguistic referent; and second, a stress on the radical contemporaneity and radical indeterminacy, in short the radical textuality, of our current constructions of the past.

Neither position is entirely without insight: our readings both of cultural texts and of history itself are indeed unavoidably plural and, equally unavoidably, made in the present. But if pluralism is inescapable, even desirable, then relativism most certainly is not. There are many truths about any particular cultural text, from the truth of its original inspiration to that of its most recent reception, and each such truth is recoverable, if at all, then only as a result of systematic empirical investigation. Such investigations require for their practical efficacy a certain methodological pluralism; but they are predicated, as a condition of their very possibility, on the epistemological postulate of a past or present reality existing quite independently of any knowledge construction we may place upon it. This was the central lesson of Thompson's famous Epistle to the Althusserians,[127] and it is one that might equally be readdressed to the deconstructionists.

By comparison with theoretical culturalisms, whether of the left or of the right, post-structuralism often appears both pedagogically and politically inconsequential. Its retreat into an indefinite pluralism that is neither historical nor properly speaking critical (since criticism presupposes some real object external to itself) can easily entail a kind of textual frivolity as intellectually self-indulgent as Leavisism was intellectually censorious. Its textual erotics increasingly mimic the licensed hedonisms of the officially established utilitarian culture of the (post)modern Occident. The human sciences are today increasingly threatened by the imposition of criteria of value defined almost exclusively in terms of economic gain and supposed "national interest". But if the best that the radical intelligentsia can manage by way of an alternative is state-subsidised *jouissance*, as a minority privilege, then it is one that will neither succeed nor even deserve to succeed.

The speed with which structuralist and post-structuralist discourse has been accorded academic recognition and legitimacy powerfully attests to the eminently co-optable nature of even the most apparently radical of semiotic enterprises. For this was structuralism's own hidden secret: that, in its scientism, in its near-universal espousal of a modernist aesthetic,[128] in its deprecation of the possibilities for collective human agency, in its almost impossibly constricted sense of the scope for an adversarial intellectual practice, it provided the intellectual class itself with an almost ideally effective ideological legitimation for its own peculiar position as both subordinate partner and loyal opposition to the dominant classes. Post-structuralism holds out the promise of an almost identical ideological accomplishment available to an intelligentsia even more professionalized, and even less inclined to believe in the possibilities either of truth or of action. As Pierre Bourdieu says of Derrida: "Because he never withdraws from the philosophical game, whose conventions he respects, even in the ritual transgressions at which only traditionalists could be shocked, he can only philosophically tell the truth about the philosophical text and its philosophical reading, which (apart from the silence of orthodoxy) is the best way of not telling it".[129]

Chapter 5
FEMINISM

Where culturalisms and structuralisms have very often provided the intellectual class itself with its own peculiar ideologies of, respectively, revolt and accommodation, both Marxism and *feminism* have proclaimed, by contrast, their capacities to represent quite other interests, those of the labour and socialist movements on the one hand, the women's and feminist movements on the other. Neither claim is unproblematic, for, of course, the passage from first to second term is in each case not easily accomplished: labour movements are not invariably socialist, nor women's movements invariably feminist. Nor is it clear how best to understand the specific rôle of the socialist or feminist intellectual, whether as part of the movement for which he or she claims to speak, or as a particular politically motivated member of the intellectual class. If the latter, then the possibility arises that Marxism or feminism might represent, not so much the true consciousness of the exploited proletariat or the raised consciousness of oppressed women, as the false consciousness of a certain fraction of the intelligentsia. And yet, socialist ideas have on occasion undoubtedly appealed to fairly large working class audiences, and feminist ideas to significant numbers of women. The aspiration to construct a form of intellectualism directed by needs other than those of the intelligentsia itself, and of the traditionally dominant classes and groups, is without doubt entirely honourable. Whether that aspiration has been successfully realized remains to be seen.

From the first to the second wave

Women's resistance to patriarchal oppression is very probably as old as patriarchy itself, and certainly long pre-dates the various types of cultural theory and cultural politics that have concerned us here. In

Europe, a recognizably feminist political vision can be traced back at least to the French revolutionary period: witness Mary Wollstonecraft's *A Vindication of the Rights of Women* or Olympe de Gouges's *Déclaration des droits de la femme et de la citoyenne*.[1] In the United States there was a clear feminist element both in the early to mid 19th century "abolitionist" campaigns against slavery and in the later "prohibitionist" campaigns against alcohol. But organized feminist politics did not develop in Britain until towards the end of the century. Much of this early "first wave" feminism remained quite fundamentally utilitarian and liberal in theoretical disposition, its central agitational focus provided by the demand for female suffrage, for which both Harriet Taylor and John Stuart Mill had been very public advocates.[2] By the end of the 1920s, however, the battle for the suffrage had been won: women aged over 30 secured the vote in 1918, all adult women in 1928.

For an independent feminist politics to have continued would have required more precise self-definition, and hence more explicitly theoretical articulation. Insofar as it was ever achieved, such definition occurred by way of the postulated opposition between female nurturing on the one hand, and masculine violence and militarism on the other. The small minority of feminists who had opposed the First World War, Sylvia and Adela Pankhurst for example, had certainly toyed with such ideas. For the main part, however, anti-militarism was as likely to derive inspiration from socialist ideas as from feminist: Sylvia Pankhurst was close to Keir Hardie and the pacifist wing of British socialism, Adela actively involved in Australia with the Victorian Socialist Party. Such connections between radical socialism and radical feminism might perhaps have been expected to persist into the inter-war years: certainly, Sylvia Pankhurst had greeted the Russian Revolution with considerable enthusiasm. But the new Communist Party's increasing dominance over British radicalism combined with its own, and Moscow's, deep antipathy to feminist concerns so as to obstruct the development of any sustainedly feminist cultural politics. Those women intellectuals who were recruited into the orbit of British Communism, Jessica Mitford for example, seem only rarely to have been attracted to any specifically feminist version of radical politics.

Reflecting on the early history of feminism at the beginning of the second wave itself, two American feminist historians were to conclude that: "the woman's movement virtually died in 1920 and . . . feminism was to lie dormant for forty years".[3] Allowing for the peculiarities of the different national contexts, much the same could also be said of Britain. But just as the sixties' student movement had refurbished the New Left, so too it unleashed a new, "second wave", feminism. The campus milieu provided support and inspiration to both the new women's liberation groups and the new student socialist groups with which they were occasionally intertwined. In 1971 Germaine Greer, then still a lecturer in English at Warwick University, had published *The Female Eunuch*,[4] which soon became one of the key texts of the international women's movement. Techniques first acquired in student journalism were put to work to produce a plethora of feminist newspapers, magazines and journals, the most important of which would prove to be *Feminist Review*, published by the independent Feminist Review Collective from 1979 until 1987, and by Methuen and later Routledge from 1988 on. Like the New Left, second wave feminists saw themselves very much as part of an international and internationalist political movement. Like the New Left, second wave feminists aspired to a level of theoretical articulacy and sophistication unimagined by previous radical movements.

Like the New Left, second wave feminists also came increasingly to define cultural theory itself as a matter of both particular concern and peculiar political relevance. My major focus for the remainder of this chapter will, then, be provided by the various types of feminist cultural theory which developed alongside the women's liberation movements of the sixties and after. This is not to suggest that "real" feminism began only in the 1960s, nor to deny the existence of a first wave, but only to insist that, to a quite remarkable extent, the later movement was obliged to pull itself up by its own theoretical bootstraps. If the feminist movement has indeed rediscovered the legacy of Aphra Behn or of Mary Wollstonecraft, then this has been much more obviously a consequence than a cause of its own initiatives. Contemporary feminism has had no clearly acknowledged intellectual precursors, no equivalent to what Marx has meant for Marxism, Arnold for (Anglo-) culturalism, or Saussure for structuralism. So effectively had patriarchal culture repressed the collective memory of women's history that the women's movement had no real choice but to begin virtually from scratch.

Types of feminism

Virtually, but not quite. Two widely acknowledged sources of intellectual inspiration for second wave feminism, referred to as such in text after text, have been: Virginia Woolf (1882–1941), the modernist novelist and critic, and member of the Bloomsbury Group, whose *A Room of One's Own* was first published in 1929; and Simone de Beauvoir (1908–86), the leading French existentialist philosopher and novelist, whose *The Second Sex* was first published in 1949. Woolf initiated an enduringly feminist concern with the material constraints on women's cultural production; and also a novel redefinition of Arnoldian disinterestedness as androgynous, which, though by no means uncontroversial amongst feminists, has nonetheless been seen by some as representing a first, tentative, step toward a distinctively feminist aesthetic.[5] She also registered the possibility of a peculiarly female type of writing, characterized by a sentence "of a more elastic fibre . . . capable of stretching to the extreme, of suspending the frailest particles, of enveloping the vaguest shapes".[6] In both her criticism and her fiction a connection is more or less deliberately forged between women's consciousness and modernist literary technique. It is a connection which has continued to fascinate feminist intellectuals.[7]

For de Beauvoir's feminism, as for Sartre's Marxism, the central theoretical conundrum became that of explaining how it is that a human nature characterized quite fundamentally by radical freedom, in which humans make themselves only in conscious practice, can nonetheless be betrayed into the bad faith of unfreedom. How can it be that woman, "a free and autonomous being like all human creatures . . . finds herself living in a world where men compel her to assume the status of the Other"?[8] De Beauvoir's explanation of femininity as a masculine project, in which men construct women as objects, a project in which women themselves are often complicit,[9] clearly anticipates much recent feminist debate. Her hope that socialism might ultimately provide a solution to the problems of women's oppression, a hope which she herself later came to qualify,[10] has continued to inspire a certain interest in the possibilities for a socialist feminism, though much more so in Britain than in France.

Woolf and de Beauvoir were both novelists and both also what we might well term cultural theorists, or at least cultural critics. Writing about culture, very often quite specifically about literature, has in fact occupied a highly salient position within second wave feminist discourse. Michèle Barrett insists that she "can find no sustained argument as to *why* feminists should be so interested in literature".[11] Perhaps so. But parts of the answer are provided: firstly, by the fact that feminist intellectuals have happened to be already employed disproportionately in teaching in the humanities, and especially in literature; secondly, by the widespread feminist perception of women's oppression as having cultural, rather than biological, roots; and thirdly, by the way in which feminists have very often seen women's cultural production as central to "consciousness raising", and hence to social change.

Despite the occasionally "separatist" ambitions of certain types of feminist politics, recent feminist cultural theory has been far from self-contained. K. K. Ruthven may indeed be "the Crocodile Dundee of male feminism", as Elaine Showalter describes him, but he is right nonetheless to stress the extent to which feminist thought has been influenced by Marxism, structuralism and post-structuralism.[12] We might add, moreover, as Ruthven does not, that much other feminist writing often remains covertly indebted to kinds of culturalism much more traditional to literary studies. To recognize as much is not to detract from the originality of the central feminist argument: that all hitherto existing societies, except perhaps the very early gynocentric societies discussed by Merlin Stone,[13] have been patriarchally organized around the oppression of women by men; and that the dominant cultures of those societies have therefore been necessarily androcentric, that is, male-centred, and quite possibly positively misogynist. It is, however, to recognize the versatility and the eclecticism with which feminism has rifled through the patriarchal cultural legacy, in search of theories, methods and concepts that might be put to new, gynocentric, use. Hence the way in which feminist cultural theory has proved able to recycle concepts of ideology, of signification, and of culture.

We should, then, alert ourselves to the influence of Marxism on socialist feminist writers, such as those associated with the British Marxist-feminist Literature Collective; and to that of structuralism and post-structuralism, and especially the work of Derrida and Lacan, on many of the writers associated with what was once the "new French feminism". We should also, of course, note the often unacknowledged influence of culturalist notions of tradition and disinterestedness in much Anglo-American, and especially American, feminist scholarship. The obvious instance here is that provided by Elaine Showalter herself. Showalter is Professor of English at Princeton and has been a declared opponent of all such dependence on masters, a dependency she has noted in French and British feminisms, but not in her own work. But she nicely registers the differences in approach when she observes that: "English feminist criticism, essentially Marxist, stresses oppression; French feminist criticism, essentially psychoanalytic, stresses repression; American feminist criticism, essentially textual, stresses expression. All, however, have become gynocentric".[14] By this last remark, she meant only to stress the way in which second wave feminism had evolved from an initial critique of androcentrism into a later celebration of gynocentrism. Doubtless, this wasn't in fact a uniform trajectory, but it was indeed very common, and more particularly so in the English-speaking world.

Anglo-American feminism

Certainly, Kate Millett's *Sexual Politics*, the single most important pioneering work of anglophone feminist cultural theory, had been concerned precisely to develop a critique of sexist culture. Millett argued that the period between 1930 and 1960 had been characterized by a sexual counter-revolution, a reactionary response to the protracted sexual revolution of the previous hundred years, a response entailing, above all, a reassertion of patriarchy.[15] She traced the presence of this sexual counter-revolution in Soviet and Nazi family policies and in sexually conservative ideologies such as Freudian psychoanalysis and functionalist sociology. The book culminated, however, in a sustained critique of the work of three male novelists, "counter-revolutionary sexual politicians",[16] as she termed them: D. H. Lawrence, Henry Miller and Norman Mailer. Millett's purpose here was to expose as deeply patriarchal the fundamental images of male–female relations which informed their work. Thus she wrote of Lawrence that in *Lady Chatterley* he "uses the words 'sexual' and 'phallic' interchangeably, so that the celebration of sexual passion for which the book is so renowned is largely a celebration of the penis of Oliver Mellors . . . This is . . . the transformation of masculine ascendancy into a mystical religion".[17]

Millett's work initiated a whole range of studies into the various ways in which an androcentric culture had constructed persistently negative images of women, studies which extended beyond her own initial focus on masculine high culture, to include both élite and popular cultural forms, produced by and for both men and women. This interest in negative gender stereotyping also laid the groundwork for an account of male pornography as representing women in acutely misogynist form,[18] which became increasingly relevant to practical feminist politics. This critique of cultural sexism had no direct counterpart in Marxist cultural theory, which typically accepted early bourgeois culture, at least, as "progressive". Feminists generally attribute no parallel progressive rôle to patriarchy, though some might concede its historical near-inevitability. Hence, the vigour with which second wave feminism was able to prosecute its case against the masculine cultural ascendancy.

But this early critique of sexism moved quite quickly toward the recovery, and celebration, of women's own culture. The term coined by Showalter for this latter development was "gynocritics", a translation of the French word, *la gynocritique*, by which she meant the discovery of "woman as the producer of textual meaning".[19] One important line of argument here had been the attempt to discover a female tradition, and perhaps even a female Great Tradition. Showalter's own *A Literature of Their Own* and Ellen Moers's *Literary Women* both explored such notions. For Showalter, there was indeed a distinctively female tradition in English literature, a tradition which had evolved through three broad phases, those of imitation, protest, and self-discovery. The central aim for Showalter, as she made clear in her closing lines, was still to be "great" art: "if contact with a female tradition and a female culture is a center; if women take strength in their independence to act in the world, then Shakespeare's sister, whose coming Woolf asked us to await in patience and humility, may appear at last".[20] Moers, too, detected a female tradition, one perhaps less obviously proto-canonical than Showalter's, but one characterized nonetheless by a distinctively "female realism", in which "money and its making were characteristically female . . . subjects".[21] Gynocritics has had one obviously important practical corollary within the women's movement: the creation of independent feminist publishing houses such as Virago, committed to the recovery and republication of women's writing. Again, there is no real counterpart within contemporary Marxist cultural theory to this practice of the discovery and celebration of the literatures of the oppressed. Marxist writers seem surprisingly uninterested in the creativity of proletarian culture, an indifference which speaks volumes, surely, about the actual distance between their interests and those of the class they may occasionally claim to represent.

I suggested above that anglophone feminisms of the type represented by Showalter's work were frequently deeply implicated in often unacknowledged culturalist theoretical assumptions. Let us return to this matter for a moment. Culturalism, we have seen, typically posits an organicist notion of culture, incorporating both anthropological and literary understandings of culture as, respectively, the embodiment of a whole way of life and a repository of superior value. For all her antipathy to the French masters, Showalter's work clearly incorporated each of these elements. For her, both the culture of women and the culture that women share with men have each to be conceived in holistic and organicist terms: "women's culture forms a collective experience within the cultural whole, an experience that binds women writers to each other over time and space".[22] Her model of culture was derived quite explicitly from anthropology,[23] and though literary value is simply assumed, rather than argued for, in much of her work, there can be little doubt that she displays a penchant for "completeness, even as an unattainable ideal",[24] at least as Arnoldian as anything in Raymond Williams. Her self-confessed textualism presumably derived from a similar source.

For a culturalist thinker, such as Showalter in some significant respects most certainly has been, the question of literary and cultural value is a matter of very real importance. Perhaps the central culturalist argument for the value of culture is that it somehow reveals or expresses some vital "truth" or another. In Leavis, though not in Eliot, this had led to a positive valorization of "life" which came dangerously close to a theory of aesthetic realism. Much early second wave anglophone feminism in fact subscribed to an aesthetic of this kind. When American feminists began to articulate their own criteria of literary value, they typically tended towards either the notion of subjective authenticity, or that of objective realism, or some combination of both. As Josephine Donovan concluded, "it is . . . clear that one of the primary criteria by which feminist critics are judging works of literature is by what one might call the 'truth criterion' . . .

there are truths and probabilities about the female experience that form a criterion against which to judge the authenticity of a literary statement about women".[25] Toril Moi was surely right to detect a similar such conception in Showalter, especially in the latter's objections to Woolf's modernism.[26] Moi herself pointed by way of evidence to Showalter's passing reference to Lukács. But much more significant, surely, is the reference to Q. D. Leavis:[27] what we find in Showalter is a genuinely feminist culturalism, centred around a notion of authenticity indicative of a kind of politically charged, female, (Q. D.?) Leavisism. That this is so does not in itself invalidate Showalter's position, as Moi appears to imagine it might. It does suggest, however, that for feminists, as for others, there is simply no such thing as a theoretically innocent reading.

Socialist feminism

Where the majority of Anglo-American, and especially American, feminists had found culture, a female literary tradition and female realism, those mainly British feminists who had attempted to work with concepts drawn from the Marxist tradition discovered ideology and the subsequent impress within ideology of the mode of material production. As the Marxist-feminist Literature Collective announced at Essex University in 1977: "Literary texts are . . . ideological in the sense that they cannot give us a knowledge of the social formation; but they do give us . . . an imaginary representation of real relations".[28] This was almost exactly the Althusserian formulation of the theory of ideology. It should come as little surprise, then, that the Collective's preferred reading strategy, which sought to "analyse the incoherences and contradictions in the texts",[29] and to relate these to historical developments in the social formation, derived explicitly from that of the French Althusserian literary theorist, Pierre Macherey. The point to note is that the literary texts under discussion here were themselves by women writers, that is, that they were all, in fact, examples of precisely that female tradition which Showalter by implication exempted from such "ideological" analysis.[30] As in Althusserian Marxism, so too in much British Marxist feminism, experiential authenticity was simply, or perhaps even complexly, reduced to ideology.

These British feminist appropriations of the Marxian notion of ideology took on a surprisingly uniform Althusserian coloration. Michèle Barrett, herself a member of the Marxist-feminist Literature Collective, explained in the first edition of her *Women's Oppression Today* that any such appropriation required the postulate: either that gender differences are separate from class divisions, but that Althusser's method is nonetheless applicable to both (in effect, that sexist ideology reproduces patriarchal relations of dominance); or that gender divisions can be analytically integrated into the class structure and can therefore be explained in terms of the substance of Althusser's position.[31] Both strategies were pursued, and Barrett herself was often acute on the strengths and weaknesses of each. But in 1980 at least, she still had no real doubts as to the fundamental adequacy of the Althusserian notion that ideology is somehow integrally related to the relations of production – which for her, as a feminist, involved not only a class division of labour but also a sexual division of labour.[32]

Barrett's own account of the process by which textual representations reproduce gender ideology identified four central such mechanisms: stereotyping; compensation, via the discourse about the supposed moral value of femininity; collusion, that is, manipulation of consent; and recuperation, that is, the negation of challenges to the dominant gender ideology.[33] It is not at all difficult to recognise each of these at work in both canonical and popular cultural texts. But the danger with such heavily structuralist accounts was that they so very easily conjured up the impression of a self-sealing, functional system of oppression, a system which, were it indeed such, would be effectively unchallengeable. If the world is changeable, rather than merely changing (as Althusser supposed), then it can be changed only by the agency of some human subject. But Marxist-feminism appeared to inherit from Althusserianism a deep antipathy to the notion of the subject. So much so, in fact, that another member of the Collective, Cora Kaplan, came to define the opposition between socialist and liberal (actually, the term she uses is "humanist') feminisms almost entirely in such anti-humanist terms:

> literary texts . . . centre the individual as object and subject of
> their discourse . . . The problem for socialist feminists is . . . the
> romantic theory of the subject so firmly entrenched within the
> discourse. Humanist feminist criticism does not object to the
> idea of an immanent, transcendent subject but only to the ex-

clusion of women from these definitions which it takes as an accurate account of subjectivity rather than as a historically constructed ideology.[34]

There were undoubtedly real strengths in the Marxist-feminist approach: they were right, surely, to refuse the obvious post-Marxist temptation simply to substitute gender for class, and to insist, to the contrary, that cultural forms such as the novel, drama and poetry are "discourses in which the fused language of class, race and gender are both produced and re-represented".[35] They were right, surely, to insist on the crucial relevance to the analysis of gender ideology of an elaborated account of the modes of material and cultural production. But if feminists are to make use of Marxist concepts, then why not of those which provide more, rather than less, scope for creative human initiative? In short, why not of Williams's reading of Gramsci, say, rather than that of Althusser? The obverse of this theoretical predilection for structuralism was often a practical suspicion of popular feminist writing inexplicable except as a function either of *avant-gardiste* cultural élitism or of vanguardist political immobilism. Witness Rosalind Coward's notorious dismissal of novels like Marilyn French's *The Women's Room* as essentially unfeminist simply by virtue of their fidelity to the conventions of realist literary narrative: "women-centred novels are *not* the product of a feminist audience. Nor can we say that the structures of the realist novel are neutral and that they can just be filled with a feminist content . . . It is quite clear that there are compelling similarities between 'novels that change lives' and contemporary fictional conventions, which should warn us against any simple designation of these novels as feminist".[36]

While Coward happily described her own position as coming "from within Marxism and feminism",[37] the major theoretical resources, both here and elsewhere in her work, very obviously derived not simply from Althusserianism, but from the structuralist tradition more generally, as for example in her resort to Barthesian semiology.[38] This conflation of Marxist and structuralist categories marked one of the defining features of British socialist feminism as much as of British Marxism during much of the 1970s: as we observed in Chapter 4, the British reception of French structuralism was, as it were, over-determined by the prior reception of Althusserianism. Socialist feminist analysis was thus increasingly preoccupied with the mechanisms by which the subject is interpellated as gendered. Writing in *Screen*, Laura

Mulvey argued that the general structure of conventional narrative cinema, quite apart from the particular contents of particular films, itself positions the male as active, the female as passive, or as she herself succinctly summarized it: "Woman as image, man as the bearer of the look".[39] An analogously Althusserian understanding informed Judith Williamson's *Decoding Advertisements*, for example, as also much of the work of the Women's Studies Group at Birmingham.[40] More distinctly post-structuralist thematics, deriving both from malestream deconstruction and from the new French feminism, were to become more prominent in both British and American feminism during the 1980s. We shall return to this matter very shortly. For the moment, however, let us proceed to a much more direct encounter with French feminism.

French feminisms

In her "Feminist Criticism in the Wilderness" essay, Showalter identifies four main models of sexual difference: the biological, the linguistic, the psychoanalytic and the cultural.[41] The implication here is that all four are practised both in France and in the United States. The explicit judgement, moreover, is that: "They overlap but are roughly sequential in that each incorporates the one before".[42] This latter judgement clearly functioned as a legitimation for Showalter's own culturalism, and was almost certainly false: cultural explanation had been chronologically prior in the anglophone feminist movement, as Millett's work surely attests.[1] So also, however, is the implication: the first three models had each, in fact, been much more characteristic of French feminism than of American. But Showalter was entirely right to identify these as the four such models practically available to gynocritics. Thus far, we have considered both culturalist formulations proper and also those versions of Marxist-feminism which, though redefining culture as ideology, nonetheless adopted a quite fundamentally "cultural" model of difference. It is in French feminism that we find the more persuasive instances of the biological, linguistic and psychoanalytical models.[43]

Much anglophone feminism had been desperately concerned to refute that whole range of essentially conservative arguments which had insisted upon the biological necessity of sexual difference. Hence the early centrality to its discourse of the analytical distinction between biological sex on the one hand, and socially produced gender on the other.[44] But if the female is to be celebrated positively, as in gynocritics it must be, then difference becomes much less of a political and theoretical liability. In the work of Hélène Cixous and in that of Luce Irigaray, female difference is at once both itself cause for celebration and also irretrievably biological in origin. Between the male and female body, and between male and female sexuality, is the source of that difference which for Cixous explains women's writing, and for Irigaray women's language. If Cixous and Irigaray each experiment, in different ways, with both biological and linguistic models of difference, then the best known French feminist application of a psychoanalytic model is almost certainly that of Julia Kristeva. Let us consider each in a little more detail.

In Cixous, a quasi-Derridean antipathy to the dualisms of logocentric thought becomes combined with de Beauvoir's strong sense of woman as subordinate term so as to produce a kind of feminist deconstruction. Thus, for Cixous, logocentrism is inextricably connected to phallocentrism: "the logocentric plan had always, inadmissably, been to create a foundation for (to found and fund) phallocentrism".[45] As for Derrida, it is *différance* in writing, the difference of *écriture féminine*, as Cixous terms it, that is subversive of all such dualisms. While Cixous is certainly prepared to concede that not all men repress their femininity, and even that some women "more or less strongly, inscribe their masculinity",[46] she nonetheless pursues the notion that women's writing somehow articulates the female body. Like the later Barthes, she connects writing to *jouissance*: "the difference . . . becomes most clearly perceived on the level of *jouissance*, inasmuch as a woman's instinctual economy cannot be identified by a man or referred to the masculine economy".[47] In her 1975 essay, "The Laugh of the Medusa", Cixous argued for a much more explicitly physiological connection between *écriture féminine* and the female body as a site of decentred eroticism: "A woman's body, with its thousand and one thresholds of ardor . . . will make the old single-grooved mother tongue reverberate with more than one language . . . More so than men . . . women are body. More body, hence more writing".[48]

Like Cixous, Irigaray too stresses the *jouissance* of the female body, and its connectedness to that type of deconstructive pluralism so highly prized in post-structuralist thought. "Her sexuality . . . is *plural*", she writes, "Is this the way texts write themselves/are written now? . . . *woman has sex organs more or less everywhere* She finds pleasure almost everywhere . . . the geography of her pleasure is far more diversified, more multiple in its differences, more complex, more subtle, than is commonly imagined – in an imaginary rather too narrowly focused on sameness".[49] And this is a matter not only of writing, but also of speech. For Irigaray, the female body gives rise to a distinctive women's language, *parler femme*, in which "'she' sets off in all directions . . . in what she says . . . woman is constantly touching herself".[50]

Showalter's insistence that "there can be no expression of the body which is unmediated by linguistic, social, and literary structures"[51] is, of course, true, but is nonetheless much less pertinent to the kind of argument advanced by Cixous and Irigaray than it might at first appear. What is at issue is not biological determinism, as Showalter supposed, but rather the nature of writing and of female sexuality, and of their possible connections, *given* the undoubtedly mediated ways in which the body finds cultural expression. A more serious objection, surely, is that which Juliet Mitchell directs at Kristeva, but which could easily be turned toward Cixous and Irigaray: that, insofar as femininity is indeed like this, then it is so only by virtue of the effects of patriarchal oppression. This "is just what the patriarchal universe defines as the feminine," Mitchell writes "all those things that have been assigned to women – the heterogeneous, the notion that women's sexuality is much more one of a whole body, not so genital, not so phallic. It is not that the carnival cannot be disruptive of the law; but it disrupts only within the terms of that law".[52]

Mitchell and Kristeva share a common interest in the work of Jacques Lacan, the post-structuralist psychoanalyst whose work had aspired to a synthesis between Freud and Saussure. Lacan's fundamental insight that *"the unconscious is structured like a language"*[53] had led him to the notion that language and sexual identity are simultaneously acquired, or better perhaps, simultaneously required. For Lacan, the child originally inhabits a pre-Oedipal "imaginary" characterized by speechless identity between child, mother and world. Entry into the symbolic order of language, and the acquisition of subjectivity, are achieved only at the price of a loss of this imaginary identity with the mother. The symbolic order is thus masculine, it is, in short, the law of the father. Lacan is clear that the imaginary must be superseded by the symbolic, but that that supersession nonetheless creates the unconscious, as a result of this repression of the earlier desire for the mother. Because identity with the mother, and with the world, can never be recovered (except in death), desire moves restlessly thereafter from object to object, from signifier to signifier. Like meaning itself, desire too can have no ultimate meaning.

Julia Kristeva is, in many respects, the very model of a modern Parisian intellectual: a practising psychoanalyst with a chair in linguistics; a key figure in the group of intellectuals which produced the journal, *Tel Quel*; her youthful enthusiasm for both Althusserianism and Maoism had given way to a much more apolitical, and potentially even conservative, set of psycho-semiotic preoccupations. Her work is "difficult", in what has become almost the habitual French fashion, and there can be little doubt that part, at least, of its appeal to Francophile, anglophone feminists arose simply as a result of her status as a properly "mandarin" intellectual. Hence the way in which the English-speaking reception of her work[54] was accompanied by much the same sort of "theoretical heavy breathing" as Thompson detected in the initial British response to Althusser.[55]

The key Kristevan text is almost certainly *Revolution in Poetic Language* (1974). Her central analytical framework here is essentially Lacanian, though she renames Lacan's "imaginary" as the "semiotic". The semiotic, moreover, is not necessarily repressed, but is, rather, an alternative mode of signification. Kristeva borrows from Plato the term *chora*, meaning womb or enclosed space, to refer to the pre-Oedipal pulsions with which the semiotic is linked. "Our discourse – all discourse – moves with and against the *chora*", she writes, "in the sense that it simultaneously depends upon and refuses it . . . The *chora* . . . is not a sign . . . it is not yet a signifier either . . . it is, however, generated in order to attain to this signifying position . . . the *chora* precedes and underlies figuration . . . and is analogous only to vocal or kinetic rhythm".[56] Once the symbolic order is entered, the semiotic is repressed but, according to Kristeva, not thereby superseded. Rather, it continues to constitute the heterogeneous and disruptive aspects of language. Where the symbolic is masculine, the semiotic is, not so much feminine, as like the feminine, that is, repressed and marginal. The semiotic is thus subversive: it deconstructs the binary oppositions that are fundamental to the structures of symbolic language. This position is very similar to that of Cixous and Irigaray. But in Kristeva, the sources of textual *jouissance* are located neither in the female body nor in female sexuality, but in the universally human experience of the pre-Oedipal semiotic. Masculinity and femininity are constructed by way of different routes out of this experience, and are thus in principle negotiable.

Since for Kristeva masculinity and femininity are essentially social constructs, it follows, then, that biologically male poets can in fact be as marginal to, and as subversive of, the symbolic order as are women. And, indeed, Kristeva's revolution in poetic language – in effect, the birth of the modern avant-garde – is a surprisingly male affair. Witness the rôle of Mallarmée and Lautréamont.[57] What is at issue here is a positive valorization, not of women's writing as such, but of modernist poetry. Cixous's much more explicitly gynocentric *écriture féminine* is similarly partisanly modernist and it too, surely more surprisingly, can accommodate the occasional biologically male writer. Thus the text of Genet has ascribed within it, according to Cixous, "a proliferating, maternal, femininity".[58] Male poets have certainly subverted the phallocentric order, Cixous insists, adding significantly, but "only the poets – not the novelists, allies of representationalism".[59] Thus French feminism effectively consigns virtually the whole of Showalter's female tradition, a novelists' tradition and an overwhelmingly representationalist tradition, to the camp of patriarchy.

Feminism and cultural politics

In themselves, these variously cultural, biological, linguistic and psychoanalytic models of difference remain compatible, and especially so if culture is understood as ultimately determining, as it is, paradoxically, both for Showalter and for Kristeva. Astonishingly, what most clearly divided American culturalist feminism from French feminist deconstruction, and what most clearly divided Marxist-feminists against each other, as it had divided Marxists, was the question of modernism. Where French feminism had tended to valorise modernist linguistic subversion, American feminism had tended to valorize the capacity of more representational forms to provide a more authentic account of women's experience. Drawing upon an analogy between the women's revolution and the colonial revolution, Showalter would argue that: "The language issue in feminist criticism has emerged, in a sense, after our revolution, and it reveals the tensions in the women's

movement between those who would stay outside the academic estab-
lishments and the institutions of criticism and those who would enter
and even conquer them".[60] This is, perhaps, fair comment on the difference between those such as Showalter, who have certainly stooped
to conquer, and those other American writers such as Mary Daly, who
most certainly have not. But it fails to explain that between Showalter
and Kristeva, for *both* of whom a central frame of reference was that
provided by the intellectual norms of the relevant national intellectual
culture and the relevant national academic institutions.

As to the politics of cultural realism and modernism, it seems to
me that no necessary relationship actually exists between either and
feminism, or, for that matter, between either and socialism. Both are
capable of subversive effect, but neither inherently so. As Juliet
Mitchell quite rightly observes, Kristeva's choice of exclusively masculine, and often proto-fascist, texts, was essentially apolitical: "Dis-
ruption itself can be . . . from the right as easily as from the left".[61]
The political potential of representational and non-representational
cultural forms is much more obviously determined by their immediate socio-political context than by any immanently textual properties
they may each possess. The gendered nature of our cultures seems to
me indisputable, but this is as true of our modernismsas of our realisms. As Janet Wolff has astutely observed, the feminine stroller, the
"flâneuse" as distinct from the Baudelaire's masculine "flâneur", has
no place in literary modernism.[62] And the "founding monuments" of
modernist painting appear similarly masculinist in provenance.[63] In
any case, the Kristevan programme at its fullest reach, in its positive
insistence on the necessarily subversive powers of the semiotic, seems
to me clearly misleading. For, as Mitchell argues: "the only way you
can challenge the church, challenge both the Oedipal and its pre-
Oedipal, is from within an *alternative symbolic universe* . . . So that politically speaking, it is only the symbolic, a new symbolism, a new law,
that can challenge the dominant law".[64]

For Mitchell herself the decentring of the (bourgeois/patriarchal)
subject produces, not the end of the subject as such, but "a heterogeneous area of the subject-in-process". She adds: "*in the process of becoming
what?* In deconstructing . . . history, we can only construct other histories. What are we in the process of becoming?".[65] The short answer is
that different feminists are in the process of becoming different things,
and that, for some at least, it is not so much a question of becoming,

as of already having become. For the most significant phrase, surely, in Showalter's comment on the language issue, is that disarmingly casual, throw-away line, "after our revolution". The United States, we may perhaps admit, has proceeded further in the direction of greater sexual equality than has either France or Britain. But to imagine the American women's revolution as having been completed – despite the failure of the Equal Rights Amendment, and despite that feminization of poverty which accompanied the Reagan and Bush administrations' cut-backs in welfare – was to imagine a women's revolution which had a great deal more to do with the career paths of a particular, feminist, fraction of the American intelligentsia, than with any kind of more general women's liberation. When Showalter did eventually acknowledge the threat of an anti-feminist backlash from the American New Right, she chose to represent it, all too predictably, as directed against "too *much* black and female power", not so much in society at large, but quite specifically, "in the university".[66]

Feminism and post-structuralism

As the 1980s proceeded, structuralist and post-structuralist claims became increasingly pressing upon anglophone feminisms. When Showalter herself came to produce an updated account of the evolution of recent feminist theory, she would recognize the gynocritical moment as having been succeeded, though not supplanted, by feminist post-structuralism, or "gynesic" criticism, as she terms it.[67] In the United States, new styles of feminist deconstruction had indeed acquired a very considerable importance, especially in the field of literary studies: obvious instances include the work of Gayatri Spivak, for example, or that of Barbara Johnson.[68] The enthusiasm for French post-structuralism amongst Australian feminists went so far as to prompt Michèle Barrett's description of the synthesis between Lacanian psychoanalysis and Barthesian semiology as the "New Australian Feminism"[69]. Barrett's own extensive retractions of her earlier Althusserian Marxist feminism, canvassed in the "Introduction" to the 1988 edition of *Women's Oppression Today*, clearly suggest the wider significance of such Australo-French feminisms within the international arena. Indeed, Verso's "Questions for Feminism" series, which Barrett co-edited from London, briefly became a major conduit for Australian post-structuralist, post-Marxist feminism into the broader English speaking world.

British feminists too had come to celebrate the apparently happy marriage between post-structuralist theory and feminist practice.[70] The editors of *Feminist Review*, which had formally announced itself a socialist feminist journal in its eighth issue, would reflect ruefully in its 23rd that: "some of us are very conscious that socialist-feminism is regarded by many as a dead political perspective".[71] The politico-intellectual effects of the developing union between feminism and post-structuralism were essentially twofold: firstly, a shift in general feminist preoccupations away from political economy and sociology, and towards literary and cultural studies, what Barrett nicely terms "feminism's turn to culture';[72] and secondly, a shift within feminist cultural studies itself away from a characteristically structuralist interest in the way the patriarchal text positions women, and toward a new interest in how women readers produce their own resistant, or at least negotiated, pleasures from such texts. Influential examples of the latter include Teresa de Lauretis's *Alice Doesn't* and Laura Mulvey's public rethinking of her own earlier structuralism.[73]

The sheer scale of this anglophone feminist enthusiasm for French post-structuralism became very nearly such as to marginalize alternative approaches within feminism. Such psycho-semiotic feminisms were to prove especially persuasive, moreover, to scholars working in philosophy or in the more cosmopolitan areas of literary and cultural studies. Indeed, the philosopher Elizabeth Grosz would effectively define contemporary feminist theory, as distinct from the feminism of the 1960s, in terms of a set of quite specifically "French" and post-structuralist thematics: as aspiring to autonomy (difference) rather than equality; as engaged theoretically not with "Marx, Reich, Marcuse", but "Freud, Lacan, Nietzsche, Derrida, Deleuze, Althusser, Foucault";[74] and as contesting singular or universal concepts of truth so as to "encourage a proliferation of voices . . . a plurality of perspectives and interests".[75] Such feminisms have often been ferociously and uncompromisingly "intellectual" in character. Hence, the not uncommon activist doubt that an intellectual practice centred on the deconstruction of male-dominated academic knowledges, rather than on the empirical reality of women's life in patriarchy, might prove both élitist and unfeminist. Grosz herself confronts this objection head-on: "feminist struggles are . . . occurring in many different practices, including the practice of the production of meanings, discourses and knowledges . . . This struggle for the right to write, read and know differently is not merely a minor or secondary task within feminist politics".[76]

As in the debates over multiculturalism and post-colonialism, the appeal of post-structuralism for feminists owes much to its status as somehow peculiarly "postmodern". But, just as in the debates over multiculturalism and post-colonialism, the relativizing logic of post-structuralism threatens precisely to undermine the ground from which any specifically feminist critique of patriarchal culture might actually be mounted. Hence Showalter's own determined insistence that:

> Feminist criticism can't afford . . . to give up the idea of female subjectivity, even if we accept it as a constructed or metaphysical one . . . Despite our awareness of diversity and deconstruction, feminist critics cannot depend on gynesic ruptures in discourse to bring about social change . . . The Other Woman may be transparent or invisible to some; but she is still very vivid, important, and necessary to us.[77]

Barrett makes very much the same point, albeit with a rather less assured sense of her own political certainties: "If we replace the given self with a constructed, fragmented self, this poses . . . the obvious political question of who is the I that acts and on what basis, . . . who is the I that is so certain of its fragmented and discursively constructed nature".[78]

A recent intervention into the feminist debates over popular fiction serves nicely to illustrate the dilemma. As we have seen, whereas early anglophone culturalist feminisms had sought to establish quasi-realist criteria of literary value, the later French-inspired post-structuralist feminism would privilege the subversively contradictory modernist text. But as Yvonne Tasker rightly notes, such invocation of the supposedly "feminine" text actually "stabilizes meaning once more", and illegitimately so, since "all texts are marked by contradiction".[79] Tasker follows through the logic of her own argument thus: "This is . . . only the appearance of something radical, and feminist cultural criticism needs to look beyond the terrain of this debate. . . . to shift from a discourse of textual value, whether of greatness or political correctness, would be a positive step".[80] Laura Kipnis, the American feminist video artist, has astutely observed that "the policies of *écriture féminine* and its practice of displacing politics to the aesthetic refer us back to that very modernist tradition that these . . . theorists are presumed to transcend; . . . their repudiation of representation, subjectivity, and history clearly set up the same antinomies with the popular that constituted aesthetic modernism from its inception".[81] Moreover, as Kipnis again rather astutely observes, this particular "configuration of politics, aesthetics, and theoretical autonomy" is not only generally modernist in character, it also much more specifically replicates the theoretical contours of an earlier Western Marxist enthusiasm for modernism.[82]

Kipnis herself proceeds to counterpose a postmodernist "renegotiation of the popular" to the "avant-gardist strategies of negation" which underlie French feminist theory;[83] and to argue that feminism must understand the popular as an access to hegemony rather than simply as an instrument of domination. The general failure to explore the political implications of postmodernism as distinct from modernism, she concludes, has allowed American anti-feminism, as represented for example by Phyllis Schafly, successfully to re-articulate the rhetoric of empowerment so as to produce a popular women's mobilization against the Equal Rights Amendment.[84] Kipnis's argument seems to me as pertinent to Britain as it is to the United States. Whatever may be true of malestream post-structuralism, Kristeva, Irigaray and Cixous remain committed to the archetypically modernist notion that modern life can indeed be redeemed through high culture, through writerly writing, in fact. This is an aestheticized redemptive politics, certainly, but it is still nonetheless a redemptive politics, and is as such quite distinct from the work both of Derrida and of the later Barthes. The theoretico-political import of post-structuralist feminism is thus ironically much more akin to that of the Frankfurt School than to late Barthesian hedonism: interestingly, Sigrid Weigel has drawn attention to the theoretical affinities between Kristevan semiotics and Benjamin's concept of the "dialectical image".[85]

This kinship is as much contextual as textual, especially so insofar as their anglophone receptions are concerned, as distinct from their variously continental European points of origin. In both cases, the moment of reception is structured by the immediate prehistories of the New Left and of second wave feminism respectively: their more or less contemporaneous emergence during the 1960s; their attainment to the status of near mass-movement by the early 1970s; their characteristic subversively postmodernist initial cultural politics; their later extensive and creative use of various kinds of imported European theory; and their protracted decline and degeneration into an academic theoreticism during the 1980s. As Kipnis summarizes the process: "This recourse to psychoanalysis . . . in both Marxist and feminist theory seems to take place at a particular theoretical juncture: one marked primarily by the experience of political catastrophe and defeat. The political appropriation of psychoanalysis appears to signal, then, a lack – of a mass movement or of successful counterhegemonic strategies . . . the current rearticulation of modernism by feminist theorists working at the intersections of deconstruction and psychoanalysis . . . suggests a repetitive tendency toward cultural modernism in marginalized vanguard political movements".[86]

There is an important implication here that feminist post-structuralism represents, in some significant sense, a kind of theoretical false consciousness distinctive to the women's movement in retreat. The possibility that this might be so is posed both more directly and more philosophically by those (often socialist) feminists who have insisted that feminism remains unavoidably involved in precisely that broader (liberal, socialist, rationalist) Enlightenment project against which post-structuralism has chosen to define itself. Thus, where post-structuralist feminists have come to understand Enlightenment reason as inherently patriarchal, others have insisted to the contrary that feminism is itself a part of the rationalist programme: "feminism . . . aspires to *end the war between men and women* and to replace it with communicative transparency, or truthfulness".[87] The same writer continues: "The idea of subjectivity as socially (or discursively) constructed . . . opens up a world of possibilities . . . But if feminism disowns . . . the impulse to 'enlighten', it will be at a loss to speak the wish to make these possibilities real. Subjectivity can be as fluid as you please, but this insight – once decoupled from the feminist ambition to *reconstruct* sensibility in the interest of women – will no longer be of any specifically political interest".[88]

Doubtless, the historical Enlightenment was indeed often "gender blind" or gender exclusive (just as it was also often class specific). But Enlightenment carries with it at least the promise of some more general emancipation. If Enlightenment liberalism and Enlightenment socialism have failed to date to produce any lasting women's liberation, it is nonetheless still true, as Kate Millett recognized, that both Mill and Engels faced the issue of patriarchy "courageously and intelligently".[89] What Bentham and Mill have been to liberalism, and

Marx and Engels to socialism, so is Nietzsche, the grand philosopher of nineteenth century irrationalism, to post-structuralism itself. Yet to read Nietzsche is to be confronted by an anti-feminism bordering on misogyny. Thus Nietzsche (and there is much more where this came from): "a man who has depth of spirit as well as of desires . . . can only think of woman as *Orientals* do: he must conceive of her as a possession, as confinable property, as a being predestined for service and accomplishing her mission therein – he must take his stand in this matter . . . as the Greeks did formerly; those best heirs and scholars of Asia – who . . . with their *increasing* culture and amplitude of power, from Homer to the time of Pericles, became gradually *stricter* towards woman".[90] Doubtless, feminist deconstruction already knows the source from which much of its critique of the Enlightenment is derived. But perhaps Amazons, as much as Trojans, should beware Greeks bearing gifts.

Feminism and postmodernism

Following on from Laura Kipnis's argument against too easy an assimilation of postmodernism to post-structuralism, the question arises as to what exactly a distinctly postmodern feminism might consist in. From Craig Owens on,[91] there has in fact been a tendency amongst male theorists to link the feminist to the postmodern. Despite the understandable suspicion which such linkage can excite amongst socialist feminists,[92] there is at least one important sense in which it does indeed seem apposite. As Andreas Huyssen has stressed, high modernism established itself partly by way of an opposition to mass culture in which the latter was effectively gendered "as feminine and inferior".[93] And insofar as postmodernism has decentred such high modernisms, then this has entailed a "recentring", not simply of the popular and of the female, but of the marginalized in general. Postmodern culture becomes thereby quite fundamentally subversive of all certainties, not least those of patriarchy. The liberating effects of the new languages of difference and decentring – part postmodernist, part post-structuralist – thus arise precisely "because the centre used to function as the pivot between binary oppositions which always privileged one half: white/black, male/female, self/other, intellect/ body, west/east, objectivity/subjectivity".[94]

Huyssen himself pays little attention to explicitly feminist theori- zations of the postmodern, except in his concluding invocation of a "postmodernism of resistance", which concedes the contribution made by the women's movement to an emergently postmodern "prob- lematic of 'otherness'".[95] For Huyssen, postmodern culture is at once both incorporated and oppositional, commodified and subversive. Writing from a more explicitly feminist perspective, Ann Kaplan has described these twin faces of postmodernism as, respectively, the "commercial" and the "utopian".[96] They are connected primarily by virtue of their shared antipathy to the binary trope in modernist (and more especially structuralist) thought. Where the capitalist mass-mar- ket has deconstructed the opposition between élite and popular cul- tures, postmodern feminism and the women's movement deconstruct that between masculinity and femininity. These vastly differing con- ceptions of postmodernism, a largely feminist utopianism and a deeply capitalist commercialism, can coexist in a single cultural space, accord- ing to Kaplan, only because they each respond to a similar cultural situation, that of the 1960s.[97]

But it seems to me that Kaplan here confuses two quite distinct moments within second wave feminism itself: that of a largely anglophone, often American, politically interventionist, and often pseudo-popular, feminist cultural practice which has indeed often been subversively postmodernist (as, for example, with Barbara Kruger); and that of a largely French, theoretical, feminist post-struc- turalism, which is, as Kipnis argues, almost classically modernist in its politico-cultural character. No doubt, the antithesis can be over- drawn. But one can distinguish nonetheless between the more strictly post-structuralist aestheticisms of feminist high theory on the one hand, and the more eclectic, postmodern political engagements of much feminist cultural studies, on the other. Good examples of the latter can be found in the more recent work of Judith Williamson and in that of Meaghan Morris, perhaps the most interesting and certainly one of the most widely cited of the new Australian feminists.

Williamson herself rejects the term "postmodernism", judging it the "academic parent-concept" of much that she has disliked in the accounts of "New Times" developed by the now defunct British Com- munist journal *Marxism Today*.[98] The essays collected in her *Consuming Passions* nonetheless constitute in many respects a characteristically postmodern text, busily subverting the boundaries between art and politics, semiotics and sociology, "high" and "low" culture, journalism and "theory", wit and passion. Simultaneously, however, her work defines itself against much of what has been most fashionable in academic post-structuralism. "The subject most avidly consumed in academic work over recent years", she writes, "has been 'desire' . . . But passion – passion is another story. It is to be written *about*, but not *with*: for the essence of all this academic work on 'desire' is to *stay cool* . . . And the bourgeois etiquette whereby any violent display of feeling is automatically taboo . . . merely sets out the pattern of . . . the consensus by which any form of the 'extreme' is outlawed".[99] In a provocative critique of Laura Mulvey's film, *Riddles of the Sphinx*, Williamson argues that the recent "discovery" of a language of the unconscious has allowed feminist women to seize "on something they may call their own . . . with all the ardour of a proud housewife who assumes total command of the only area allowed her".[100] Echoing Juliet Mitchell, she insists to the contrary that: "We need to claim consciousness, not unconsciousness".[101]

Williamson is similarly sceptical of the kind of consumerist "politics" suggested by the notion of resistant readings. "The idea that . . . consumer fads . . . are increasingly 'cut loose' from the economic 'base' has become more and more fashionable on the academic left," she writes, "at a time when these levels have . . . rarely been more obviously connected'.[102] Elsewhere, she remarks cuttingly on the ways in which capitalist mass-marketing itself constructs consumption as difference: "the ideology of difference is not, in fact, different from the ideologies that imprison us all".[103] In their efforts to "be" popular, the radical intelligentsia, both feminist and socialist, have increasingly abandoned their own erstwhile political vocabularies, she argues, celebrating "subversion" in almost any aspect of popular culture![104] Williamson herself is clear that this overlap between cultural studies, post-structuralism, postmodernism and the politics of *Marxism Today* actually tended to "take over, rather than to transform, the agenda of the right".[105] Here, then, is a convincingly radical version of radical semiotics, operating in and against the cultural space of postmodernity, indebted to post-structuralism certainly, but engaged with the practical politics of a more generally socialist and feminist emancipatory project, and much more interested in the meanings and effects of postmodern popular culture than with the textual resistances of the high modernist text.

Meaghan Morris's work is similarly indebted to French post-structuralism, and as much to malestream thinkers like Barthes[106] as to the new French feminism itself. For Morris, a post-structuralist semiotics enables not the discovery of the truth of some deep structure inherent in the text, but rather the production of new readings, that is, of new strategic rewritings; such rewritings can be of value in her view only by virtue of their relationship to the political discourses of feminism;[107] but nonetheless, there can still be no appeal beyond signification to the supposed reality of a referent.[108] Like Williamson, Morris retains a more than residual commitment, to the notion of a left which is socialist as well as feminist.[109] Politically engaged and engagingly writerly, her work also often runs directly against the apparent drift toward apolitical academicism within post-structuralist feminism. Indeed, much of the creative dynamic in Morris's writing seems to derive from its own unresolved tensions between the aspiration to a subversively postmodernist cultural politics on the one hand, and a more generally post-structuralist theoretical framework on the other.

There is a happy eclecticism at work theoretically in Morris which surely derives in part from her obvious discomfort at the more sectarian intellectual habits not only of the left but also of the academy. Hence, her declared antipathy to Felperin's proposed post-structuralist rationale for the literary canon,[110] as also her parallel enthusiasm for "the kind of 'mixed' public to be encountered at events organized on thematic or political, rather than purely professional, principles".[111] Hence, too, the characteristically defiant insistence that: "it doesn't follow for one moment that I consider the activity of 'transforming discursive material' as sufficient to, or coextensive with, the tasks of feminist political struggle".[112] Interestingly, Morris's usage of the Foucauldian notion of the "specific intellectual" is quite deliberately broadened in scope so as to preclude the "myth of institutional and discursive *closure* which may emerge from the . . . academic attempt to 'know your limitations'".[113] Quite unlike Tony Bennett, Morris remains a cultural critic in an almost fully culturalist sense of the term. She insists, for example, on the need for a "critical vocabulary available to people . . . to theorize the discriminations . . . they make in relation to . . . popular culture",[114] thus simultaneously rejecting both the kind of "fatalistic theory" characteristic of left pessimism and structuralism, and the "making the best of things" approach more commonly found in celebratory postmodernism.[115]

Morris herself seems all too aware of the potential for depoliticiz-ation immanent within the post-structuralist stress on resistant read-ings. Borrowing from a friend, she nicely summarizes the position as "the discovery that washing your car on Sunday is a revolutionary event".[116] Elsewhere, Morris speculates wittily as to the existence of a possible English master-disk "from which thousands of versions of the same article about pleasure, resistance, and the politics of con-sumption are being run off under different names with minor varia-tions".[117] And the point of such arguments, she is clear, and with it "one of the immediate political functions" of the present boom in cultural studies, is precisely to discredit "grumpy feminists and cranky leftists".[118] From her Australian vantage point, Morris is also able to show how an initially British left populism, "still . . . at least nominally . . . attempting to salvage a sense of life from the catastrophe of Thatcherism", becomes radically depoliticized when recycled into the quite "different political cultures" of Australia and America.[119] Mor-ris herself cites[120] as relevant instances John Fiske's "British Cultural Studies and Television" and Iain Chambers's *Popular Culture*.[121] But one could just as well add Fiske, Hodge and Turner's enthusiastically postmodern celebration of the banalities of Australian suburban life,[122] or Cathy Switchenberg's dazzlingly uncritical invocation of Madon-na's supposedly "postmodern feminism".[123]

There is much in post-structuralism, it seems to me, that is in itself theoretically wrong-headed, and little that bears anything but the most tangential of practical relations to any liberationist politics. It has be-come one of a number of theoreticist manoeuvres by which substan-tial sections of an erstwhile progressive radical intelligentsia have sought to theorize, and dramatize, their own emergent depoliticiz-ation. Postmodernism, by contrast, is much better understood as a con-temporary condition we all share simply by virtue of our status as in-habitants of liberal-democratic polities and late-capitalist societies. Insofar as feminism has sought to work in and against this new postmodern reality, then it has very often attained a more fully contem-porary relevance than any available to other kinds of cultural theory. But insofar as feminism has become merely another post-structuralist academicism, "just another way of talking about books",[124] as Ruthven sees it, then it becomes deeply complicit with the dominant politico-cultural logics of a society still not only deeply utilitarian and deeply capitalist but also deeply patriarchal in character.

This is not to suggest that feminism has somehow become non-adversarial. To the contrary: its attempt to challenge the cultural legitimacy of, quite literally, millennia of patriarchy, represents as grand an adversarial gesture as any in the intellectual history of the West. But both second wave feminism and contemporary Western Marxism inhabit peculiarly divided selves, torn between the claims of their respective communities of the oppressed (women, the working class) on the one hand, and those of the academic intelligentsia, to which their intellectual representatives typically belong as a matter of objective class membership, on the other. An earlier generation of socialist and feminist intellectuals normally gained its employment, as journalists, from the political movements they sought to serve. But the expansion of the modern system of higher education, the central institutional site of the powers and privileges of the intellectual class, has provided an almost irresistible source of attraction for much of the contemporary socialist and feminist intelligentsia. In the academy, both Marxism and feminism can be much more fairly, and much more reasonably, discussed and debated than elsewhere in the society. But, without repeated and continuing exposure to the countervailing force of some organized and non-academic counter culture, such Marxisms and feminisms become perilously exposed to the dangers of colonization by more conventionally intellectual forms of oppositionism, be they culturalist, structuralist or post-structuralist.

Chapter 6
POSTMODERNISM

In this concluding chapter we turn to what Meaghan Morris has described, without undue irony, as contemporary cultural theory's "own version of cinema's blockbuster: the state-of-the-globe, state-of-the-arts, Big Speculation",[1] that is to *postmodernism*. The five types of cultural theory we have discussed thus far, utilitarianism, culturalism, Marxism, structuralism and feminism, each pursue their own kinds of strategy toward the analysis of cultural artefacts in *general*. Postmodernism is not a cultural theory of this kind, indeed it is not properly speaking a theory at all. Rather, the term denotes: primarily, a whole set of contemporary literary and cultural movements (for example, in painting or architecture) which self-consciously define themselves in opposition to earlier, equally self-consciously modernist such movements; and only secondarily, a set of efforts from within cultural theory to define the specific nature of these movements in relation to other equally specific aspects of contemporary society and culture. The former is postmodernism; the latter, as it were, the "postmodern debate".[2]

Postmodernism and Late Capitalism

Like all blockbusters, postmodernism's success derives in part from its capacity to appeal to as wide an audience as possible, high philosophy in the art house cinemas of the academy and middlebrow multi-screen literary criticism as much as local fleapit sociology. If not exactly meaning all things to all people, the term very obviously signifies differently within different discourses: in short, it is as polysemic a sign as they come. An apparently enduring postmodern trope, however, is that of "being after". Postmodernism, Zygmunt Bauman wittily reminds us, is the "morning after" modernism, simultaneously a "sobering up and a headache".[3] "*Post*modernism," Ferenc Fehér writes, "like many of its conceptual brethren, *post*-revolutionary or *post*-industrial society, *post*-structuralism and the like, understand themselves not in terms of what they are but in terms of what they come after".[4] But after what? After modernism certainly, after modernity perhaps, and crucially also after "the War". For the generations that would eventually attempt to theorize these many and varied postmodern conditions had grown up in a world that considered itself quite decisively "post-War".

Here, surely, is the trope *in initio*: to quote Meaghan Morris yet again, "the postmodern era could be said to begin in 1945, at Hiroshima and Nagasaki".[5] Such early datings of the beginnings of "postmodernity" are by no means uncontroversial: the more typical focus in recent cultural theory has fallen on the supposedly more radical transformations of the late 1950s and the early 1960s, as in Fredric Jameson's *Postmodernism, or, The Cultural Logic of Late Capitalism*,[6] or even those of the 1970s and 1980s, as in the analyses of "New Times" developed by the journal *Marxism Today*.[7] These later datings often call attention to quite significant changes within post-war society and culture, for example the rise of the "new social movements" or the development of new "post-industrial" technologies. But the more fundamental shift is that registered by Morris, that to a distinctively post-war world, the more general characteristics of which continue to structure our contemporary reality.

That shift is peculiarly visible in precisely the "high cultural" social sub-sector from which the "postmodernist" debate derives much of its vocabulary. Both modernist high culture in general and the cultural avant-garde in particular were the creations of the great cities of continental Europe – Berlin and Vienna, Moscow and St Petersburg, above all Paris[8] – and as such, they were fated to become direct casualties of the twin totalitarianisms of Nazism and Stalinism. What survived into post-war New York was an increasingly commodified imitation of avant-garde style, increasingly bereft of avant-garde social purpose. This is post-modernism in the most obvious of senses, that of the "high" culture that survived after modernism, and it is a culture which clearly dates from the 1940s. This is a "post-modernism" grudgingly acknowledged by even those most hostile to the notion itself: Alex Callinicos, for example, agrees that the "postwar stabilization of capitalism left the few still committed to avant-garde

objectives beached";[9] Perry Anderson that "the Second World War
. . . cut off the vitality of modernism".[10] And as Jameson nicely observes of the latter, "whatever Perry Anderson . . . thinks of the utility
of the period term – postmodernism – his paper demonstrates that
. . . the conditions of existence of modernism were no longer present.
So we are in something else".[11] This something else is postmodernism.

The historical fate of the avant-garde aside, at least three other
characteristic features of contemporary politico-economic "postmodernity" also date from the 1940s: a prodigiously consumerist
economy of affluence, initially confined to the United States, later
dispersed throughout the West; the rapid collapse of the older European imperialisms and the development of new transnational cultural
and economic forms; and a dynamically expansionist global hypermilitarism, very visibly represented in nuclear weapons systems, but
also in the more general growth of high-tech military capacities.
This, then, is our starting point: a distinction between post-modernism as culture and postmodernity as political economy, a definition
of postmodernism as the successor culture to a chronologically prior
modernism, and a periodization which specifies the postmodern era
as co-extensive with the post-war. We might add that, although this
periodization is not always that preferred by Jameson himself, it is
the one most obviously implied in his reliance on Ernest Mandel's
Late Capitalism,[12] for which late capitalism is precisely post-war capitalism.

If postmodernism is not in this account a specific type of cultural
theory, in the sense of post-structuralism or neo-Marxist critical theory,
then nor is it a specific type of politics, in the sense of feminism or
socialism. It is, rather, a particular cultural space available for analysis to many different kinds of contemporary cultural theory and for
intervention to many different kinds of contemporary cultural politics. As Michèle Barrett has observed: "postmodernism is not something that you can be for or against: the reiteration of old knowledges
will not make it vanish . . . it is a cultural climate as well as an intellectual position, a political reality as well as an academic fashion".[13]
The term is best understood, then, as denoting a "cultural dominant",
in Jameson's phrase, or even, in Williams's terms, a "structure of feeling". At this most general of levels, it is quite simply the dominant
culture of the post-war West. In this sense, Habermas's sustained
polemic against the implied neo-conservatism of French post-struc-

turalism[14] can be read as an intervention within postmodernism as much as an argument against it. There is even less point, then, in Callinicos's argument *against* the very idea of postmodernism than in that of Lukács against the substance of modernism. As Fehér asks, echoing Andreas Huyssen, "who wants to become the Lukács of post-modernism?"[15]

Yet a complication does indeed enter as we acknowledge not only that some cultural theory affects to be itself "postmodernist", but also that postmodernist art is often very much aware of such postmodernist theory and often seeks to position itself in relation to the latter. It becomes possible, then, to disagree with "postmodernist" theories of culture or of society, while nonetheless accepting that important instances in our cultural life are indeed postmodern, while nonetheless recognising that the latter may indeed by informed by the former. Callinicos actually distinguishes very nicely between postmodernist art, post-structuralist theory and post-industrialist sociology,[16] but proceeds thence to the judgement that of the three, post-structuralist theory alone can "offer partial insights of great value".[17] This seems to me peculiarly perverse for a self-declared Marxist, since it is post-structuralist theory itself, rather than post-industrialist sociology, still less postmodernist art, that most directly challenges the most fundamental of Marxist and other pretensions to the theoretical authority of "science". My own position is much closer to Scott Lash: like him I am no postmodernist, like him my own modes of procedure are I hope rationalist, like him I admit that postmodernist culture has proved on balance unfavourable to the left. But, like Lash, I acknowledge too "that the cultural terrain on which we now all live, work, love, and struggle is pervaded by postmodernism . . . it would be unwise for the left to ignore it".[18]

Transgression, marginality and post-imperialism

Celebratory postmodernism as a major academic event dates from the 1970s, from the first publication of Jean-François Lyotard's *The Postmodern Condition*, a specifically Canadian text originally prepared for the Conseil des Universitiés of the government of Quebec. For Lyotard, modernism and modernity had been characterized above all by the co-presence of science and of a series of universalizing and legitimating meta-narratives, which ultimately derived from the Enlightenment. These meta-narrative paradigms had run aground, he argued, in the period since the Second World War: "In contemporary society and culture – postindustrial society, postmodern culture – the . . . grand narrative has lost its credibility, regardless of what mode of unification it uses, regardless of whether it is a speculative narrative or a narrative of emancipation".[19] The postmodern condition's "incredulity towards meta-narratives", whether in aesthetics or science or politics, is for Lyotard in part a consequence of the internal logic of the meta-narratives themselves, which proceed from scepticism to pluralism, in part also a correlate of post-industrialism, in which knowledge itself becomes a principal form of production, thereby shifting emphasis "from the ends of action to its means".[20] Lyotard's slightly later "What is Postmodernism?", first published in 1982, recapitulates much of the earlier analysis, despite its, in my view very unhelpful, retreat from the initial attempt at cultural periodization.[21] Here, the postmodern continues to be understood as that which "denies itself the solace of good forms, the consensus of a taste which would make it possible to share collectively the nostalgia for the unattainable; that which searches for new representations . . . in order to impart a strong sense of the unpresentable".[22] The postmodern, Lyotard tells us, will "wage a war on totality", that "transcendental illusion" of the nineteenth century, the full price of which has proved to be "terror".[23]

The term "postmodern" was by no means an original coinage, however. To the contrary, Lyotard's initial argument is quite deliberately inserted into an already existing North American discourse: as he explained, "the word *postmodern* . . . is in current use on the American continent among sociologists and critics".[24] One of Lyotard's North American sources was Daniel Bell, whose *The Coming of Post-Industrial Society*[25] figures in the text's very first footnote. Curiously, Lyotard makes no reference to Bell's more specific attempts at a cultural sociology of postmodernism *per se*, especially *The Cultural Contradictions of Capitalism*,[26] which had been published only three years previously, and the even more recent essay, "Beyond Modernism, Beyond Self".[27] For Bell, following Lionel Trilling,[28] modernism represented a radically "adversary culture", opposed not merely to this society but to any and all conceivable societies. As the capitalist economic system had developed, he argued, it had rendered the older Puritan values progressively obsolescent, thereby unleashing an increasingly unrestrained modernism, the simultaneous product of Hobbesian individualism on the one hand, corporate capitalism on the other.[29] The "postmodernism" of the 1960s – and this is the term Bell actually uses – finally subverts all restraints: "It is a programme to erase all boundaries, to obliterate any distinction between the self and the external world, between man and woman, subject and object, mind and body".[30] "In doctrine and cultural life-style," he concludes, "the anti-bourgeois has won . . . The difficulty in the West . . . is that bourgeois society – which in its emphasis on individuality and the self gave rise to modernism – is itself culturally exhausted".[31]

By and large, contemporary cultural criticism has found Lyotard's celebration of the postmodern much more interesting than Bell's indictment. But note their common origins in a specifically North American, rather than European, perception of the postmodern as at once uniquely contemporary and uniquely transgressive. Where Lyotard cries liberty and Bell finds licence, both mean transgression, in the sense of the continuous disturbance and subversion of pre-existing cultural norms. Which leads us to the proposition, first, that postmodernism is above all a culture of transgression; and secondly that, whatever the current fashion for French theory, this is a culture which remains peculiarly visible from a New World, extra-European vantage point. Lyotard's various accounts of the postmodern are stories told by a Frenchman, it is true, but they are told in the first place to Canadians nonetheless. They are also, no doubt, in themselves grand narratives of dissolution, which bespeak a political and cultural history at once much richer and much more fraught than any endured to date by the European colonies of settlement in North America or Australasia. For Lyotard, modernity is quite specifically European, its transcendental illusion explicitly that of Hegel and Marx, its terror that of Stalin and Hitler. Doubtless, the settler colonies have had their own philosophers and their own terrors: yet theirs has been a different experience from the European, provincial in origin rather than metropolitan, often suburban rather than urban, civilizing rather than cultured, terrorizing rather than terrorized. This too is a postmodern condition, perhaps the paradigmatically postmodern condition which provides both Bell and Lyotard with their original empirical datum. It is one often named as "post-colonialism", but better understood, I suspect, as "post-imperialism".

Modernism, postmodernism and the popular

Discounting Lyotard's conceit that postmodernism is "modernism . . . in the nascent state",[32] we need to define postmodernism in terms of its own difference from a modernism to which it is, if not chronologically then at least logically, subsequent. High modernism can, in turn, best be characterized substantially in terms of its own antithetical relationship not only to bourgeois realism, the predecessor culture, but also to contemporary "mass", that is, popular, culture. Relatively distinct élite and popular cultures are, of course, an almost invariable accompaniment to the socio-cultural combination of structured social inequality with the cultural technology of writing. It is only in relatively classless, tribal societies that one finds relatively unitary, oral cultures (and even these are internally differentiated by age and gender). Once writing becomes technically available, cultural differentiation becomes virtually unavoidable, since writing is, as Williams observes, "wholly dependent on forms of specialized training, not only . . . for producers but also, and crucially, for receivers".[33] The historical and anthropological record in fact provides us with very little warrant for any understanding of traditional, pre-modern, literate cultures as generally unitary. And yet, this was a recurrent theme, not only in Hegel and (sometimes) in Marx, but also in much of both German sociology, where it appeared as the distinction between *Gemeinschaft* and *Gesellschaft*,[34] and French anthropology, where it appeared as that between mechanical and organic solidarity.[35]

In English studies, the opposition was troped as that between Eliot's medieval common culture or the Leavises' pre-industrial organic community, on the one hand, and the dissociated sensibilities of industrialized mass civilization, on the other.[36] As history, this was very obvious nonsense: Wat Tyler and John Ball would hardly have led a popular revolt against any truly common culture; and John Bunyan, F. R. Leavis's own preferred instance of the unity of élite and popular cultures,[37] was also, and by no means coincidentally, a soldier in the armies of the English Revolution. The literary canon handed down by "English" was in reality the product and the possession of an extremely small and socially exclusive cultural élite. As late as 1839, only 58.4 per cent of those married during that year in Great Britain were able to sign the marriage register:[38] it seems unlikely that very many of the illiterate majority can have had much of a taste for Metaphysical poetry. Truly popular pre-modern cultures have been essentially non-literate folk cultures, and the record we have of them is often both imprecise and patchy. That they were significantly differentiated from contemporaneous élite cultures nonetheless seems almost certain to have been the case.

We can be rather more definite about élite culture. In pre-modern Europe, such cultures were overwhelmingly defined, constructed and regulated either by the church or by the court. If the former had a popular dimension, the latter by and large did not. And even then, popular Catholicism was very often distinctly heretical and normally distinctly heterogeneous: it was never a part of the seamless web of some ideal Christian social organism.

The new more fully modern cultures of the 18th and 19th centuries – or at least what was distinctively modern about them – were quintessentially "bourgeois" in form: democratic, realistic, and prosaic. The exemplary instance here is that of the rise of the realist novel.[39] Formally democratic though the realist novel may have been, it was not, however, in any sense a truly popular literary form: in the 18th century, the "price of a novel . . . would feed a family for a week or two".[40] Throughout the 18th century, and across Europe, print runs were generally still well below 2,000;[41] by way of contrast, Orwell's *1984* sold 360,000 copies in the United States and 50,000 in Britain during its first year of publication.[42]

It is only in the late 19th century, in fact, that we are able to observe the more or less simultaneous emergence of both a new modernist high culture and a new mass popular culture. The new modernism was characterized above all by its aesthetic self-consciousness, by a formalist experimentalism that recurred in painting and drama, poetry and music, the novel and sculpture; the new mass culture by the rapid development of a whole range of technically novel cultural forms each of which was in principle almost universally available (yellow journalism, penny dreadful and later paperback fiction, radio, cinema, and so on). Whenever we date the beginnings of modernism, whether from 1890, as does one standard academic text,[43] or from December 1910, as rather more interestingly did Virginia Woolf,[44] there can be no doubt that high modernism and mass culture are indeed contemporaneous. However we may characterize the cultural avant-garde, whether as integral to high modernism, as do Bradbury and McFarlane,[45] or as internally opposed to it, as does Peter Bürger,[46] there can be no doubt that both stand in essentially adversarial relation not only to bourgeois realism but also to mass culture.

Bürger himself argues that bourgeois art consists in a celebration in form of the liberation of art from religion, from the court, and eventually even from the bourgeoisie.[47] Modernist art thus emerges as an autonomous social "institution", the preserve and prerogative of an increasingly autonomous intellectual class, and thereby necessarily counterposed to other non-autonomous arts. In short, both high modernism and the historical avant-garde ascribe some real redemptive function to high art. And as the historical memory of bourgeois realism recedes, it is hostility to contemporary popular culture in particular which develops into perhaps the most characteristic topos, or stock theme, in 20th century intellectual life – whether overt, as in the Leavisite opposition between mass civilization and minority culture (of which Eliot's modernism is a central instance), or that of the Frankfurt School between the culture industries and autonomous art; or covert, as in the structuralist distinction between readerly and writerly texts, the text of *plaisir* and the text of *jouissance*. Whether as degraded culture for the conservative intelligentsia or as manipulated culture for the radical intelligentsia, mass culture remained the Other, or at least an Other, of modernist high culture.

Which brings us to postmodernism. For, however else we might care to characterize the postmodern, there can be little doubt that postmodernist art typically attempts, or at least results from, the collapse precisely of this antithesis between high and low, élite and popular. It is this boundary, as much as any other, that is transgressed in postmodern culture. Almost all the available theorizations of postmodernism, whether celebratory or condemnatory, whether or not themselves postmodernist, agree on the centrality of this progressive deconstruction and dissolution of what was once, in Bourdieu's phrase, "distinction".[48] Huyssen goes so far as to locate postmodernism quite specifically "after the great divide" between modernism and mass culture.[49] But even for Bell, postmodernism was a kind of "porno-pop" which "overflows the vessels of art . . . tears down the boundaries and insists that *acting out*, rather than making distinctions, is the way to gain knowledge".[50]

For Lyotard, the postmodern incredulity towards meta-narratives applies not only to the meta-narratives of science and politics, but also to that of art as enlightenment. For Baudrillard, postmodernity is characterized by "the disappearance of aesthetics and higher values in kitsch and hyperreality . . . the disappearance of history and the real in the televisual".[51] For Bürger, postmodernism is initiated essentially by the failure of the historical avant-garde to subvert from within the cultural institutions of high modernism, a failure which results nonetheless in the final loss of criteria for determining the paradigmatic work of art[52] and, hence, in a loss of criteria for distinguishing between art and non-art. For Jameson, postmodernism is above all a kind of aesthetic populism, in which pastiche eclipses parody, constituted within a "field of stylistic and discursive heterogeneity without a norm", a culture "fascinated by this whole 'degraded' landscape of schlock and kitsch, of TV series and Readers' Digest culture, of advertising and motels, of the late show and the grade-B Hollywood film, of so-called paraliterature".[53] For Lash, postmodernist "de-differentiation" is present in the transgression "between literature and theory, between high and popular culture, between what is properly cultural and properly social".[54]

Whichever account we adopt, we should note that what is being charted here is primarily an endogenous transformation, internal to élite culture, rather to any wider, mass or popular culture. Postmodernism has doubtless entered the vocabulary of popular style, much as did French existentialism, for example, in the years immediately after the Second World War.[55] But such popular borrowings from élite, or in this case "quasi-élite", cultures are by no means in themselves peculiarly postmodernist: as Bakhtin reminds us, the carnivalesque is as characteristic a feature of medieval popular culture as any.[56] Postmodernism proper is neither a popular culture, nor, in any sense that Leavis or even Williams might have understood, a common culture: it is post-modernist, but not necessarily post-popular. Postmodernism may well "quote" from mass culture, but it is nonetheless not in itself a popular culture: Campbell's soup is indeed a mass commodity, but Warhol prints are not. What postmodernism provides us with, then, is an index of the range and extent of the Western intelligentsia's own internal crisis, that is, its collective crisis of faith in its own previously proclaimed adversarial and redemptive functions. Historically, cultural institutions have typically been staffed by Gramscian "traditional" intellectuals. But their pretensions to cultural authority have also been replicated by counter-cultural intelligentsias, such as those associated in the early 20th century with both the literary and artistic avant-garde and the revolutionary political party. It is the collapse of all such pretensions, whether traditional, avant-garde or vanguardist, that most clearly marks the moment of postmodernism.

Certain aspects of this collective crisis of faith are no doubt very specific: to the European intellectual confronted by America; to the literary intellectual confronted by the mass media; to the male intellectual confronted by the female. But their sum adds up to a Jamesonian cultural dominant, rather than to any particular literary or artistic style. Indeed, much effort to define a distinctively postmodernist style serves only so as to remind us of the latter's deeply derivative relation to high modernism. It is the general crisis of faith, rather than any particular set of cultural techniques, which is truly defining. Here, Zygmunt Bauman's distinction between the rôle of the intellectual as legislator and that as interpreter, as also his account of the ways in which the latter function progressively displaces the former, becomes instructive.[57] As Bauman concludes: "The postmodernity/modernity opposition focuses on the waning of certainty and objectivity grounded in the unquestioned hierarchy of values ... and on the transition to a situation characterized by a coexistence or armistice between values ... which makes the questions of objective standards impracticable and hence theoretically futile".[58]

Apocalyptic hedonism and the decline of the legislative intellectual

The central social functions of the post-war, postmodern Western intelligentsia have, then, become primarily interpretive rather than legislative. The novelty of this situation is registered both in Foucault's distinction between the "universal" and "specific" intellectual and in the only limited applicability of the Gramscian distinction between "traditional" and "organic" intellectuals to the cultural sociology of the post-war West. No doubt there are still Gramscian traditional intellectuals at work within the clergy or the judiciary, perhaps even within academia. No doubt there are still Gramscian organic intellectuals: the bourgeoisie have their economists, engineers and accountants, the proletariat its trade union officials and Labour politicians. Gramsci, however, clearly envisaged both kinds of intellectual as performing an essentially legislative or universal function, whereas in fact the dominant rôle of each has now become primarily interpretive and specific. If the changing rôle and self-perception of the Western intelligentsia is indeed itself central to the postmodernist reorientation of cultural discourse, as Bauman argues, then the very generality of that reorientation nonetheless bespeaks the possibility that postmodernist culture might still have deep structural roots in some distinctively postmodern socio-political reality, whether characterizable as post-industrialism, consumerism, late capitalism, or whatever.

There is some agreement as to the more characteristic features of this new way of life: new mass media; new post-industrial technologies; mass marketing and an increasingly affluent mass market; new systems of fast transport and communication; some would add to the list the distinctly American,[59] or at least "post-European",[60] character of this postmodern "hyper-reality". For both liberal and conservative analysts, the new society is essentially post-industrial, and thus by implication post-capitalist: despite their respectively antipathetic and enthusiastic responses to postmodernism, both Bell and Lyotard are agreed as to the general significance of the coming of post-industrial society.[61] By contrast, Jameson's Marxism leads him to insist that this "late capitalism" constitutes something very close to capitalism in its purest form.[62] Postmodernism, Jameson argues, represents the final and full commodification of art: "What has happened is that aesthetic production today has become integrated into commodity production generally: the frantic economic urgency of producing fresh waves of ever more novel-seeming goods . . . at ever greater rates of turnover, now assigns an increasingly essential structural function and position to aesthetic innovation and experimentation".[63] Thus understood, postmodernism is a commodity culture in a double sense: both as a set of commodified artefacts actually available for sale in the culture market, and as a set of texts the very textuality of which often affirms their own commodity status. As Jameson insists, "the various postmodernisms . . . all at least share a resonant affirmation, when not an outright celebration, of the market as such".[64]

Here, it seems to me, Jameson captures much of what it is that is truly distinctive about our contemporary culture. The more commodified that culture has become, the less plausible the intelligentsia's erstwhile pretensions to legislative cultural authority have appeared, both to themselves and to their prospective audiences. As Bauman has observed: "within the context of a consumer culture no room has been left for the intellectual as legislator. In the market, there is no one centre of power, nor any aspiration to create one . . . There is no site from which authoritative pronouncements could be made, and no power resources concentrated and exclusive enough to serve as the levers of a massive proselytizing campaign".[65] Nineteenth and early 20th century conceptions, whether literary-critical, anthropological or sociological, had almost invariably envisaged culture, not simply as distinct from economy and polity, but also as itself the central source of social cohesion: human society as such appeared inconceivable without culture. But it is so *now*: postmodern capitalism is held together, not by culture, understood as a normative value system, but by the market.

As Jameson writes: "ideologies in the sense of codes and discursive systems are no longer particularly determinant . . . ideology . . . has ceased to be functional in perpetuating and reproducing the system".[66] Leavis and the Leavisites were mistaken, we can now recognize: there *is* a substitute for culture, and it is the one that Leavis himself feared it might be, "*More* jam tomorrow".[67] In short, postmodern intellectual culture is at once both peculiarly normless and peculiarly hedonistic. The hedonism arises very directly out of the commodity cultures of affluence, as they impinge both on the wider society and on the intelligentsia in particular. The normlessness, however, may well have its origins elsewhere: on the one hand, in a recurring apocalyptic motif within post-war culture, which must surely bear some more or less direct relation to the threat of nuclear extinction; and on the other, in the radically internationalizing nature of post-war society and culture, which progressively detached erstwhile national intelligentsias from the national cultural "canons" of which they had hitherto been the custodians.

Let us say a little more about the apocalypse. Jameson himself has argued that Mandel's *Late Capitalism* represents the "single exception" to a general tendency within the Marxist tradition to resist with vehemence any attempt at a theorization of the historical novelty of post-industrial capitalism[68] and has sought to justify his own position, as also that of Mandel, as replicating the method, though not the substance, of Lenin's earlier analysis of imperialism, by "for the first time" theorizing "a third stage of capitalism from a usably Marxian perspective".[69] This judgement on Mandel seems to me over-generous. I am familiar with at least three other attempts to theorize something like a third "stage" in the history of capitalism: E. P. Thompson's famous essay on exterminism, Michael Kidron's account of the post-war permanent arms economy and Baran and Sweezy's *Monopoly Capital*.[70] Interestingly, the latter had served much the same function in Jameson's earlier *Marxism and Form*[71] as does Mandel in *Postmodernism* itself.

All three of these analyses have the merit of pointing to the deep complicity between the post-war political-economy and post-war militarism. If postmodernism is indeed the cultural dominant of late capitalism, then late capitalism itself has been not only consumerist, computerized and televisual, but also, as Jameson sometimes appears to forget, hypermilitarized. Though Mandel himself certainly recognized the sheer scale of the permanent war economy and conceded that it substantially accelerated, but did not fundamentally shape, the pattern of post-war capital accumulation,[72] Jameson appears virtually indifferent to the phenomenon. Postmodernism, we must insist, has been underwritten throughout by the arms economy, the visual symbol of which – the mushroom cloud, not the missile – has become so universally culturally available as to have in effect displaced the phallus as the ultimate signifier. As such, it has signified the ultimate hurt, the ultimate refusal of desire. No matter how much it is able to consume, a civilization permanently confronted by the prospect of its own extinction, such as ours has been, is understandably tempted by the notion that history might come to an end. That global environmental catastrophe comes increasingly to substitute for large-scale nuclear warfare in no way diminishes the power of the trope. The postmodernist effacement of history by "the random cannibalization of . . . the past, the . . . increasing primacy of the 'neo'", which Jameson also records,[73] thus runs in close counterpoint to a powerfully apocalyptic element in the post-war culture of the West.

This hypermilitarism is itself only one, peculiarly significant, aspect of the more generally internationalizing nature of socio-economic postmodernity. Here, Jameson is especially acute: "it is precisely this . . . original new global space which is the 'moment of truth' of postmodernism", and which will require an "aesthetic of cognitive mapping – a pedagogical political culture which seeks to endow the individual subject with some new heightened sense of its place in the global system".[74] It is one of the weaknesses of Bell's approach, for example, that it remains quite extraordinarily preoccupied with parochially American concerns, to the near exclusion of an equivalent consideration of the wider international system. A parallel weakness informs much of Baudrillard's more naive enthusiasm for America: at the very moment when radical revisions of the European political map seem likely to effect an equally radical, and almost certainly irreversible, decentring of the political economy of the West away from the United States and towards a much more genuinely transnational homelessness, it seems utterly absurd (but also somehow utterly characteristic of much recent French thought) to declaim that "all the myths of modernity are American".[75]

The politics of postmodernism

As we noted in Chapter 5, postmodernist culture is at once both incorporated and oppositional, commodified and subversive, commercial and utopian. The coexistence of these twin faces of postmodernism is not so much a feature of the sixties in particular as of the post-war period in general. It arises, moreover, not so much as the effect of a presence as that of an absence. Where Marxists have detected commodification and post-structuralists difference, we actually find both, connected to each other not by any positive content, such as the beneficence of the market, but by a negativity, that of the prior collapse of the high culture of the traditional intelligentsia. In itself this can easily be welcomed: neither traditional minority culture nor avant-garde modernism are in any obvious sense at all compatible with cultural democracy. But it remains an absence, or perhaps an opening, a space in which new options might be explored, others foreclosed, a problem rather than its resolution.

When academic cultural theory bought into structuralism and post-structuralism, and into the radically "theoreticist" version of Marxism represented by Althusserianism, it effectively relinquished its more traditionally "culturalist" function of policing the boundaries of cultural authority. True, the relatively arcane language by which the manoeuvre was effected somewhat obscured its culturally populist import. But the import was real enough: the only boundaries academics police these days are those of critical rigour itself, their only sacred texts theoretical ones. At one level, all of this seems absolutely welcome. The old literary humanism had, by the time of its demise, ossified into an irredeemable élitism, its public face that of a near permanent sneer – at "mass culture", at women's writing, at foreign literature, at creative writing, at community arts. Its ideal of a common culture can best be understood as "ideology", in the most pejorative of senses. But this is, nonetheless, not the whole story. European Romanticism in general developed by way of reaction against the European Enlightenment, British culturalism in particular by way of reaction against utilitarian political economy. And in each case, it is not the former term but the latter which most properly characterizes "the dominant ideology". The dominant classes and élites in societies such as ours are in fact very much as Romanticism construed them: children of civilization rather than culture, servants of utility rather than beauty, industry rather than art. By virtue of that very organicism which seems so reprehensibly monocultural to our contemporary post-Marxist, post-structuralist, post-feminist, postmodernist sensibilities, Romantic and post-Romantic conceptions of culture actually did set up deep resistances to the driving cultural imperatives of a capitalist civilization that was indeed, in its dominant modes, utilitarian, competitive, acquisitive and individualistic.

The new postmodern pluralism, with its play of differences, clearly does allow at least some of the hitherto culturally marginalized some opportunity to assert something of their own specificity. But how has this decentring of cultural authority actually arisen? It has certainly not been the "new social movements" that have achieved such decentring of the cultural authority of the traditional intelligentsia. The achievement belongs solely to the market and to the commodity aesthetics it enjoins. In short, the cultures of difference are sustained, not so much by the existence of effectively organized political counter-cultures, as by an effective monetary demand for commodifiable counter-cultural texts. Those of us who formed part of a once highly profitable market for Che Guevara posters will recall just how vulnerable to fluctuations in demand such "cultures" can be.

Romantic and post-Romantic culturalisms envisaged culture, not simply as separate from economy and polity, but also as in itself the central source of social cohesion: society as such was inconceivable without culture. Each also, in one way or another, counterposed the claims of culture, understood as a repository of superior values, to those of utilitarian capitalist civilization, understood as driven by the dynamics of profitable exchange. But in these terms postmodernism clearly represents a triumph of civilization over culture. Let us be clear what is at stake here. Any society will possess some institutional arrangement or another for the regulation of symbolic artefacts and practices; in that sense, society is indeed inconceivable without culture. But these institutions may themselves be either "political", that is, based on the ultimate threat of coercion wielded by the state; or "economic", that is, organized through commodity exchange in a more or less (normally less) competitive market; or "cultural", in the "culturalist" sense, that is, based on theoretically (though often not actually) consensual arrangements for the generation of authoritative, but not in fact politically coercive, judgements of value.

Soviet socialist realism provided us with an extreme instance of the first, contemporary postmodernism the second. But most cultures, we may agree, have been much more properly "cultural". No doubt, the old literary humanist "common culture" was neither common nor consensual: most people were very effectively excluded from its deliberations on grounds of lack of taste. But its rhetoric nonetheless captured an important part of what many of us still experience as the most basic of truths about our "culture': that our art, our religion, our morals, our knowledge, our science, are not simply matters of private revealed preference, but rather possess an "objectivity" the validity of which is ultimately "social'; in short, that we belong to our culture very much more than it belongs to us. The problem with any radical commodification of culture, such as is entailed in postmodernism, is not simply the perennial failing of all markets, that they confer the vote not on each person but on each dollar and thereby guarantee undemocratic outcomes, but also the much more specific failing that the market undermines precisely what it is that is most cultural about culture, that is, its sociality.

George Stauth and Bryan Turner conclude an essay on postmodernism and mass culture thus: "The cultural elite, especially where it has some pretention to radical politics, is . . . caught in a constant paradox . . . To embrace enthusiastically the objects of mass culture involves the cultural elite in pseudo-populism; to reject critically the objects of mass culture involves distinction, which in turn draws the melancholic intellectual into nostalgic withdrawal from contemporary culture".[76] Melancholia I take to be the characteristically modernist stance, what Lyotard berates as "the nostalgia of the whole and the one, for the reconciliation of the concept and the sensible, of the transparent and the communicable experience".[77] But it is pseudo-populism, the more properly postmodernist stance, which most characteristically defines the contemporary radical intellectual culture. This is evident in the kinds of theoretical post-structuralism that have become widely current in contemporary cultural theory: in psycho-semiotic feminism; in post-structuralist rewritings of multiculturalism as discourse; in the new post-colonial theory's misrecognition of post-imperial literatures. Each of these almost invariably endorses the cultural pluralism of the postmodern condition, and with it the collapse of older, institutionalized claims to authoritative cultural judgement.

Pseudo-populism is evident too in the enthusiasm of much recent writing about popular culture itself: in Tony Bennett's determination to open up popular reading to a radical politics that can transcend the élitist antinomy between fiction and Literature/Science;[78] and in Meaghan Morris's insistence that the "dead cleverness" of *Crocodile Dundee* should alert radical criticism to the need not only for a cultural politics but for a political politics.[79] For Bennett and for Morris, popular culture is too important for the discard tray marked "mass civilization/culture industry", to which traditional intellectuals both of the left and of the right have habitually consigned it. Their intentions are in each case indisputably, and honourably, subversive of the cultural pretensions of the intellectual class to which they themselves belong. The danger remains, however, that such deconstruction of the élite/popular boundary might unwittingly confirm the incorporative dynamics of commercial postmodernism, that is, of multinational late capitalism itself.

To be more specific, I do not doubt that the contempt of left-wing, pessimistic intellectuals for mass audiences is at once both élitist and self-interested. But it does *not* thereby follow that films or TV programmes are somehow politically innocent. It is naïve in the extreme to pretend either that such texts are themselves the products of working-class solidarity or informality, or that they are amenable to some kind of indefinite reappropriation by their audiences. Films and TV programmes are manufactured either by the state or by private capitalism in the interests either of profit or of hegemony, they are often quite deliberately intended as manipulative, and there is no good reason at all to suppose that such intentions are never or even rarely satisfied. This is not to advise a return to high modernism; it is simply to caution against the dangers of a postmodernism that can easily become properly speaking pseudo-populist, as distinct from simply popular. There is, however, a third position which remains both theoretically available and politically preferable: it is possible to recognize that much of the erstwhile modernist high culture is indeed élitist,*and* to recognize that much of mass culture is indeed manipulative,*and* to insist nonetheless on the desirability and possibility of an as yet to be made, democratic common culture. This was, of course, the central politico-cultural trajectory projected in Raymond Williams's *The Long Revolution*.

Towards 2000

Whatever the possible appeal either of postmodernist sensibility in general or of post-structuralist critical theory in particular, their refusal of history remains both disabling and debilitating. For, as Jameson quite rightly insists, history is not a text, though it is nonetheless inaccessible to us except in textual form.[80] "History is what hurts," he writes, "it . . . sets inexorable limits to individual as well as collective praxis . . . we may be sure that its alienating necessities will not forget us, however much we might prefer to ignore them".[81] History is also often progress, although it is currently very unfashionable to admit as much. This too Jameson recognizes: the mystery of the cultural past can be re-enacted, he observes, "only if the human adventure is one", that is, only if its apparently long dead issues can be "retold within the unity of a great collective story; only if, in however disguised and symbolic form, they are seen as sharing a single fundamental theme . . . the collective struggle to wrest a realm of Freedom from a realm of Necessity".[82] Orwell's "struggle of the gradually awakening common people against the lords of property"[83] is but one local instance of this same single human adventure. So too is Williams's long revolution, simultaneously an industrial revolution, a democratic revolution, a revolution in the social relations of class, and in the extension of culture.

In its original formulation, Williams had almost certainly erred on the side of evolutionism, both in the sense of an excessive reliance on the inevitability of gradualism and that of an over-confident expectation of continuing progress. Hence, the conclusion to *The Long Revo-*

lution itself: "The nature of the process indicates a perhaps unusual revolutionary activity: open discussion, extending relationships, the practical shaping of institutions. But it indicates also a necessary strength . . . for and with the people who in many different ways are keeping the revolution going".[84] The dismal political failings of the British Labour governments of the 1960s and 1970s, and the darkly utilitarian rationalisms of the Conservative governments that succeeded them, would provoke in Williams, however, a growing awareness that: "If there are no easy answers there are still available and discoverable hard answers".[85] Williams's two major works of the 1980s, his 1983 reworking of the long revolution analysis, *Towards 2000*, and his last unfinished work, *The Politics of Modernism*, both quite explicitly address the cultural politics of postmodernity. They each attempt to reformulate the original culturalist project, its aspiration to community and culture as a whole way of life, by way of a critique both of modernism and of postmodernism, a critique which rejects, in principle, in theory, and in practice, the antithesis between mass civilization and minority culture, without thereby becoming trapped in the cultural logic of commodification.

In *The Long Revolution* itself, as in *Culture and Society*, Williams had respectfully but determinedly aired his differences with the guardians of the old minority culture. By *Towards 2000*, he had become much more dismissive: "There are very few absolute contrasts left between a 'minority culture' and 'mass communications'";[86] "many minority institutions and forms have adapted, even with enthusiasm, to modern corporate capitalist culture".[87] Moreover, Williams is insistent that the older modernisms, which once threatened to destabilize the certainties of bourgeois life, have become transformed into a new "'postmodernist' establishment" which "takes human inadequacy . . . as self-evident'; and that the deep structures thereof have already been transferred into effectively popular cultural forms in film, TV and fiction.[88] The work both of monopolizing corporations and élite intellectuals, "these debased forms of an anguished sense of human debasement . . . have become a widely distributed 'popular' culture that is meant to confirm both its own and the world's destructive inevitabilities".[89] That there are resistances to this culture goes without saying for a thinker as fundamentally optimistic as Williams. But these are much more obviously present in popular life itself, in the "very general area of jokes and gossip, of everyday singing and dancing, of occasional dressing-up and extravagant outbursts of colour",[90] than in the mass media.

A second site of cultural resistance is, of course, that provided by the radical intelligentsia. But, as early as 1983, Williams was already deeply sceptical of the type of "pseudo-radical" intellectual practice in which a nominally revolutionary radicalism is turned back into the confusions of "bourgeois subjectivism" by "the negative structures of post-modernist art".[91] In *The Politics of Modernism* he would state the case much more forcefully:

> Are we now informed enough, hard enough, to look for our own double edges? Should we not look, implacably, at those many formations, their works and their theories, which are based practically only on their negations and forms of enclosure, against an undifferentiated culture and society beyond them? . . . Are we not obliged to distinguish these reductive and contemptuous forms, these assayers of ugliness and violence, which in the very sweep of their negations can pass as radical art, from . . . very different forms of relating or common exploration, articulation, discovery of identities, in . . . consciously extending and affiliating groups . . . ? Can theory not help in its refusal of the rationalizations which sustain the negations, and in its determination to probe actual forms, actual structures of feeling, actually lived and desired relationships, beyond the easy labels of radicalism which even the dominant institutions now incorporate or impose?[92]

To affirm as much, it is clear, would be to break decisively with the predominantly modernist and postmodernist cultural forms, and their variously structuralist, post-structuralist, post-Marxist, and post-structuralist feminist theoretical legitimations, which currently construct so much of the radical intelligentsia in the image of Williams's "New Conformists".[93]

To speak or to write of actually lived and desired relationships amongst real human beings, as distinct from amongst the rationally maximizing monads of utilitarian fantasy (whether it be in the guise of economics or of semiotics), is to invoke immediately that "solidarity effect" to which I referred in Chapter 4. For, even in the midst of alienation, the vast majority of human beings still live out considerable portions at least of their lives through face to face networks of kinship and community, identity and obligation, friendship and love.

Indeed, this is what most of us mean by "life". The ideal of a common culture which Williams here invokes is, in my view, neither inherently reactionary nor inherently utopian. Quite the contrary, it represents the only possible alternative, within the space of postmodernity, to a radical commodification which will eventually entail the effective absorption of the cultural into the economic. At one level, it registers little more than the truth of an already existing commonality, evident in language and in the most fundamental of moral proscriptions. At another, it registers the "ideals" of community and solidarity, as standards against which to measure the actual deficiencies of our culture and our society. A democratic common culture cannot be made from within the intellectual class itself, but only from within those exploited and oppressed classes and groups the cultural lives of which have proved, by turn, the objects of realist neglect, modernist disdain and postmodernist pastiche. Doubtless, both international communism, as represented in the late, unlamented barracks socialism of Eastern Europe, and international socialism, as in the pernicious pragmatism of the modern Labour Party, have each proved false starts in the politics of the long revolution. But history is a long time; and it is not over yet. As Williams himself concludes: "If we are to break out of the non-historical fixity of *post*-modernism, then we must search out and counterpose an alternative tradition . . . which may address itself . . . to a modern *future* in which community can be imagined again".[94]

NOTES

Chapter 1

1. M. Green, "Cultural studies!", said the magistrate, *News From Nowhere*, 8, 1990, p. 30.
2. A. Easthope, *British post-structuralism since 1968* (London, Routledge, 1988), p. 74.
3. L. Grossberg et al., *It's a sin: essays on postmodernism, politics and culture* (Sydney, Power Publications, 1988), p. 8.
4. G. Turner, *British cultural studies: An introduction* (London, Unwin Hyman, 1990), p. 76.
5. S. Hall, Cultural studies: two paradigms, *Media, Culture and Society*, 2, 1, 1980; R. Johnson, Histories of culture/theories of ideology: notes on an impasse, in *Ideology and cultural production*, eds. M. Barrett et al. (London, Croom Helm, 1979).
6. Hall, Cultural studies: two paradigms, pp. 62–3.
7. *Ibid.*, pp. 67–9.
8. S. Hall, Cultural studies and the Centre: some problematics and problems, in *Culture, media, language*, eds. S. Hall et al. (London, Hutchinson/Centre for Contemporary Cultural Studies, 1980), p. 19.
9. F. R. Leavis & D. Thompson, *Culture and environment* (London, Chatto & Windus, 1960), p. 87.
10. K. Marx, *Early writings* (Harmondsworth, Penguin, 1975), p. 425.
11. M. Weber, *From Max Weber: essays in sociology*, eds. H. H. Gerth & C. W. Mills (London, Routledge & Kegan Paul, 1948), pp. 180–95.
12. As Lévi-Strauss reminds us, "primitive" knowledge can indeed be understood as a kind of science. cf. C. Lévi-Strauss, *The savage mind* (Chicago, University of Chicago Press, 1966), pp. 13–16.
13. L. Febvre & H.-J. Martin, *The coming of the book: the impact of printing 1450–1800*, tr. D. Gerard, eds. G. Nowell-Smith & D. Wootton (London, New Left Books, 1976), p. 249.
14. W. Benjamin, The work of art in the age of mechanical reproduction, in *Illuminations*, tr. H. Zohn (Glasgow, Fontana, 1973).
15. R. Williams, *Culture* (Glasgow, Fontana, 1981), pp. 36–8.
16. R. Escarpit, *The sociology of literature*, tr. E. Pick (London, Cass, 1971), p. 38.
17. Williams, *Culture*, pp. 38–44.
18. P. Bürger, *Theory of the avant-garde*, tr. M. Shaw (Minneapolis, University of Minnesota Press, 1984), p. 47.
19. This is not to suggest that cultural theory is not itself political, only that the politics of contemporary cultural theory are neither reducible to nor the effect of political theory proper (in the sense, that is, of the theory of the state and of state power).
20. Bürger, *Theory of the avant-garde*, p. 49.
21. H. Marcuse, The affirmative character of culture, in *Negations*, tr. J. J. Shapiro (Bos-

ton, Beacon Press, 1968).

22. Williams, *Culture*, p. 102.

23. A. Gramsci, *Selections from prison notebooks*, tr. Q. Hoare & G. Nowell Smith (London, Lawrence & Wishart, 1971), pp. 5–8.

24. C. B. Macpherson, *The political theory of possessive individualism: Hobbes to Locke* (Oxford, Oxford University Press, 1962), pp. 53–4.

25. *Ibid.*, p. 51.

26. D. Hume, *Of the standard of taste and other essays* (Indianapolis, Bobbs-Merrill, 1965), p. 17.

27. *Ibid.*, p. 7.

28. J. Bentham, The rationale of reward, in *The works of Jeremy Bentham*, vol. II (New York, Russell & Russell, 1962), p. 253.

29. J. S. Mill, *Utilitarianism* (Glasgow, Fontana, 1962), pp. 258, 260.

30. *Ibid.*, p. 260.

31. *Ibid.*, p. 259.

32. T. Parsons, *The structure of social action* (New York, Free Press, 1949), p. 44.

33. *Ibid.*, p. 56.

34. *Ibid.*

35. *Ibid.*, pp. 60–1.

36. *Ibid.*, p. 469.

37. Though it seems much less offensively so at present. As one sociologist has recently argued: "In our current social situation, where economists are seeking to apply utilitarian models to everything from crime and immigration to the selling of children, where utilitarian rational-choice models seem once again to be making inroads into the heart of sociology, and where methodological empiricism is stronger than ever, it is well to reread Parsons's fifty year-old demolition of these very same points of view" (M. Gould, Voluntarism versus utilitarianism: a critique of Camic's history of ideas, *Theory, culture and society*, 6, 4, 1989, p. 649).

38. A. W. Gouldner, *The coming crisis of western sociology* (London, Heinemann, 1971), pp. 61–2.

39. M. Horkheimer, *Critical theory: selected essays*, tr. M. J. O. O'Connell (New York, Seabury Press, 1972), p. 202.

40. I am well aware that capitalism and state capitalism have produced a whole series of other, much more objectionable, political forms: Bonapartism, military dictatorship, fascism, Stalinism, and so on. But these each appear to be essentially exceptional responses to moments of particular crisis. The dismantling of Iberian fascism in the 1970s, of a whole series of Latin American military dictatorships during the late 1980s, and most spectacularly of all of Eastern European Stalinism as a result of the revolutions of 1989, all seem to suggest the provisional, transitional and temporary nature of such illiberal forms. I should add that it is liberalism, rather than democracy, which is much more properly normal to capitalist society.

41. It is, of course, deeply controversial to suggest that the intelligentsia is any kind of class. My own view, however, is that it is a "social class", in Weber's sense of the term. cf. M. Weber, *The theory of social and economic organization*, tr. A. M. Henderson & T. Parsons (New York, Free Press, 1964), p. 424. It is a group possessed of sense of collective identity founded on common material interests. These interests are not those of a common relation to the means of production, such as is postulated in Marx's un-

derstanding of class, but rather of a shared access to what Pierre Bourdieu terms "cultural capital". cf. P. Bourdieu, *Outline of a theory of practice*, tr. R. Nice (Cambridge, Cambridge University Press, 1977), pp. 183–97.

42. Gouldner, *The coming crisis of western sociology*, p. 79.

43. *Ibid.*, p. 80.

44. D. Bell, *The cultural contradictions of capitalism* (London, Heinemann, 1979), p. 53.

45. *Ibid.*, pp. 80–1, 84.

46. J. Habermas, *Legitimation Crisis*, tr. T. McCarthy (Boston, Beacon Press, 1975), pp. 77–8.

47. *Ibid.*, p. 78.

Chapter 2

1. R. Johnson, Histories of culture/theories of ideology: notes on an impasse, in *Ideology and Cultural Production*, eds. M. Barrett et al. (London, Croom Helm, 1979), pp. 51–2.

2. P. B. Shelley, *A defence of poetry* (with P. Sidney, *An apology for poetry*), ed. H. A. Needham (London, Ginn, 1931), p. 109.

3. R. Williams, *Culture and society 1780–1950* (Harmondsworth, Penguin, 1963), p. 17.

4. M. Arnold, *Culture and anarchy*, ed. J. Dover Wilson (Cambridge, Cambridge University Press, 1966), pp. 48–9.

5. *Ibid.*, pp. 101–5.

6. *Ibid.*, p. 109.

7. *Ibid.*, p. 203.

8. *Ibid.*, 76.

9. Williams, *Culture and society*, p. 133.

10. Arnold, *Culture and anarchy*, p. 109.

11. J. Habermas, *The structural transformation of the public sphere: an inquiry into a category of bourgeois society* tr. T. Burger with F. Lawrence (Cambridge, Polity Press, 1989).

12. T. Eagleton, *The function of criticism: from "The Spectator" to post-structuralism* (London, Verso, 1984), p. 9.

13. *Ibid.*, pp. 34–6, 56–7, 65.

14. B. Doyle, The hidden history of English studies, in *Re-reading English*, ed. P. Widdowson (London, Methuen, 1982), pp. 21, 26–7.

15. C. Baldick, *The social mission of English criticism 1848–1932* (Oxford, Oxford University Press, 1983), pp. 61–72.

16. *Ibid.*, pp. 76–7, 80, 87–9, 93–5, 104–6.

17. T. S. Eliot, *Selected essays* (London, Faber, 1963), p. 16.

18. T. S. Eliot, *Notes towards the definition of culture* (London, Faber, 1962), p. 120.

19. T. S. Eliot, *The idea of a Christian society and other writings* (London, Faber, 1982), p. 53.

20. Eliot, *Notes towards the definition of culture*, p. 42.

21. Eliot, *Selected essays*, p. 287.

22. T. S. Eliot, *Milton: two studies* (London, Faber, 1968), p. 34.

23. Eliot, *The idea of a Christian society*, p. 66.

24. F. R. Leavis, *The common pursuit* (Harmondsworth, Penguin, 1962), p. 182.

25. *Ibid.*, p. 184.

26. F. R. Leavis, *Nor shall my sword: discourses on pluralism, compassion and social hope* (London,

Chatto & Windus, 1972), p. 15.

27. Leavis, *The common pursuit*, p. 190.

28. F. R. Leavis, *Education and the university: a sketch for an "English school"* (London, Chatto & Windus, 1948), p. 145.

29. F. R. Leavis, *Revaluation* (Harmondsworth, Penguin, 1972), p. 58.

30. The phrase is originally Nietzsche's, but has been borrowed by Fredric Jameson to describe structuralist and Formalist theories of literature. cf. F. Jameson, *The prison-house of language* (Princeton, Princeton University Press, 1972).

31. F. R. Leavis, *New bearings in English poetry* (London, Chatto & Windus, 1938), pp. 213–14.

32. Leavis, *The common pursuit*, p. 184.

33. Thus Leavis: "to aim at solving the problems of civilization in terms of the 'class war' is to aim . . . at completing the work of capitalism and its products" – F. R. Leavis, *For continuity* (Cambridge, Minority Press, 1933), p. 172.

34. P. Anderson, Components of the national culture, in *Student power* eds. R. Blackburn & A. Cockburn (Harmondsworth, Penguin, 1970), p. 276. Interestingly, this passage is omitted from the revised version of the essay included in Anderson's *English questions*, presumably because he now considers it "some of the bombast and excess of the period" – P. Anderson *English questions* (London, Verso, 1992), Acknowledgements page.

35. Anderson, *English questions*, p. 102.

36. F. Mulhern, *The moment of "Scrutiny"* (London, Verso, 1981), p. 322.

37. Eagleton, *The function of criticism*, p. 75.

38. D. J. Palmer, *The rise of English studies* (Oxford, Oxford University Press, 1965), p. 99.

39. Leavis, *Nor shall my sword*, p. 94.

40. *Ibid.*, ch.1.

41. F. R. Leavis, *Two cultures?* (London, Chatto & Windus, 1962), p. 30.

42. Mulhern, *The moment of "Scrutiny"*, p. 326.

43. Anderson, *English questions*, p. 99.

44. Leavis, *Revaluation*, pp. 58, 53.

45. M. Green, British decency, *Kenyon Review*, 21, 4, 1959, pp. 506–7.

46. R. Hoggart & R. Williams, Working class attitudes, *New Left Review*, 1, 1960.

47. E. P. Thompson, *William Morris: romantic to revolutionary* (London, Lawrence & Wishart, 1955).

48. E. P. Thompson, *The making of the English working class* (London, Victor Gollancz, 1963), p. 832.

49. *Ibid.*

50. R. Hoggart, *The uses of literacy* (Harmondsworth, Penguin, 1958), p. 343.

51. Williams, *Culture and society*, p. 311.

52. *Ibid.*, p. 313.

53. *Ibid.*, p. 311.

54. R. Williams, *The long revolution* (Harmondsworth, Penguin, 1965), p. 68.

55. Williams, *Culture and society*, p.322.

56. *Ibid.*, p. 318.

57. *Ibid.*, p. 311.

58. Williams, *The long revolution*, p. 64.

59. *Ibid.*, pp. 64–5.

60. R. Williams, *The English novel: from Dickens to Lawrence* (St Albans, Paladin, 1974).

61. R. Hoggart, *Speaking to each other, vol. 2 about literature* (London, Chatto & Windus, 1970), p. 255.

62. R. Williams, *Communications*, third edn. (Harmondsworth, Penguin, 1976), p. 149.

63. R. Williams, *Communications* (London, Penguin, 1962); R. Williams, *Television: technology and cultural form* (Glasgow, Fontana, 1974).

64. Williams, *Television*, p. 151.

65. S. Hall and T. Jefferson (eds), *Resistance through rituals: youth sub-cultures in post-war Britain* (London, Hutchinson/Centre for Contemporary Cultural Studies, 1976).

66. D. Hebdidge, *Subculture: the meaning of style* (London, Methuen, 1979).

67. P. Willis, *Learning to labour: How working class kids get working class jobs* (London, Saxon House, 1977); P. Willis, *Profane culture* (London, Routledge & Kegan Paul, 1978).

68. P. Willis et al., *Common culture: symbolic work at play in the everyday culture of the young* (Milton Keynes, Open University Press, 1990).

69. J. Seabrook, *Landscapes of poverty* (Oxford, Basil Blackwell, 1985); J. Seabrook, *The leisure society* (Oxford, Basil Blackwell, 1988).

70. Thus Herder: "The cultivation of its mother tongue alone can lift a nation out of a state of barbarism" – J. G. von Herder, *Reflections on the philosophy of the history of mankind*, tr. T. O. Churchill, ed. F. E. Manuel (Chicago, University of Chicago Press, 1968), p. 328. cf. also pp. 3–78.

71. G. W. F. Hegel, *The philosophy of history*, tr. J. Sibtree (New York, Dover, 1956), p. 53.

72. E. Gellner, *Thought and change* (London, Weidenfeld & Nicolson, 1964), p. 169.

73. E. Kedourie, *Nationalism* (London, Hutchinson, 1960).

74. T. Nairn, *The break-up of Britain* (London, New Left Books, 1977).

75. B. Anderson, *Imagined communities: reflections on the origins and spread of nationalism* (London, Verso, 1983), p. 15.

76. *Ibid.*, pp. 30, 41, 46–7, 50–128.

77. R. Williams, *Resources of hope: culture, democracy, socialism*, ed. R. Gable (London, Verso, 1989), pp. 117–18.

78. R. Williams, *Towards 2000* (London, Chatto & Windus, 1983), p. 181.

79. R. Williams, *What I came To say*, eds. N. Belton et al. (London, Hutchinson Radius, 1989), p. 59.

80. Williams, *Towards 2000*, p. 197.

81. M. Morris & A. Freadman, Import rhetoric: semiotics in/and Australia, in *The foreign bodies papers*, eds. P. Botsman et al. (Sydney, Local Consumption Publications, 1981), pp. 126–7.

82. R. Williams, *Second generation* (London, Chatto & Windus, 1964), p. 322.

83. T. Eagleton, Nationalism: irony and commitment, in T. Eagleton et al., *Nationalism, colonialism and literature* (Minneapolis, University of Minnesota Press, 1990), p. 23.

Chapter 3

1. A. Salomon, German sociology, in *Twentieth century sociology*, eds. G. Gurvitch & W. E. Moore (New York, Philosophical Library, 1945), p.596.

2. M. Merleau-Ponty, *Adventures of the dialectic*, tr. J. Bien (London, Heinemann, 1974), ch. 2.

NOTES

3. K. Marx, *Early writings* (Harmondsworth, Penguin, 1975), pp. 327–30.

4. *Ibid.*, p. 328.

5. *Ibid.*, p. 329.

6. K. Marx & F. Engels, *The communist manifesto*, tr. S. Moore (Harmondsworth, Penguin, 1967), p. 82.

7. K. Marx, *Capital*, vol. I, tr. S. Moore & E. Aveling (London, Lawrence & Wishart, 1970), p. 72.

8. K. Marx & F. Engels, *The German ideology*, part one, tr. W. Lough, C. Dutt & C. P. Magill, ed. C. J. Arthur (London, Lawrence & Wishart, 1970), p. 47.

9. *Ibid.*, p. 64.

10. *Ibid.*, pp. 65–6.

11. Marx, *Early writings*, p. 425.

12. *Ibid.*, p. 426.

13. The terms are Althusser's. cf. L. Althusser and É. Balibar, *Reading Capital*, tr. B. Brewster (London, New Left Books, 1970), pp. 186–7. Althusser's discussion is deliberately intended to promote a third model, that of structural causality, an intention which clearly colours the account of expressive causality in particular. But the distinction between mechanical and expressive models of causation nonetheless remains valid. It is possible, of course, that all three types of causation actually occur empirically.

14. Thus Marx's warning to new readers in the "Preface" to the first French edition of *Capital*: "There is no royal road to science, and only those who do not dread the fatiguing climb of its steep paths have a chance of gaining its luminous summits" – Marx, *Capital*, vol. I, p. 21.

15. G. Plekhanov, Art and social life, tr. E. Hartley et al., in *Art and social life* eds. P. Davison et al. (Cambridge, Chadwyck Healey, 1978), p. 23.

16. *Ibid.*, pp. 19–20.

17. *Ibid.*, p. 63.

18. *Ibid.*, pp. 53–5.

19. A. A. Zhdanov, Soviet literature – the richest in ideas, the most advanced in literature, in M. Gorky et al., *Soviet Writers' Congress 1934: the debate on socialist realism and modernism* (London, Lawrence & Wishart, 1977), p. 18.

20. *Ibid.*, p. 19.

21. P. Bourdieu, *Distinction: a social critique of the judgement of taste* tr. R. Nice (London, Routledge & Kegan Paul, 1984), p. 32.

22. Zhdanov, Soviet literature, p. 21.

23. Of course, this is not literally true: Russian communists spoke Russian, and British communists English. But the Comintern did evolve an international style of its own. Hence the way in which British communist publications, written by British activists, very often read as if translated from the Russian. It was this international style which meant very different things to Western and Eastern communisms.

24. L. Trotsky, *On literature and art*, ed. P. N. Seigel (New York, Pathfinder Press, 1970), p. 106.

25. cf. U. Sinclair, *The jungle* (Harmondsworth, Penguin, 1965); F. Hardy, *Power without glory* (London, Panther, 1975); R. Williams, *Border country* (London, Chatto & Windus, 1960); R. Williams, *Second generation* (London, Chatto & Windus, 1964).

26. C. Caudwell, *Illusion and reality* (London, Lawrence & Wishart, 1946), p. 201.

27. *Ibid.*, p. 130.

28. *Ibid.*, p. 55.

29. *Ibid.*, p. 30.

30. *Ibid.*, p. 124.

31. *Ibid.*, p. 261

32. *Ibid.*, p. 121.

33. *Ibid.*, p. 297.

34. *Ibid.*, p. 288.

35. A. West, *Crisis and criticism* (London, Lawrence & Wishart, 1975), p. 99.

36. *Ibid.*, p. 102.

37. R. Fox, *The novel and the people* (London, Lawrence & Wishart, 1979), p. 37.

38. *Ibid.*, p. 138.

39. R. Williams, *Politics and letters: interviews with New Left Review* (London, New Left Books, 1979), p. 45.

40. M. Weber, *The Protestant ethic and the spirit of capitalism*, tr. T. Parsons (London, Unwin, 1930), p. 183.

41. *Ibid.*, p. 91.

42. On capitalism, cf. M. Weber, *The theory of social and economic organization*, tr. A. M. Henderson & T. Parsons (New York, Free Press, 1964), p. 279; on bureaucracy, cf. M. Weber, *From Max Weber: essays in sociology*, eds. H. H. Gerth & C. W. Mills (London, Routledge & Kegan Paul, 1948), pp. 215–16; on Protestantism, cf. Weber, *The Protestant ethic*, pp. 153–4; on music, cf. M. Weber, *The rational and social foundations of music*, tr. D. Martindale et al. (Carbondale, Southern Illinois University Press, 1958), pp. 82–8.

43. Weber, *The Protestant ethic*, p. 181.

44. A. Giddens, *Capitalism and modern social theory* (Cambridge, Cambridge University Press, 1971), p. 193.

45. A. W. Gouldner, *The two Marxisms: contradictions and anomalies in the development of theory* (London, Macmillan, 1980), pp. 368–87.

46. M. Weber, *Economy and society*, vol. 3, tr. E. Fischoff et al. (New York, Bedminster, 1968), pp. 1401–2.

47. Weber, *Theory of social and economic organization*, p. 115.

48. *Ibid.*, pp. 152–3, 324–52.

49. *Ibid.*, p. 328.

50. P. Anderson, *Considerations on western Marxism* (London, New Left Books, 1976), pp. 75–6.

51. A. Gramsci, *Selections from political writings 1910–1920*, tr. J. Mathews (London, Lawrence & Wishart, 1977), pp. 34–7.

52. G. Lukács, *History and class consciousness*, tr. R. Livingstone (London, Merlin Press, 1971), pp. 27–8.

53. *Ibid.*, pp. 83–110.

54. *Ibid.*, pp. 6–7.

55. *Ibid.*, p. 20.

56. *Ibid.*, p. 51.

57. cf. G. Lukács, *The meaning of contemporary realism*, tr. J. &nd N. Mander (London, Merlin Press, 1963).

58. Zhdanov, Soviet Literature, pp. 21–2; Lukács, *Meaning of contemporary realism*, pp. 124–7.

59. cf. G. Lukács, *Solzhenitsyn*, tr. W. D. Graf (London, Merlin Press, 1970).

60. Lukács, *Meaning of contemporary realism*, p. 45.

61. T. Adorno & M. Horkheimer, *Dialectic of enlightenment*, tr. J. Cumming (London, Verso, 1979), p. 9.

62. *Ibid.*, p. 131.

63. cf. W. Benjamin, The work of art in the age of mechanical reproduction, in *Illuminations*, tr. H. Zohn (Glasgow, Fontana, 1973).

64. T. Adorno, Letters to Walter Benjamin, tr. J. Zohn, in E. Bloch et al., *Aesthetics and politics* (London, Verso, 1980), pp. 122–3.

65. T. Adorno, Reconciliation under duress, tr. R. Livingstone, in Bloch, *Aesthetics and politics*, pp. 151–76.

66. The alliance between Trotskyism and surrealism was of Trotsky's making as well as Breton's. cf. Trotsky, *On literature and art*, pp. 122–4.

67. Anderson, *Considerations*, pp. 92, 88.

68. L. Goldmann, *The hidden God*, tr. P. Thody (London, Routledge & Kegan Paul, 1964); L. Goldmann, *Towards a sociology of the novel*, tr. A. Sheridan (London, Tavistock, 1975).

69. J-P. Sartre, *Critique of dialectical reason*, tr. A. Sheridan-Smith (London, New Left Books, 1976), pp. 43–7; J-P. Sartre, Socialism in one country, *New Left Review*, 100, 1976/1977, p. 162.

70. A. Gramsci, *Selections from prison notebooks*, tr. Q. Hoare & G. Nowell Smith (London, Lawrence & Wishart, 1971), p. 263.

71. *Ibid.*, p. 12.

72. *Ibid.*, p. 5.

73. *Ibid.*, p. 7.

74. R. Williams, *Marxism and literature* (Oxford, Oxford University Press, 1977), p. 108.

75. L. Althusser, *For Marx*, tr. B. Brewster (London, New Left Books, 1977), pp. 32–7.

76. Althusser and Balibar, *Reading Capital*, p. 186.

77. L. Althusser, *Lenin and philosophy and other essays*, tr. B. Brewster (London, New Left Books, 1971), pp. 143–71.

78. *Ibid.*, p. 122.

79. Althusser and Balibar, *Reading Capital*, pp. 30–4.

80. P. Macherey, *A theory of literary production*, tr. G. Wall (London, Routledge & Kegan Paul, 1978).

81. P. Sedgwick, The two New Lefts, in *The Left In Britain 1956–1968*, ed. D. Widgery (London, Penguin, 1976).

82. In his *Arguments Within English Marxism*, Perry Anderson explicitly denies the charge that the *New Left Review* adopted an essentially Althusserian stance – P. Anderson, *Arguments Within English Marxism* (London, Verso, 1980), p. 133. No doubt the *Review* and New Left Books did indeed devote resources to the (more or less) critical appraisal of each of the major schools of Western Marxism. But they also exercised a very real discrimination in the ways in which those resources were allocated. For much of the late 1960s and the 1970s the *Review*'s theoretical interests and sympathies were in fact defined primarily in relation to Althusserianism. Sufficiently so at least for the North American "Hegelian Marxist" journal *Telos* to complain of the *Review*'s "inability to come to terms with its own culture, opting instead for the most sterile version of post-Althusserian word games" – Toronto *Telos* Group, Short journal reviews, *Telos*, 27, 1976, p. 258.

83. P. Anderson, *English questions* (London, Verso, 1992), pp. 15–47, 48–104; T. Nairn, The british political elite, *New Left Review*, 23, 1964; T. Nairn, The english working class, *New Left Review*, 24, 1964; T. Nairn, The anatomy of the Labour Party, *New Left Review*, 27 and 28, 1964.

84. T. Nairn, *The break-up of Britain* (London, New Left Books, 1977).

85. Anderson, *Arguments*, pp. 138–9.

86. T. Nairn, *The enchanted glass: Britain and its monarchy* (London, Picador, 1990), pp. 371–6.

87. Anderson, *English questions*, pp. 196–7, 199–200.

88. T. Eagleton, *Criticism and ideology* (London, New Left Books, 1976), pp. 44–63.

89. *Ibid.*, pp. 64–101.

90. *Ibid.*, p. 27.

91. *Ibid.*, p. 26.

92. *Ibid.*, pp. 33–4.

93. *Ibid.*, p. 25.

94. E. P. Thompson, *The poverty of theory and other essays* (London, Merlin Press, 1978), p. 205.

95. Eagleton, *Criticism and ideology*, pp. 162–3.

96. H. Felperin, *Beyond deconstruction: the uses and abuses of literary theory* (Oxford, Oxford University Press, 1985), p. 57.

97. Thompson, *The poverty of theory*, p. ii.

98. *Ibid.*, p. 358.

99. *Ibid.*, p. 384.

100. Williams, *Marxism and literature*, p. 4.

101. R. Williams, *Problems in materialism and culture: selected essays* (London, New Left Books, 1980), p. 243.

102. R. Williams, *Culture* (Glasgow, Fontana, 1981).

103. G. Turner, *British cultural studies: an introduction* (London, Unwin Hyman, 1990), p. 65.

104. A. O'Connor, *Raymond Williams: writing, culture, politics* (Oxford, Basil Blackwell), p. 103.

105. Williams, *Marxism and literature*, p. 110.

106. *Ibid.*, p. 111.

107. *Ibid.*, p. 125.

108. *Ibid.*, pp. 121–7.

109. *Ibid.*, p. 122.

110. *Ibid.*, p. 123.

111. *Ibid.*, p. 126.

112. Williams, *Culture*, p. 205.

113. Williams, *Marxism and literature*, p. 126.

114. *Ibid.*, pp. 133–4.

115. *Ibid.*, p. 93.

116. *Ibid.*

117. T. Eagleton, Introduction, in *Raymond Williams: critical perspectives*, ed. T. Eagleton (Cambridge, Polity Press, 1989), p. 6.

118. J. Dollimore, Introduction: Shakespeare, cultural materialism and the new historicism, in *Political Shakespeare: new essays in cultural materialism* eds. J. Dollimore & A. Sinfield (Manchester, Manchester University Press, 1985), p. 15. cf. T. Lovell, *Pictures of reality: aesthetics, politics, pleasure* (London, British Film Institute, 1980); J. Wolff, *The social*

production of art (London, Macmillan, 1981); A. Sinfield, Literary theory and the "crisis" in English studies, *Critical Quarterly*, 25, 3, 1983; T. Eagleton, *Literary theory: an introduction* (Oxford, Basil Blackwell, 1983).

119. T. Lovell, *Consuming fiction* (London, Verso, 1987); J. Wolff, *Feminine sentences: essays on women and culture* (Cambridge, Polity Press, 1990).

120. T. Eagleton, Base and superstructure in Raymond Williams, in *Raymond Williams*, ed. Eagleton, p. 169.

121. A. Sinfield, *Literature, politics and culture in postwar Britain* (Oxford, Basil Blackwell, 1989), pp. 26–7, 31, 35.

122. C. Hampton, *The ideology of the text* (Milton Keynes, Open University Press, 1990); A. Sinfield, *Faultlines: cultural materialism and the politics of dissident reading* (Oxford, Oxford University Press, 1992).

123. R. Collins et al., Introduction, in *Media, culture and society: a critical reader*, eds. R. Collins et al. (London, Sage, 1986), p. 4.

124. *Ibid.*, pp. 4–5.

125. Turner, *British cultural studies*, pp. 194–5.

126. R. Williams, *Communications* (Harmondsworth, Penguin, 1962); R. Williams, *Television: technology and cultural form* (Glasgow, Fontana, 1974).

Chapter 4

1. D. Robey, Introduction, in *Structuralism: an introduction*, ed. D. Robey (Oxford, Oxford University Press, 1973), pp. 1–2.

2. Comte subscribed to a radically positivistic notion of science. Indeed, the term "positivism" derives from his "positive philosophy". And, unlike the utilitarians, he conceived this science in, equally radical, holistic terms. cf. R. Aron, *Main currents in sociological thought*, vol. 1, tr. R. Howard & H. Weaver (London, Weidenfeld & Nicholson, 1965), ch. 2.

3. E. Durkheim, *The rules of sociological method*, tr. S. A. Solovay & J. H. Mueller (New York, Free Press, 1964), p. 3.

4. E. Durkheim, *The elementary forms of the religious life*, tr. J. W. Swain (London, George Allen & Unwin, 1976), p. 433.

5. *Ibid.*, pp. 423–4.

6. *Ibid.*, p. 40.

7. *Ibid.*, p. 47.

8. F. de Saussure, *Course in General Linguistics*, tr. W. Baskin (Glasgow, Fontana, 1974), p. 14.

9. *Ibid.*, p. 67.

10. *Ibid.*, p. 66.

11. *Ibid.*, p. 120.

12. *Ibid.*, p. 87.

13. Thus Durkheim: "we cannot arrive at an understanding of the most recent religions except by following the manner in which they have been progressively composed in history" – Durkheim, *Elementary forms*, p. 3.

14. Saussure, *Course*, p. 16.

15. C. Lévi-Strauss, *Structural anthropology*, tr. C. Jacobson & B. Grundfest Schoepf

(Harmondsworth, Penguin, 1972).

16. cf. E. Durkheim, *The division of labor in society*, tr. G. Simpson (New York, Free Press, 1964), bk. 2, ch. 2.

17. T. Todorov, *Théorie de la littérature: textes des formalistes russes* (Paris, Éditions du Seuil, 1965).

18. V. Shklovsky, Art as technique, tr. L. Lemon & M. Reis, in *Russian formalist criticism: four essays*, eds. L. Lemon & M. Reis (Lincoln, University of Nebraska Press, 1965), p. 12.

19. R. Jakobson, Closing statement: linguistics and poetics, in *Style in language*, ed. T. A. Sebeok (Cambridge, Mass., MIT Press, 1960), pp. 356–7.

20. R. Barthes, *Mythologies*, tr. A. Lavers (St Albans, Paladin, 1973), pp. 114–15.

21. *Ibid.*, p. 142.

22. *Ibid.*, p. 148.

23. R. Barthes, *Elements of semiology*, tr. A. Levers & C. Smith (New York, Hill & Wang, 1968); R. Barthes, *The fashion system*, tr. M. Ward & R. Howard (New York, Hill & Wang, 1983).

24. R. Barthes, To write: an intransitive verb?, tr. R. Macksey & E. Donato, in *The languages of criticism and the sciences of man*, eds. R. Macksey & E. Donato (Baltimore, The Johns Hopkins University Press, 1970), pp. 141–2.

25. *Ibid.*, p. 144.

26. R. Barthes, *Image-music-text*, tr. S. Heath (New York, Hill & Wang, 1977), p. 148.

27. U. Eco, *The role of the reader: explorations in the semiotics of texts* (London, Hutchinson, 1981).

28. Barthes, *Image-music-text*, p. 148.

29. M. Foucault, *Power/knowledge: selected interviews and other writings 1972–1977*, ed. C. Gordon (Brighton, Harvester Press, 1980), p. 114.

30. M. Foucault, *Madness and civilization: a history of insanity in the age of reason*, tr. R. Howard (New York, Vintage Books, 1965), ; M. Foucault, *The birth of the clinic*, tr. A. M. Sheridan (London, Tavistock, 1973).

31. M. Foucault, *The order of things: an archaeology of the human sciences* (New York, Vintage Books, 1973); M. Foucault, *The archaeology of knowledge*, tr. A. M. Sheridan (London, Tavistock, 1972).

32. Foucault, *The order of things*, p. 379.

33. M. Foucault, *Language, counter-memory, practice*, ed. D. F. Bouchard, tr. D. F. Bouchard & S. Simon (Ithaca, Cornell University Press, 1977), pp. 113–38.

34. Foucault, *The archaeology of knowledge*, p.205.

35. R. Barthes, *S/Z*, tr. R. Miller (New York, Hill & Wang, 1974), p.4.

36. *Ibid.*, p. 77.

37. R. Barthes, *The pleasure of the text*, tr. R. Miller (New York, Hill & Wang, 1975), p. 62.

38. *Ibid.*, p. 9.

39. J. Derrida, Structure, sign and play in the discourse of the human sciences, tr. R. Macksey, in *The languages of criticism and the sciences of man*, eds. R. Macksey & E. Donato (Baltimore, The Johns Hopkins University Press, 1970).

40. J. Derrida, *Writing and difference*, tr. A. Bass (Chicago, University of Chicago Press, 1978), p. 25.

41. J. Derrida, *Speech and phenomena and other essays on Husserl's theory of signs*, tr. D. B. Allison (Evanston, Northwestern University Press, 1973), p. 129.

42. J. Derrida, *Of grammatology*, tr. G. C. Spivak (Baltimore, The Johns Hopkins Univer-

sity Press, 1976), p. 159.

43. Derrida, Structure, sign and play, p. 265.

44. M. Foucault, *Histoire de la folie á l'âge classique* (Paris, Éditions Gallimard, 1972), p. 602.

45. Foucault, *Power/knowledge*, p. 114.

46. M. Foucault, *Discipline and punish: the birth of the prison*, tr. A. M. Sheridan (Harmondsworth, Allen Lane, 1977).

47. Foucault's last major project was the three volume *History of sexuality*. Its original focus on power-knowledge regimes becomes displaced, in the second and third volumes, by a historical and quasi-historicist account of the development of the sexual subject. cf. M. Foucault, *The history of sexuality*, tr. R. Hurley (New York, Random House, 1978); M. Foucault, *The use of pleasure*, tr. R. Hurley (New York, Pantheon Books, 1985); M. Foucault, *The case of the self*, tr. R. Hurley (New York, Pantheon Books, 1986).

48. Foucault, *Power/knowledge*, p. 39.

49. *Ibid.*, p. 119.

50. P. Anderson, *In the tracks of historical materialism: the Wellek Library lectures* (London, Verso, 1983), p. 54.

51. Foucault, *Power/knowledge*, p. 117.

52. *Ibid.*, p. 126.

53. *Ibid.*, p. 130.

54. J. Culler, *Structuralist poetics: structuralism, linguistics and the study of literature* (London, Routledge & Kegan Paul, 1975).

55. G. Hartman (ed.), *Deconstruction and criticism* (New York, Seabury Press, 1979).

56. A. Easthope, *British post-structuralism since 1968* (London, Routledge, 1988), pp. 21–2, 161–4.

57. *Ibid.*, p. 210.

58. T. Hawkes, *Structuralism and semiotics* (London, Methuen, 1977).

59. T. Hawkes, *That Shakespeherian rag: essays on critical process* (London, Methuen, 1986); T. Hawkes, *Meaning by Shakespeare* (London, Routledge, 1992).

60. J. Fiske, *Introduction to communication studies* (London, Methuen, 1982); J. Fiske, *Reading the popular* (London, Unwin Hyman, 1989); J. Fiske, *Understanding Popular Culture* (London, Unwin Hyman, 1989).

61. P. Widdowson, The crisis in English studies, in *Re-reading English*, ed. P. Widdowson (London, Methuen, 1982).

62. A. Easthope, *Literary into cultural studies* (London, Routledge, 1991), p. 11.

63. S. Hall, Cultural studies and the Centre: some problematics and problems, in *Culture, media, language*, eds. S. Hall et al. (London, Hutchinson/Centre for Contemporary Cultural Studies, 1980), p. 35.

64. S. Hall, Encoding/decoding, in *Culture, media, language* eds. Hall et al.

65. S. Hall, Cultural studies: two paradigms, *Media, culture and society*, 2, 1, 1980.

66. S. Hall, The toad in the garden: Thatcherism among the theorists, in *Marxism and the interpretation of culture*, eds. C. Nelson & L. Grossberg (London, Macmillan, 1988), p. 56.

67. *Ibid.*, pp. 51–3.

68. Easthope, *British post-structuralism*, p. 153.

69. *Ibid.*

70. H. Felperin, *Beyond deconstruction: the uses and abuses of literary theory* (Oxford, Oxford University Press, 1985), pp. 71–2.

71. F. Lentricchia, *After the new criticism* (Chicago, University of Chicago Press, 1980).

72. Easthope, *British post-structuralism*, pp. 134–5.

73. C. MacCabe, *Theoretical essays: film, linguistics, literature* (Manchester, Manchester University Press, 1985), pp. 33–57; S. Heath, *Questions of cinema* (London, Macmillan, 1981), pp. 19–75.

74. F. Barker, *The tremulous private body: essays on subjection* (London, Methuen, 1984).

75. C. Belsey, *The subject of tragedy: identity and difference in Renaissance drama* (London, Methuen, 1985).

76. J. Dollimore, Introduction: Shakespeare, cultural materialism and the new historicism, in *Political Shakespeare: new essays in cultural materialism* (Manchester, Manchester University Press, 1985), p. 3.

77. Easthope, *Literary into cultural studies*, pp. 119–23.

78. T. Bennett et al. (eds.), *Popular culture and social relations* (Milton Keynes, Open University Press, 1986), p. vii.

79. Easthope, *Literary into cultural studies*, p. 74.

80. T. Bennett, *Outside literature* (London, Routledge, 1990).

81. T. Bennett, *Formalism and Marxism* (London, Methuen, 1979).

82. Bennett, *Outside literature*, p. 195.

83. *Ibid.*, p. 10.

84. *Ibid.*, p. 270.

85. B. Ashcroft et al., *The empire writes back: theory and practice in post-colonial literatures* (London, Routledge, 1989).

86. I. Adam & H. Tiffin (eds), *Past the last post: theorizing post-colonialism and post-modernism* (London, Harvester Wheatsheaf, 1991).

87. Ashcroft et al., *The empire writes back*, p. 12.

88. *Ibid.*, p. 33.

89. S. Gunew, Australia 1984: A moment in the archaeology of multiculturalism, in *Europe and its others*, vol. I, eds. F. Barker et al. (Colchester, University of Essex, 1985), p. 188.

90. E. W. Said, *Orientalism* (New York, Pantheon Books, 1978), p. 3.

91. S. Hall et al., *Policing the crisis: mugging, the state, and law and order* (London, Macmillan, 1978).

92. G. C. Spivak, Can the subaltern speak?, in *Marxism and the interpretation of culture*, eds. Nelson & Grossberg, p. 273.

93. C. MacCabe, Foreword, in G. C. Spivak, *In other worlds: essays in cultural politics* (London, Methuen, 1987), p. ix.

94. Spivak, *In other worlds*, pp. 206–7.

95. *Ibid.*, p. 209.

96. N. Fraser, The french Derrideans: politicizing deconstruction or deconstructing the political?, *New German Critique*, 33, 1984, p. 133.

97. Spivak, *In other worlds*, p. 208.

98. E. P. Thompson, The long revolution, *New Left Review*, 9 and 10, 1961.

99. E. Showalter, A criticism of our own: autonomy and assimilation in Afro-American and feminist literary theory, in *The future of literary theory*, ed. R. Cohen (London, Routledge, 1989), p. 369.

100. cf. H. K. Bhabha, The other question: difference, discrimination and the discourse of colonialism, in *Literature, politics and theory*, eds. F. Barker et al. (London, Methuen,

1986); H. K. Bhabha, DissemiNation: time, narrative, and the margins of the modern nation, in *Nation and narration*, ed. H. K. Bhabha (London, Routledge, 1990); D. Chakrabarty, *Rethinking working-class history, Bengal 1890–1940* (Princeton, NJ, Princeton University Press, 1989).

101. A. Ahmad, *In theory: classes, nations, literatures* (London, New Left Books, 1992), pp. 92–3.

102. *Ibid.*, p. 94.

103. cf. E. W. Said, *After the last sky: Palestinian lives* (London, Faber, 1986); E. W. Said, *The question of Palestine* (New York, Pantheon Books, 1979).

104. T. Eagleton, A culture in crisis, *The Guardian 3*, 27 November 1992, p. 6.

105. Ashcroft et al., *The empire writes back*, p. 2.

106. In the closing lines of an 1823 sonnet addressed to Britannia herself, William Charles Wentworth had imagined his country's future thus:

And Australasia float, with flag unfurled,
A NEW BRITANNIA IN ANOTHER WORLD!

– W. C. Wentworth, Australasia, in *The heritage of Australian Poetry*, ed. G. Dutton (Melbourne, Currey O'Neil, 1984), p. 24.

107. S. Rushdie, *Imaginary homelands: essays and criticism 1981–1991* (London, Granta Books, 1991), p. 70.

108. S. During, Postmodernism or post-colonialism today?, in *Postmodern conditions*, eds. A. Milner et al. (Oxford, Berg Publishers, 1990), pp. 128–9.

109. Ashcroft et al., *The empire writes back*, p. 2.

110. S. During, Literature – nationalism's other? The case for revision, in *Nation and narration*, ed. Bhabha, pp. 139, 151.

111. *Ibid.*, p. 139.

112. S. Gunew, Denaturalizing cultural nationalisms: multicultural readings of "Australia", in *Nation and narration*, ed. Bhabha, p. 116.

113. During, Literature – nationalism's other?, p. 139.

114. E. W. Said, Yeats and decolonization, in T. Eagleton et al., *Nationalism, colonialism and literature* (Minneapolis, University of Minnesota Press, 1990), p. 74.

115. F. R. Leavis, *Nor shall my sword: discourses on pluralism, compassion and social hope* (London, Chatto & Windus, 1972), p. 93.

116. E. Grosz, Feminism and anti-humanism, in *Discourse and difference: post-structuralism, feminism and the moment of history*, eds. A. Milner & C. Worth (Melbourne, Centre for General and Comparative Literature, 1990), p. 74.

117. S. Lash, *Sociology of postmodernism* (London, Routledge, 1990), p. 153.

118. D. Bell, *The cultural contradictions of capitalism* (London, Heinemann, 1979); J. Habermas, *The philosophical discourse of modernity*, tr. F. Lawrence (Cambridge, Polity Press, 1987); P. Bürger, *Theory of the avant-garde*, tr. M. Shaw (Minneapolis, University of Minnesota Press, 1984); A. Huyssen, *After the great divide: modernism, mass culture and postmodernism* (London, Macmillan, 1988); F. Jameson, *Postmodernism, or the cultural logic of late capitalism* (London, Verso, 1991); A. Heller & F. Fehér, *The postmodern political condition* (Cambridge, Polity Press, 1988).

119. J. Baudrillard, *America*, tr. C. Turner (London, Verso, 1988); J-F. Lyotard, *The postmodern condition: a report on knowledge*, tr. G. Bennington & B. Massumi (Minneapolis, University of Minnesota Press, 1984).

120. Z. Bauman, *Intimations of postmodernity* (London, Routledge, 1992); M. Featherstone,

Consumer culture and postmodernism (London, Sage, 1991); B. Turner (ed.), *Theories of modernity and postmodernity* (London, Sage, 1990).

121. M. Morris, *The pirate's fiancée: feminism, reading, postmodernism* (London, Verso, 1988), pp. 11–23.

122. Foucault, *The order of things*, pp. 385–6.

123. A. Callinicos, *Against postmodernism: a Marxist critique* (Cambridge, Polity Press, 1989), p. 5.

124. Huyssen, *After the great divide*, p. 209.

125. *Ibid.*, pp. 209–10.

126. Jameson, *Postmodernism*, p. 18.

127. E. P. Thompson, *The poverty of theory and other essays* (London, Merlin Press, 1978), pp. 229–42.

128. Foucault shares in this celebration of modernism. cf. Foucault, *The order of things*, pp. 305–6.

129. P. Bourdieu, *Distinction: a social critique of the judgement of taste*, tr. R. Nice (London, Routledge & Kegan Paul, 1984), p. 495.

Chapter 5

1. cf. M. Maclean, Revolution and exclusion: the other voice, in *Discourse and difference: post-structuralism, feminism and the moment of history*, eds. A. Milner & C. Worth (Melbourne, Centre for General and Comparative Literature, 1990); M. Wollstonecraft, *A vindication of the rights of women* (New York, Norton, 1975).

2. cf. J. S. Mill and H. Taylor Mill, *Essays on sex equality* (Chicago, University of Chicago Press, 1970).

3. J. Hole and E. Levine, The first feminists, in *Notes from the third year: women's liberation*, eds. A. Koedt & S. Firestone (New York, Notes from the Second Year Inc., 1971), p. 10.

4. G. Greer, *The female eunuch* (London, MacGibbon & Kee, 1971).

5. cf. V. Woolf, *A room of one's own* (St Albans, Panther, 1977); N. T. Bazin, *Virginia Woolf and androgynous vision* (New Brunswick, Rutgers University Press, 1973).

6. V. Woolf, *Women and writing* (London, Women's Press, 1979), p. 191.

7. cf. S. M. Gilbert & S. Gubar, *No man's land: the place of the woman writer in the twentieth century, vol. 1: the war of the words* (New Haven, Yale University Press, 1988).

8. S. de Beauvoir, *The second sex*, tr. H. M. Parshley (Harmondsworth, Penguin, 1972), p. 29.

9. *Ibid.*, p. 21.

10. S. de Beauvoir, From an interview, tr. H. Eustis, in *New french feminisms: an anthology*, eds. E. Marks & I. de Courtivron (Brighton, Harvester, 1981), pp. 142–3, 150.

11. M. Barrett, *Women's oppression today: problems in Marxist feminist analysis* (London, Verso, 1980), p. 84.

12. E. Showalter, A criticism of our own: autonomy and assimilation in Afro-American and feminist literary theory, *The future of literary theory*, ed. R. Cohen (London, Routledge, 1989), p. 366; K. K. Ruthven, *Feminist literary studies: an introduction* (Cambridge, Cambridge University Press, 1984), ch. 2.

13. cf. M. Stone, *The paradise papers: the suppression of women's rites* (London, Virago, 1979).

14. E. Showalter, Feminist criticism in the wilderness, in *The new feminist criticism: essays on women, literature, and theory*, ed. E. Showalter (New York, Pantheon Books, 1985), p. 249.

15. K. Millett, *Sexual politics* (London, Virago, 1977), ch. 4.

16. *Ibid.*, p. 233.

17. *Ibid.*, p. 238.

18. cf. A. Dworkin, *Woman hating* (New York, Dutton, 1974).

19. Showalter, Feminist criticism in the wilderness, p. 128.

20. E. Showalter, *A literature of their own: British women novelists from Brontë to Lessing* (London, Virago, 1978), p. 319.

21. E. Moers, *Literary women* (London, Women's Press, 1978), p. 67.

22. Showalter, Feminist criticism in the wilderness, p. 260.

23. *Ibid.*, pp. 261–2, 266.

24. *Ibid.*, p. 266.

25. J. Donovan, Afterword: critical re-vision, in *Feminist literary criticism: explorations in theory*, ed. J. Donovan (Lexington, University Press of Kentucky, 1975), p. 77.

26. T. Moi, *Sexual/textual politics* (London, Methuen, 1985), p. 4.

27. Showalter, *A literature of their own*, pp. 295–6.

28. Marxist-feminist Literature Collective, Women's writing: *Jane Eyre, Shirley, Villette, Aurora Leigh*, in *1848: the sociology of literature*, eds. F. Barker et al. (Colchester, University of Essex, 1978), p. 185.

29. *Ibid.*, p. 186.

30. Showalter, Feminist criticism in the wilderness, p. 245.

31. Barrett, *Women's oppression today*, p. 124.

32. *Ibid.*, pp. 98–9.

33. *Ibid.*, pp. 108–12.

34. C. Kaplan, Pandora's box: subjectivity, class and sexuality in socialist feminist criticism, in *Making a difference: feminist literary criticism*, eds. G. Greene & C. Kahn (London, Methuen, 1985), p. 149.

35. *Ibid.*

36. R. Coward, Are women's novels feminist novels?, in *The new feminist criticism*, ed. Showalter, p. 234. cf. M. French, *The women's room* (London, Sphere Books, 1978).

37. *Ibid.*, p. 228.

38. *Ibid.*, p. 238n. cf. R. Coward & E. Ellis, *Language and materialism* (London, Routledge & Kegan Paul, 1977), ch. 3 and 4.

39. L. Mulvey, Visual pleasure and narrative cinema, in *Popular television and film*, eds. T. Bennett et al. (London, British Film Institute, 1981), p. 209.

40. J. Williamson, *Decoding advertisements: ideology and meaning in advertising* (London, Marion Boyars, 1978); Women's Studies Group, *Women take issue: aspects of women's subordination* (London, Hutchinson/Centre for Contemporary Cultural Studies, 1978).

41. Showalter, Feminist criticism in the wilderness, p. 249.

42. *Ibid.*, p. 250.

43. Influential might be a better term than persuasive. For there certainly are very persuasive anglophone instances of the latter two. cf. D. Spender, *Man made language* (London, Routledge & Kegan Paul, 1980); M. Daly, *Gyn/ecology: the metaethics of radical feminism* (Boston, Beacon Press, 1978); J. Mitchell, *Psychoanalysis and feminism* (London, Penguin, 1974). These are, however, much less representative of anglophone feminist discourse than are Kristeva, Cixous and Irigaray of French.

44. Millett, *Sexual politics*, pp. 28–31.
45. H. Cixous and C. Clément, *The newly born woman*, tr. B. Wing (Minneapolis, University of Minnesota Press, 1986), p. 65.
46. *Ibid.*, p. 81.
47. *Ibid.*, p. 82.
48. H. Cixous, The laugh of the Medusa, tr. K. Cohen & P. Cohen, in *New French feminisms*, eds. Marks & de Courtivron, pp. 256–7.
49. L. Irigaray, *This sex which is not one*, tr. C. Porter with C. Burke (Ithaca, Cornell University Press, 1985), p. 28.
50. *Ibid.*, p. 29.
51. Showalter, Feminist criticism in the wilderness, p. 252.
52. J. Mitchell, *Women: the longest revolution. Essays in feminism, literature and psychoanalysis* (London, Virago, 1984), p. 291.
53. J. Lacan, *The four fundamental concepts of psycho-analysis*, tr. A. Sheridan (London, Hogarth Press, 1977), p. 20.
54. cf. Moi, T. (ed.), (1986), *The Kristeva reader* (Oxford: Basil Blackwell).
55. E. P. Thompson, *The poverty of theory and other essays* (London, Merlin Press, 1978), p. 405.
56. J. Kristeva, *Revolution in poetic language*, tr. M. Waller (New York, Columbia University Press, 1984), p. 26.
57. *Ibid.*, pp. 82–5.
58. Cixous and Clément, *The newly born woman*, p. 84.
59. Cixous, Laugh of the Medusa, p. 250.
60. Showalter, Feminist criticism in the wilderness, p. 255.
61. Mitchell, *Women: the longest revolution*, p. 292.
62. J. Wolff, *Feminine sentences: essays on women and culture* (Cambridge, Polity Press, 1990), pp. 33–47.
63. G. Pollock, *Vision and difference: femininity, feminism and histories of art* (London, Routledge, 1988), p. 54.
64. Mitchell, *Women: The longest revolution*, p. 291.
65. *Ibid.*, p. 294.
66. Showalter, A criticism of our own, p. 369. To be fair, we should note that the "Feminist Criticism in the Wilderness" essay was first published as early as 1981, that is, well before the New Right backlash gathered its full momentum. But Showalter chose to republish it unamended as late as 1985 in a book she herself edited.
67. Showalter, A criticism of our own, p. 359.
68. G. C. Spivak, *In other worlds: essays in cultural politics* (London, Methuen, 1987); B. Johnson, *A world of difference* (Baltimore, The Johns Hopkins University Press, 1987).
69. M. Barrett, *Women's oppression today: the Marxist/feminist encounter* (London, Verso, 1988), p. xxix.
70. C. Weedon, *Feminist practice and post-structuralist theory* (Oxford, Basil Blackwell, 1987).
71. Editorial, *Feminist Review*, 23, 1986, p. 4.
72. M. Barrett, Feminism's turn to culture, *Woman: A Cultural Review*, 1, 1990.
73. T. de Lauretis, *Alice doesn't: feminism, semiotics, cinema* (London, Macmillan, 1984); L. Mulvey, Afterthoughts on "visual pleasure and narrative cinema" inspired by *Duel in the Sun*, in *Popular fiction: technology, ideology, production, reading*, ed. T. Bennett (London, Routledge, 1990).

74. E. Gross, Conclusion: What is feminist theory?, in *Feminist challenges: social and political theory* eds. C. Pateman and E. Gross (Boston, Northeastern University Press, 1986), pp. 190–3.

75. *Ibid.*, p. 204.

76. E. Grosz, *Sexual subversions: three french feminists* (Sydney, Allen & Unwin, 1989), p. 234.

77. Showalter, A criticism of our own, p. 369.

78. M. Barrett, Words and things: materialism and method in contemporary feminist analysis, in *Destabilizing theory: contemporary feminist debates*, eds. M. Barrett & A. Phillips (Cambridge, Polity Press, 1992), p. 208.

79. Y. Tasker, Having it all: feminism and the pleasures of the popular, in *Off centre: feminism and cultural studies*, eds. S. Franklin et al. (London, HarperCollins Academic, 1991), p. 96.

80. *Ibid.*

81. L. Kipnis, Feminism: the political conscience of postmodernism?, in *Universal abandon? the politics of postmodernism*, ed. A. Ross (Edinburgh, Edinburgh University Press, 1989), p. 154.

82. *Ibid.*, p. 155.

83. *Ibid.*, p. 164.

84. *Ibid.*

85. S. Weigel, Body and image space: problems and representations of a female dialectic of enlightenment, in *Discourse and difference: post-structuralism, feminism and the moment of history*, eds. A. Milner & C. Worth (Melbourne, Centre for General and Comparative Literature, 1990).

86. Kipnis, Feminism: the political conscience of postmodernism?, pp. 150–3.

87. S. Lovibond, Feminism and postmodernism, *New Left Review* 178, 1989, p. 17.

88. *Ibid.*, pp. 27–8.

89. Millett, *Sexual politics*, p. 89.

90. F. Nietzsche, *Beyond good and evil: prelude to a philosophy of the future*, tr. H. Zimmern (New York, Macmillan, 1907), pp. 186–7.

91. C. Owens, The discourse of others: feminists and postmodernism, in *Postmodern culture*, ed. H. Foster (London, Pluto Press, 1985).

92. cf. T. Moi, Feminism, postmodernism and style: recent feminist criticism in the United States, *Cultural Critique* 9, 1988.

93. A. Huyssen, *After the great divide: modernism, mass culture and postmodernism* (London, Macmillan, 1988), p. 62.

94. L. Hutcheon, *A poetics of postmodernism* (London, Routledge, 1988), p. 62.

95. Huyssen, *After the great divide*, pp. 219–20.

96. E. A. Kaplan, Introduction, in *Postmodernism and its discontents: theories, practices*, ed. E. A. Kaplan (London, Verso, 1988), p. 4.

97. *Ibid.*, p. 5.

98. J. Williamson, Even new times change, *New Statesman* 7 July 1989, p. 35.

99. J. Williamson, *Consuming passions: the dynamics of popular culture* (London, Marion Boyars, 1986), pp. 11–12.

100. *Ibid.*, p. 142.

101. *Ibid.*, p. 143.

102. *Ibid.*, p. 233.

103. J. Williamson, Woman is an island, in *Studies in entertainment*, ed. T. Modleski

(Bloomington, Indiana University Press, 1986), p. 116.

104. cf. J. Williamson, The problems of being popular, *New Socialist* 41, 1986.

105. Williamson, Even new times change, pp. 33–4.

106. M. Morris, *The pirate's fiancée: feminism, reading, postmodernism* (London, Verso, 1988), pp. 123–36.

107. *Ibid.*, p. 5.

108. *Ibid.*, p. 7.

109. *Ibid.*, pp. 173–86.

110. *Ibid.*, pp. 127–9.

111. *Ibid.*, p. 8.

112. *Ibid.*, p. 5.

113. *Ibid.*, p. 10.

114. M. Morris, Banality in cultural studies, *Block* 14, 1988, p. 25.

115. *Ibid.*, p. 24.

116. M.Morris, Things to do with shopping centres, in *Grafts: feminist cultural criticism*, ed. S. Sheridan (London, Verso, 1988), pp. 213–14.

117. Morris, Banality in cultural studies, p. 20.

118. *Ibid.*, p. 20.

119. *Ibid.*, p. 23.

120. *Ibid.*, p. 20.

121. J. Fiske, British cultural studies and television, in *Channels of discourse: television and contemporary criticism*, ed. R. C. Allen (London, Methuen, 1987); I. Chambers, *Popular culture: the metropolitan experience* (London, Methuen, 1986).

122. J. Fiske et al., *Myths of Oz: reading Australian popular culture* (Sydney, Allen & Unwin, 1987).

123. C. Switchenberg, Madonna's postmodern feminism: bringing the margins to the centre, in *The madonna connection: Representational politics, subcultural identities and cultural theory*, ed. C. Switchenberg (Boulder, Westview Press, 1993).

124. Ruthven, *Feminist literary studies*, p. 6.

Chapter 6

1. M. Morris, *The pirate's fiancée: feminism, reading, postmodernism* (London, Verso, 1988), p. 242.

2. *Ibid.*

3. Z. Bauman, What is post and what is modern in postmodernity?, Centre for Cultural Studies Research Seminar, University of Leeds, 25 November 1992.

4. F. Fehér, The pyrrhic victory of art in its war of liberation: remarks on the postmodernist intermezzo, in *Postmodern Conditions*, eds. A. Milner et al. (Oxford, Berg, 1990), p. 87.

5. Morris, *The pirate's fiancée*, p. 186.

6. F. Jameson, *Postmodernism, or the cultural logic of late capitalism* (London, Verso, 1991), p. 1.

7. *Marxism Today*, special issue on "New Times", October 1988.

8. M. Bradbury, The cities of modernism, in *Modernism 1890–1930*, eds. M. Bradbury & J. McFarlane (London, Penguin, 1976).

9. A. Callinicos, *Against postmodernism: a Marxist critique* (Cambridge, Polity Press, 1989), p. 60.

NOTES

10. P. Anderson, Modernity and revolution, in *Marxism and the interpretation of culture*, eds. C. Nelson & L. Grossberg (London, Macmillan, 1988), p. 326.

11. F. Jameson, Discussion, in *Marxism and the interpretation of culture*, eds. Nelson & Grossberg, p. 359.

12. E. Mandel, *Late capitalism*, tr. J. De Bres (London, New Left Books, 1975).

13. M. Barrett, *Women's oppression today: the Marxist/feminist encounter* (London, Verso, 1988), p. xxxiv.

14. J. Habermas, Modernity – an incomplete project, in *Postmodern culture*, ed. H. Foster (London, Pluto Press, 1985); J. Habermas, *The philosophical discourse of modernity* tr. F. Lawrence (Cambridge, Polity Press, 1987).

15. Fehér, The pyrhhic victory of art, p. 92.

16. Callinicos, *Against postmodernism*, pp. 2–3.

17. *Ibid.*, p. 5.

18. S. Lash, *Sociology of postmodernism* (London, Routledge, 1990), p. 3.

19. J-F. Lyotard, *The postmodern condition: a report on knowledge*, tr. G. Bennington & B. Massumi (Minneapolis, University of Minnesota Press, 1984), p. 37.

20. *Ibid.*

21. *Ibid.*, p. 79.

22. *Ibid.*, p. 81.

23. *Ibid.*, pp. 81–2.

24. *Ibid.*, p. xxiii.

25. D. Bell, *The coming of post-industrial society* (New York, Basic Books, 1973).

26. D. Bell, *The cultural contradictions of capitalism* (London, Heinemann, 1976).

27. D. Bell, Beyond modernism, beyond self, in *Art, politics and will: essays in honour of Lionel Trilling*, eds. Q. Anderson et al. (New York, Basic Books, 1977).

28. L Trilling, *Beyond culture* (Harmondsworth, Penguin, 1967).

29. Bell, *Cultural contradictions of capitalism*, pp. 80–1, 84.

30. Bell, Beyond modernism, beyond self, p. 243.

31. *Ibid.*, pp. 250–2.

32. Lyotard, *Postmodern condition*, p. 79.

33. R. Williams, *Culture* (Glasgow, Fontana, 1981), p. 93.

34. F. Tönnies, *Community and association*, tr. C. P. Loomis (London, Routledge & Kegan Paul, 1955), pp. 37–9.

35. E. Durkheim, *The division of labor in society*, tr. G. Simpson (New York, Free Press, 1964), pp. 129–32.

36. cf. T. S. Eliot, *Notes towards the definition of culture* (London, Faber, 1962); F. R. Leavis & D. Thompson, *Culture and environment* (London, Chatto & Windus, 1960).

37. F. R. Leavis, *The common pursuit* (Harmondsworth, Penguin, 1962), pp.188–190.

38. R. Williams, *The long revolution* (Harmondsworth, Penguin, 1965), p. 187.

39. Terry Lovell has argued very persuasively for the significance of female as distinct from male writers, and fantastic as distinct from realist motifs, in the early history of the novel. cf. T. Lovell, *Consuming fiction* (London, Verso, 1987). This clearly invalidates certain central theses originally advanced by Watt in 1957, but not, I think, the general notion of an early bourgeois, male preference for formal realism. cf. I. Watt, *The rise of the novel: studies in Defoe, Richardson and Fielding* (Harmondsworth, Penguin, 1963, ch.2).

40. Watt, *The rise of the novel*, p. 43.

41. L. Febvre and H-J. Martin, *The coming of the book: the impact of printing 1450-1800*, tr. D. Gerard, eds. G. Nowell-Smith & D. Wootton (London, New Left Books, 1976), p. 220.

42. B. Crick, *George Orwell: a life* (London, Secker & Warburg, 1980), p. 393.

43. M. Bradbury & J. McFarlane (eds), *Modernism 1890-1930* (Harmondsworth, Penguin, 1976).

44. V. Woolf, Mr Bennett & Mrs Brown, *Collected essays* I, (London, Hogarth Press, 1966), p. 321.

45. Bradbury & McFarlane, p. 29.

46. P. Bürger, *Theory of the avant-garde*, tr. M. Shaw (Minneapolis, University of Minnesota Press, 1984), p. 22.

47. *Ibid.*, pp. 46-9.

48. P. Bourdieu, *Distinction: a social critique of the judgement of taste*, tr. R. Nice (London, Routledge & Kegan Paul, 1984).

49. A. Huyssen, *After the great divide: modernism, mass culture and postmodernism* (London, Macmillan, 1988).

50. Bell, *Cultural contradictions of capitalism*, pp. 51-2.

51. J. Baudrillard, *America*, tr. C. Turner (London, Verso, 1988), p. 101.

52. Bürger, p. 63.

53. Jameson, *Postmodernism*, pp. 17, 2.

54. Lash, *Sociology of postmodernism*, pp. 173-4.

55. cf. A. Heller, Existentialism, alienation, postmodernism: cultural movements as vehicles of change in the patterns of everyday life, in *Postmodern conditions*, eds. A. Milner et al. (Oxford, Berg, 1990).

56. M. Bakhtin, *Rabelais and his world*, tr. H. Iswolsky (Bloomington, Indiana University Press, 1984), pp. 4-17.

57. Z. Bauman, *Intimations of postmodernity* (London, Routledge, 1992), pp. 1-24.

58. *Ibid.*, p. 24.

59. cf. Baudrillard, *America*; U. Eco, *Travels in hyperreality*, tr. W. Weaver (San Diego, Harcourt Brace Jovanovich, 1986).

60. Fehér, The Pyrrhic victory of art, pp. 91-2.

61. cf. Bell, *Coming of post-industrial society*; Lyotard, *Postmodern condition*, pp. 46-7.

62. Jameson, *Postmodernism*, p. 3.

63. *Ibid.*, pp. 4-5.

64. *Ibid.*, p. 305.

65. Z. Bauman, *Legislators and interpreters: on modernity, post-modernity and intellectuals* (Cambridge, Polity Press, 1987), p. 167.

66. Jameson, *Postmodernism*, p. 398.

67. F. R. Leavis, *Nor shall my sword: discourses on pluralism, compassion and social hope* (London, Chatto & Windus, 1972), p. 58.

68. Jameson, *Postmodernism*, p. 3.

69. *Ibid.*, p. 400.

70. cf. E. P. Thompson, Notes on exterminism, the last stage of civilization, *New Left Review* 121, 1980); M. Kidron, *Capitalism and theory* (London, Pluto Press, 1974), pp. 124-67; P. Baran & P. Sweezy, *Monopoly capital* (Harmondsworth, Penguin, 1968).

71. F. Jameson, *Marxism and form* (Princeton, NJ, Princeton University Press, 1971), pp. 35-36.

NOTES

72. Mandel, *Late capitalism*, p. 306.

73. Jameson, *Postmodernism*, p. 18.

74. *Ibid.*, pp. 49, 54.

75. Baudrillard, *America*, p. 81.

76. G. Stauth & B. Turner, Nostalgia, postmodernism and the critique of mass culture, *Theory, Culture and Society* 5, 2–3, 1988, p. 524.

77. Lyotard, *Postmodern condition*, pp. 81–2.

78. T. Bennett, Marxism and popular fiction, in *Popular fictions: essays in literature and history*, eds. P. Humm et al. (London, Methuen, 1986), p. 264.

79. M. Morris, Tooth and claw: tales of survival and *Crocodile Dundee*, in *Universal abandon? the politics of postmodernism*, ed. A. Ross (Edinburgh, University of Edinburgh Press, 1989), pp. 124–5.

80. F. Jameson, *The political unconscious: narrative as a socially symbolic act* (London, Methuen, 1981), p. 35.

81. *Ibid.*, p. 102.

82. *Ibid.*, p. 19.

83. G. Orwell, *Collected essays, journalism and letters: vol. 2* (Harmondsworth, Penguin, 1970), p. 305.

84. Williams, *The long revolution*, p. 383.

85. R. Williams, *Towards 2000* (London, Chatto & Windus, 1983), pp. 268–9.

86. *Ibid.*, p. 134.

87. *Ibid.*, p. 140.

88. *Ibid.*, p. 141.

89. *Ibid.*, pp. 141–2.

90. *Ibid.*, p. 146.

91. *Ibid.*, p. 145.

92. R. Williams, *The politics of modernism: against the new conformists*, ed. T. Pinkney (London, Verso, 1989), pp. 175–6.

93. The projected, but sadly unwritten, last chapter of *The politics of modernism* was to bear the title "Against the new conformists". Whether the New Conformists were specifically postmodernist or more generally modernist is immaterial. For Williams was clear that there was no technically distinct postmodernism: "Modernism being the terminus, everything afterwards is counted out of development. It is *after*, stuck in the post" — *Ibid.*, p. 35.

94. *Ibid.*

FURTHER READING

Chapter 1: Utilitarianism

J. Bentham, *The works of Jeremy Bentham*, vol. II (New York, Russell & Russell, 1962).

D. Hume, *Of the standard of taste and other essays* (Indianapolis, Bobbs-Merrill, 1965).

C. B. Macpherson, *The political theory of possessive individualism: Hobbes to Locke* (Oxford, Oxford University Press, 1962).

J. S. Mill, *Utilitarianism* (Glasgow, Fontana, 1962).

T. Parsons, *The structure of social action* (New York, Free Press, 1949).

Chapter 2: Culturalism

Arnold, Eliot and the rise of english studies

M. Arnold, *Culture and anarchy*, ed. J. Dover Wilson (Cambridge, Cambridge University Press, 1966).

C. Baldick, *The social mission of English criticism 1848–1932* (Oxford, Oxford University Press, 1983).

B. Doyle, *English and Englishness* (London, Routledge, 1989).

T. S. Eliot, *Notes towards the definition of culture* (London, Faber, 1962).

T. S. Eliot, *The idea of a Christian society and other writings* (London, Faber, 1982).

D. J. Palmer, *The rise of English studies* (Oxford, Oxford University Press, 1965).

Leavis and Leavisism

F. R. Leavis, *Education and the university: a sketch for an 'English School'* (London, Chatto & Windus, 1948).

F. R. Leavis, *The common pursuit* (Harmondsworth, Penguin, 1962).

F. R. Leavis, *Nor shall my sword: discourses on pluralism, compassion and social hope* (London, Chatto & Windus, 1972).

F. R. Leavis & D. Thompson, *Culture and environment* (London, Chatto & Windus, 1960).

F. Mulhern, *The Moment of 'Scrutiny'* (London, Verso, 1981).

Left culturalism and British cultural studies

R. Hoggart, *The uses of literacy* (Harmondsworth, Penguin, 1958).

J. Seabrook, *Landscapes of poverty* (Oxford, Basil Blackwell, 1985).

E. P. Thompson, *William Morris: romantic to revolutionary* (London, Lawrence & Wishart, 1955).

E. P. Thompson, *The making of the English working class* (London, Victor Gollancz, 1963).

R. Williams, *Culture and society 1780–1950* (Harmondsworth, Penguin, 1963).

R. Williams, *The long revolution* (Harmondsworth, Penguin, 1965).

P. Willis, *Learning to labour: how working class kids get working class jobs* (London, Saxon House, 1977).

4. Nationalism and culture

B. Anderson, *Imagined communities: reflections on the origins and spread of nationalism* (London, Verso, 1983).

E. Gellner, *Thought and change* (London, Weidenfeld & Nicolson, 1964).

J. G. von Herder, *Reflections on the philosophy of the history of mankind*, tr. T.O. Churchill, ed. F. E. Manuel (Chicago, University of Chicago Press, 1968).

E. Kedourie, *Nationalism* (London, Hutchinson, 1960).

T. Nairn, *The break-up of Britain* (London, New Left Books, 1977).

Chapter 3: Marxism

Classical and communist Marxism

C. Caudwell, *Illusion and reality* (London, Lawrence & Wishart, 1946).

R. Fox, *The novel and the people* (London, Lawrence & Wishart, 1979).

M. Gorky et al., *Soviet Writers' Congress 1934: The debate on socialist realism and modernism* (London, Lawrence & Wishart, 1977).

K. Marx, *Early writings* (Harmondsworth, Penguin, 1975).

K. Marx and F. Engels, *The German ideology*, part one, tr. W. Lough et al., ed. C. J. Arthur (London, Lawrence & Wishart, 1970).

G. Plekhanov, Art and social life, tr. E. Hartley et al., in *Art and social life*, eds. P. Davison et al. (Cambridge, Chadwyck Healey, 1978).

A. West, *Crisis and criticism* (London, Lawrence & Wishart, 1975).

German sociology

R. Aron, *Main currents in sociological thought*, vol. 1, tr. R. Howard & H. Weaver (London, Weidenfeld & Nicholson, 1965).

A. Salomon, German sociology, in *Twentieth century sociology*, eds. G. Gurvitch & W. E. Moore (New York, Philosophical Library, 1945).

F. Tönnies, *Community and association*, tr. C. P. Loomis (London, Routledge & Kegan Paul, 1955).

M. Weber, *The Protestant ethic and the spirit of capitalism*, tr. T. Parsons (London, Unwin, 1930).

M. Weber, *From Max Weber: essays in sociology*, eds. H. H. Gerth & C. Wright Mills (London, Routledge & Kegan Paul, 1948).

Western Marxism

T. Adorno & M. Horkheimer, *Dialectic of enlightenment*, tr. J. Cumming, (London, Verso, 1979).

P. Anderson, *Considerations on western Marxism* (London, New Left Books, 1976).

E. Bloch et al., *Aesthetics and politics* (London, Verso, 1980).

L. Althusser, *Lenin and philosophy and other essays*, tr. B. Brewster (London, New Left Books, 1971).

M. Bakhtin, *Rabelais and his world*, tr. H. Iswolsky (Bloomington, Indiana University Press, 1984).

W. Benjamin, *Illuminations*, tr. H. Zohn, (Glasgow, Fontana, 1973).

L. Goldmann, *The hidden God*, tr. P. Thody (London, Routledge & Kegan Paul, 1964).

A. Gramsci, *Selections from prison notebooks*, tr. Q. Hoare & G. Nowell Smith (London, Lawrence & Wishart, 1971).

J. Habermas, *Legitimation crisis*, tr. T. McCarthy (Boston, Beacon Press, 1975).

J. Habermas, *The structural transformation of the public sphere: an inquiry into a category of bourgeois society*, tr. T. Burger (Cambridge, Polity Press, 1989).

M. Horkheimer, *Critical theory: selected essays*, tr. M. J. O. O'Connell (New York, Seabury Press, 1972).

G. Lukács, *The meaning of contemporary realism*, tr. J. & N. Mander (London, Merlin Press, 1963).

G. Lukács, *History and class consciousness*, tr. R. Livingstone (London, Merlin Press, 1971).

H. Marcuse, *Negations*, tr. J. J. Shapiro (Boston, Beacon Press, 1968).

J-P. Sartre, *Critique of dialectical reason*, tr. A. Sheridan-Smith (London, New Left Books, 1976).

The New Left

P. Anderson, *Arguments within English Marxism* (London, New Left Books, 1980).

P. Anderson, *English questions* (London, Verso, 1992).

R. Collins et al. (eds), *Media, culture and society: a critical reader* (London, Sage, 1986).

J. Dollimore & A. Sinfield (eds), *Political Shakespeare: new essays in cultural materialism* (Manchester, Manchester University Press, 1985).

T. Eagleton, *Criticism and ideology* (London, New Left Books, 1976).

T. Eagleton, *The function of criticism: from 'The Spectator' to post-structuralism* (London, Verso, 1984).

T. Eagleton, (ed.) *Raymond Williams: critical perspectives* (Cambridge, Polity Press, 1989).

F. Jameson, *Marxism and form* (Princeton, NJ, Princeton University Press, 1971).

F. Jameson, *The political unconscious: narrative as a socially symbolic act* (London, Methuen, 1981).

A. Milner, *Cultural materialism* (London, UCL Press, 1993).

T. Nairn, *The enchanted glass: Britain and its monarchy* (London, Picador, 1990).

C. Nelson & L. Grossberg (eds), *Marxism and the interpretation of culture* (London, Macmillan, 1988).

A. Sinfield, *Literature, politics and culture in postwar Britain* (Oxford, Basil Blackwell, 1989).

D. Widgery (ed.), *The left in Britain 1956–1968* (Harmondsworth, Penguin, 1976).

R. Williams, *Marxism and literature* (Oxford, Oxford University Press, 1977).

R. Williams, *Culture* (Glasgow, Fontana, 1981).

Chapter 4: Structuralism

Structuralism

E. Durkheim, *The elementary forms of the religious life*, tr. J. W. Swain (London, George Allen & Unwin, 1976).

R. Barthes, *Elements of semiology*, tr. A. Lavers & C. Smith (New York, Hill & Wang, 1968).

R. Barthes, *Mythologies*, tr. A. Lavers (St Albans, Paladin, 1973).

R. Barthes, *Image-music-text*, tr. S. Heath (New York, Hill & Wang, 1977).

J. Culler, *Structuralist poetics: structuralism, linguistics and the study of literature* (London, Routledge & Kegan Paul, 1975).

U. Eco, *The role of the reader: explorations in the semiotics of texts* (London, Hutchinson, 1981).

M. Foucault, *Madness and civilisation: a history of insanity in the age of reason*, tr. R. Howard (New York, Vintage Books, 1965).

M. Foucault, *The archaeology of knowledge*, tr. A. M. Sheridan (London, Tavistock, 1972).

FURTHER READING

M. Foucault, *The birth of the clinic*, tr. A. M. Sheridan (London, Tavistock, 1973).

M. Foucault, *The order of things: an archaeology of the human sciences* (New York, Vintage Books, 1973).

M. Foucault, *Language, counter-memory, practice*, ed. D. F. Bouchard, tr. D. F. Bouchard & S. Simon (Ithaca, Cornell University Press, 1977).

L. Lemon & M. Reis (eds), *Russian formalist criticism: four essays* (Lincoln, University of Nebraska Press, 1965).

C. Lévi-Strauss, *The savage mind* (Chicago, University of Chicago Press, 1966).

C. Lévi-Strauss, *Structural anthropology*, tr. C. Jacobson & B. Grundfest Schoepf (Harmondsworth, Penguin, 1972).

R. Macksey & E. Donato (eds), *The languages of criticism and the sciences of man* (Baltimore, The Johns Hopkins University Press, 1970).

F. de Saussure, *Course in general linguistics*, tr. W. Baskin (Glasgow, Fontana, 1974).

Post-structuralism

R. Barthes, *S/Z*, tr. R. Miller (New York, Hill & Wang, 1974).

R. Barthes, *The pleasure of the text*, tr. R. Miller (New York, Hill & Wang, 1975).

P. Bourdieu, *Outline of a theory of practice*, tr. R. Nice (Cambridge, Cambridge University Press, 1977).

P. Bourdieu, *Distinction: A social critique of the judgement of taste*, tr. R. Nice (London, Routledge & Kegan Paul, 1984).

J. Derrida, *Speech and phenomena and other essays on Husserl's theory of signs*, tr. D. B. Allison (Evanston, Northwestern University Press, 1973).

J. Derrida, *Of grammatology*, tr. G. C. Spivak (Baltimore, The Johns Hopkins University Press, 1976).

J. Derrida, *Writing and difference*, tr. A. Bass (Chicago, University of Chicago Press, 1978).

H. Felperin, *Beyond deconstruction: the Uses and abuses of literary theory* (Oxford, Oxford University Press, 1985).

M. Foucault, *Discipline and punish: the birth of the prison*, tr. A. M. Sheridan (Harmondsworth, Allen Lane, 1977).

M. Foucault, *The history of sexuality*, tr. R. Hurley (New York, Random House, 1978).

M. Foucault, *Power/knowledge: selected interviews and other writings, 1972–1977*, ed. C. Gordon (Brighton, Harvester Press, 1980).

M. Foucault, *The use of pleasure*, tr. R. Hurley (New York, Pantheon Books, 1985).

M. Foucault, *The case of the self*, tr. R. Hurley (New York, Pantheon Books, 1986).

G. Hartman (ed.), *Deconstruction and criticism* (New York, Seabury Press, 1979).

J. Lacan, *The four fundamental concepts of psycho-analysis*, tr. A. Sheridan (London, Hogarth Press, 1977).

Structuralism, post-structuralism and British cultural studies

F. Barker, *The tremulous private body: essays on subjection* (London, Methuen, 1984).

C. Belsey, *The subject of tragedy: identity and difference in Renaissance drama* (London, Methuen, 1985).

T. Bennett, *Formalism and Marxism* (London, Methuen, 1979).

T. Bennett, *Outside literature* (London, Routledge, 1990).

A. Easthope, *British post-structuralism since 1968* (London, Routledge, 1988).

A. Easthope, *Literary into cultural studies* (London, Routledge, 1991).

J. Fiske, *Introduction to communication studies* (London, Methuen, 1982).

J. Fiske, *Reading the popular* (London, Unwin Hyman, 1989).

S. Hall, Cultural studies: two paradigms, *Media, culture and society*, 2, 1, 1980.

S. Hall et al., *Culture, media, language* (London, Hutchinson/Centre for Contemporary Cultural Studies, 1980).

S. Hall & T. Jefferson (eds), *Resistance through rituals: youth subcultures in post-war Britain* (London, Hutchinson, 1976).

T. Hawkes, *Structuralism and semiotics* (London, Methuen, 1977).

S. Heath, *Questions of cinema* (London, Macmillan, 1981).

D. Hebdidge, *Subculture: the meaning of style* (London, Methuen, 1979).

C. MacCabe, *Theoretical essays: film, linguistics, literature* (Manchester, Manchester University Press, 1985).

G. Turner, *British cultural studies: an introduction* (London, Unwin Hyman, 1990).

P. Widdowson (ed.), *Re-reading English* (London, Methuen, 1982).

Postcolonialism and multiculturalism

I. Adam & H. Tiffin (eds), *Past the last post: theorizing post-colonialism and post-modernism* (London, Harvester Wheatsheaf, 1991).

A. Ahmad, *In theory: classes, nations, literatures* (London, Verso, 1992).

B. Ashcroft et al., *The empire writes back: theory and practice in post-colonial literatures* (London, Routledge, 1989).

F. Barker et al. (eds), *Europe and its others* (Colchester, University of Essex, 1985).

H. K. Bhabha (ed.), *Nation and narration* (London, Routledge, 1990).

T. Eagleton et al., *Nationalism, colonialism and literature* (Minneapolis, University of Minnesota Press, 1990).

S. Rushdie, *Imaginary homelands: essays and criticism 1981–1991* (London, Granta Books, 1991).

E. W. Said, *Orientalism* (New York, Pantheon Books, 1978).

E. W. Said, *Culture and imperialism* (London, Chatto & Windus, 1993).

G. C. Spivak, *In other worlds: essays in cultural politics* (London, Methuen, 1987).

G. C. Spivak, Can the subaltern speak?, in *Marxism and the interpretation of culture*, eds. C. Nelson & L. Grossberg (London, Macmillan, 1988).

Chapter 5: Feminism

Anglo-American feminism

J. Donovan (ed.), *Feminist literary criticism: explorations in theory* (Lexington, University Press of Kentucky, 1975).

A. Dworkin, *Woman hating* (New York, Dutton, 1974).

S. M. Gilbert & S. Gubar, *No man's land: the place of the woman writer in the twentieth century, vol. 1: the war of the words* (New Haven, Yale University Press, 1988).

G. Greer, *The female eunuch* (London, MacGibbon & Kee, 1971).

J. S. Mill & H. Taylor Mill, *Essays on sex equality* (Chicago, University of Chicago Press, 1970).

K. Millett, *Sexual politics* (London, Virago, 1977).

E. Moers, *Literary women* (London, Women's Press, 1978).

E. Showalter, *A literature of their own: British women novelists from Brontë to Lessing* (London, Virago, 1978).

E. Showalter, Feminist criticism in the wilderness, in *The new feminist criticism: essays on women, literature, and theory*, ed. E. Showalter (New York, Pantheon Books, 1985).

E. Showalter, A criticism of our own: autonomy and assimilation in Afro-American and feminist literary theory, in *The future of literary theory*, ed. R. Cohen (London, Routledge, 1989).

D. Spender, *Man made language* (London, Routledge & Kegan Paul, 1980).

S. Franklin et al. (eds), *Off centre: feminism and cultural studies* (London, Harper Collins Academic, 1991).

M. Wollstonecraft, *A vindication of the rights of women* (New York, Norton, 1975).

Women's Studies Group, *Women take issue: aspects of women's subordination* (London, Hutchinson/Centre for Contemporary Cultural Studies, 1978).

V. Woolf, *Collected essays*, I (London, Hogarth Press, 1966).

V. Woolf, *A room of one's own* (St Albans, Panther, 1977).

V. Woolf, *Women and writing* (London, Women's Press, 1979).

Socialist feminism

M. Barrett, *Women's oppression today: the Marxist/feminist encounter* (London, Verso, 1988).

M. Barrett, Words and things: materialism and method in contemporary feminist analysis, in *Destabilizing theory: contemporary feminist debates*, eds. M. Barrett & A. Phillips (Cambridge, Polity Press, 1992).

C. Kaplan, Pandora's box: subjectivity, class and sexuality in socialist feminist criticism, in *Making a difference: feminist literary criticism*, eds. G. Greene & C. Kahn (London, Methuen, 1985).

T. Lovell, *Pictures of reality: aesthetics, politics, pleasure* (London, British Film Institute, 1980).

T. Lovell, *Consuming fiction* (London, Verso, 1987).

Marxist-feminist Literature Collective, Women's writing: *Jane Eyre, Shirley, Villette, Aurora Leigh*, in *1848: the sociology of literature*, eds. F. Barker et al. (Colchester, University of Essex, 1978).

J. Mitchell, *Psychoanalysis and feminism* (Harmondsworth, Penguin, 1974).

J. Mitchell, *Women: The longest revolution. Essays in feminism, literature and psychoanalysis* (London, Virago, 1984).

T. Moi, *Sexual/textual politics* (London, Methuen, 1985).

J. Williamson, *Decoding advertisements: ideology and meaning in advertising* (London, Marion Boyars, 1978).

J. Williamson, *Consuming passions: the dynamics of popular culture* (London, Marion Boyars, 1986).

J. Wolff, *The social production of art* (London, Macmillan, 1981).

J. Wolff, *Feminine sentences: essays on women and culture* (Cambridge, Polity Press, 1990).

French feminism

S. de Beauvoir, *The second sex*, tr. H. M. Parshley (Harmondsworth, Penguin, 1972).

E. Marks & I. de Courtivron (eds), *New French feminisms: an anthology* (Brighton, Harvester, 1981).

H. Cixous & C. Clément, *The newly born woman*, tr. B. Wing (Minneapolis, University of Minnesota Press, 1986).

E. Grosz, *Sexual subversions: three French feminists* (London, Unwin Hyman, 1989).

L. Irigaray, *This sex which is not one*, tr. C. Porter with C. Burke (Ithaca, Cornell University Press, 1985).

J. Kristeva, *Revolution in poetic language*, tr. M. Waller (New York, Columbia University Press, 1984).

T. Moi (ed.), *The Kristeva reader* (Oxford, Basil Blackwell, 1986).

Feminism and post-structuralism

R. Coward & E. Ellis, *Language and materialism* (London, Routledge & Kegan Paul, 1977).

T. de Lauretis, *Alice doesn't: feminism, semiotics, cinema* (London, Macmillan, 1984).

E. Grosz, *Jacques Lacan: a feminist introduction* (London, Unwin Hyman, 1990).

B. Johnson, *A world of difference* (Baltimore, The Johns Hopkins University Press, 1987).

C. Pateman & E. Gross (eds), *Feminist challenges: social and political theory* (Boston, Northeastern University Press, 1986).

M. Morris, *The pirate's fiancée: feminism, reading, postmodernism* (London, Verso, 1988).

L. Mulvey, Visual pleasure and narrative cinema, in *Popular television and film*, eds. T. Bennett et al. (London, British Film Institute, 1981).

G. Pollock, *Vision and difference: femininity, feminism and histories of art* (London, Routledge, 1988).

S. Sheridan (ed.), *Grafts: feminist cultural criticism* (London, Verso, 1988).

G. C. Spivak, *In other worlds: essays in cultural politics* (London, Methuen, 1987).

C. Switchenberg (ed.), *The Madonna connection: representational politics, subcultural identities and cultural theory* (Boulder, Westview Press, 1993).

C. Weedon, *Feminist practice and post-structuralist theory* (Oxford, Basil Blackwell, 1987).

Chapter 6: Postmodernism

J. Baudrillard, *America* tr. C. Turner (London, Verso, 1988).

Z. Bauman, *Legislators and interpreters: on modernity, post-modernity and intellectuals* (Cambridge, Polity Press, 1987).

Z. Bauman, *Intimations of postmodernity* (London, Routledge, 1992).

D. Bell, *The Coming of post-industrial society* (New York, Basic Books, 1973).

D. Bell, *The cultural contradictions of capitalism* (London, Heinemann, 1976).

P. Bürger, *Theory of the avant-garde*, tr. M. Shaw (Minneapolis, University of Minnesota Press, 1984).

A. Callinicos, *Against postmodernism: a Marxist critique* (Cambridge, Polity Press, 1989).

U. Eco, *Travels in hyperreality*, tr. W. Weaver (San Diego, Harcourt Brace Jovanovich, 1986).

M. Featherstone, *Consumer culture and postmodernism* (London, Sage, 1991).

H. Foster (ed.), *Postmodern culture* (London, Pluto Press, 1985).

J. Habermas, *The philosophical discourse of modernity*, tr. F. Lawrence (Cambridge, Polity Press, 1987).

A. Heller & F. Fehér, *The postmodern political condition* (Cambridge, Polity Press, 1988).

L. Hutcheon, *A poetics of postmodernism* (London, Routledge, 1988).

A. Huyssen, *After the great divide: modernism, mass culture and postmodernism* (London, Macmillan, 1988).

F. Jameson, *Postmodernism, or the cultural logic of late capitalism* (London, Verso, 1991).

E. A. Kaplan (ed.), *Postmodernism and its discontents: theories, practices* (London, Verso, 1988).

S. Lash, *Sociology of postmodernism* (London, Routledge, 1990).

J-F. Lyotard, *The postmodern condition: a report on knowledge*, tr. G. Bennington & B. Massumi (Minneapolis, University of Minnesota Press, 1984).

A. Milner et al. (eds), *Postmodern conditions* (Oxford, Berg, 1990).

M. Morris, *The pirate's fiancée: feminism, reading, postmodernism* (London, Verso, 1988).

A. Ross (ed.), *Universal abandon? the politics of postmodernism* (Edinburgh, Edinburgh University Press, 1989).

B. Turner (ed.), *Theories of modernity and postmodernity* (London, Sage, 1990).

R. Williams, *Towards 2000* (London, Chatto & Windus, 1983).

R. Williams, *The politics of modernism: against the new conformists*, ed. T. Pinkney (London, Verso, 1989).

INDEX

INDEX

187

INDEX

INDEX

Durkheim, E.   12, 27, 60, 77–81, 86

Eagleton, T.   24, 33, 46, 68, 70, 71, 74, 75, 92, 95, 96, 100
Easthope, A.   2, 92, 93, 95, 96
Eco, U.   85
Economic and philosophical manuscripts   50, 63
economic determinism   37, 38, 62
economic rationalism   9
economics   4, 9, 14, 18, 155
écriture féminine   119, 122, 126
Edinburgh, university of   25
education   4, 6, 12, 16, 21, 23, 25–7, 33, 43, 99
Elementary forms of the religious life, The   77, 78
Elements of semiology   84
Eliot, T. S.   21, 22, 26–32, 34, 35, 38, 39, 41, 48, 81, 114, 141, 143
emergent culture   72–3
Empire writes back, The   97
empiricism   2, 8, 69, 77
"Encoding and decoding in television discourse"   94
Engels, F.   50, 54, 57, 60, 128
English Association   25, 26
English literature   26, 34, 35
English novel   30, 39
English school   31, 32, 40
English studies   1, 21–2, 24–6, 33, 34, 40, 42, 44, 93, 95, 102, 141
Enlightenment   48, 64, 98, 128, 129, 139, 150
epistemological break   67
episteme   85–6, 104
Equal Rights Amendment   124, 127
Essex, university of   93, 115
ethnicity   45, 46
evolutionism   79, 81, 153
existentialism   144
experience   3, 7, 11, 21, 39, 69, 70, 73, 77, 114, 115, 122, 151, 152
exterminism   148

fascism   64
Fashion system, The   84
Faultlines   75

Febvre, L.   5
Fehér, F.   62, 103, 136, 138
felicific calculus   11
Felperin, H.   71, 95, 132
Female eunuch, The   109
female realism   113
female tradition   113, 115, 122
feminist anti-humanism   103
"Feminist criticism in the wilderness"   118
Feminist review   109, 125
Feminist review collective   109
feudalism   4, 10, 28, 29
first wave feminism   108–109
Fiske, J.   92, 133
Formalism   80, 82, 84
Foucauldian   93, 95, 96, 98, 132
Foucault, M.   80, 85–91, 94, 95, 104, 125, 145
Fox, R.   57, 59
Frankfurt school   62–4, 127, 143
Freeman, E. A.   34
French feminist theory   127
French, M.   117
Freud, S.   120, 125
Freudian   112

Garnham, N.   75
Gellner, E.   42
Gemeinschaft   141
gender   15, 45, 46, 113, 116, 117, 119, 123, 128, 129, 141
genealogy   89, 91
general crisis of capitalism   59
Genet, J.   122
genotype   58
German ideology, The   51, 61
Gesellschaft   141
Giddens, A.   61
Glasgow, university of   25
Goldmann, L.   62, 66
Gouges, O. de   108
Gouldner, A.   13, 17, 18, 61
Gramsci, A.   7, 16, 62, 63, 66–9, 72, 94, 117, 145
Gramscian   67, 144, 145
Gramscianism   94

INDEX

INDEX

Kant, I. 61
Kaplan, C. 116
Kaplan, E. A. 130
Kautsky, K. 49, 60
Kedourie, E. 42
Kidron, M. 148
Kipnis, L. 126–30
Knights, L. C. 29
knowable community 40
knowledge function 67
knowledge/power relation 87
Korsch, K. 62
Kreiswirth, M. 93
Kristeva, J. 119–23, 127
Kristevan 121, 123, 127
Kruger, B. 130

labour movement 48, 76, 107
Labour Party 38, 69, 154, 156
Lacan, J. 87, 111, 120, 121, 125
Lacanian 87, 93, 121, 124
Lady Chatterley's lover 112
Lancaster, university of 1
language 15, 30–32, 35, 39, 41, 43, 77–9, 82–4, 88, 89, 104, 117, 119–22, 124, 129, 131, 156
langue 78, 83, 88
Lash, S. 103, 138, 144
late capitalism 92, 133, 135, 137, 146, 148, 152
Late capitalism 137, 147
"Laugh of the Medusa, The" 119
Lauretis, T. de 125
Lautréamont, comte de 122
Lawrence, D. H. 39, 112
Leavis, F. R. 3, 22, 29–35, 37–40, 42, 59, 74, 81, 91, 103, 114, 141, 144, 147
Leavis, Q. D. 29, 115, 141
Leavisism 26, 32–7, 40, 59, 93, 105, 115
Leavisite 3, 29–32, 34–7, 41, 42, 102, 143, 147
Leeds, university of 1
left culturalism 36, 37, 40, 41, 43, 47, 71, 93, 102
left deconstruction 95, 96
left-Leavisite 94
Legitimation crisis 17, 18

legitimation 61–3, 66, 83, 106, 155
Lenin, V. I. 147
Lentricchia, F. 95
Les mots et les choses 85
Lévi-Strauss, C. 80, 86
Lévy-Bruhl, L. 80
liberalism 9, 128
"life" 30, 37, 114, 156
linguistic sign 30, 78
linguistics 31, 76, 77, 79, 82, 121
literariness 82–4
literary canon 35, 71, 74, 92, 104, 113, 116, 132, 141, 147
literary criticism 3, 24, 26, 29, 32, 33, 59, 74, 80, 89, 135, 147
literary form 64, 66, 142
literary realism 55
literary studies 47, 74, 93, 99, 102, 111, 124
Literary theory 74
literary tradition 38, 115
literary value 34, 54, 114, 126
Literary women 113
"literature" 36, 74, 102
Literature and history 93
Literature of their own, A 113
Locke, J. 8
logocentrism 88, 119
Long revolution, The 3, 33, 99, 153, 154, 156
Lord Herbert of Cherbury 28
Lovell, T. 74
Lukács, G. 60, 62–5, 69, 95, 115, 138
Lukácsian 65
Luxemburg, R. 49
Lyotard, J-F. 103, 138–41, 143, 146, 151

MacCabe, C. 95, 99
Macherey, P. 68, 115
Macpherson, C. B. 9, 10, 12
Madness and civilisation 85
Madonna 133
Mailer, N. 112
Making of the English working class, The 36
Mallarmée, S. 122
Manchester metropolitan university 1, 2
Manchester, university of 25

191

INDEX

INDEX

INDEX

INDEX